1993

# Reading in the Content Areas
## for Junior High
## and High School

# Reading in the Content Areas
## for Junior High
## and High School

### JUDITH A. COCHRAN
University of Texas—Permian Basin

### ALLYN AND BACON
Boston London Toronto Sydney Tokyo Singapore

Copyright © 1993 by Allyn and Bacon
A Division of Simon & Schuster, Inc.
160 Gould Street
Needham Heights, Massachusetts 02194

**Library of Congress Cataloging-in-Publication Data**


Cochran, Judith.
    Reading in the content areas for junior high and high school  /
Judith A. Cochran.
        p.   cm.
    Includes bibliographical references and index.
    ISBN 0-205-13404-1
    1. Reading (Secondary)   2.  Content area reading.   I. Title.
LB1632.C56   1993
428.4'0712—dc20                                              92-5031
                                                                CIP


Printed in the United States of America
10 9 8 7 6 5 4 3 2      96 95 94 93

# CONTENTS

**Chapter 2**     **Using Textbooks Effectively     27**

**Chapter 3**      **Testing**    **49**

**Chapter 4**  **Vocabulary Development    89**

**Chapter 5**  **Reading Comprehension    119**

**Chapter 6**      **Reading and Writing: Avenues to
Critical Thinking     155**

**Chapter 10**        **Overview of Reading Program Organization**    **271**

# PREFACE

Students in junior and senior high school have reading problems. Parents, teachers, and the students themselves recognize the problem as well as the limited resources available for help. Secondary teachers are trained in content areas and often do not believe that the teaching of elementary reading skills should be a part of their job. Most also feel unprepared to diagnose and remediate reading problems that might encompass emotional and learning disability components. Secondary teachers turn to reading specialists when they are available, but only a mere 40 percent of this country's high schools employ reading specialists. Availability of reading specialists in our junior highs is more encouraging, as most of our schools employ such an individual. But how many students can one reading teacher remediate? Obviously, he or she can help only so many students—those who have the most severe problems. Those students with "minor" problems, who seem to fall between the cracks year after year, continue to fall further behind as their deficiencies go unaddressed.

When the school is unable to help their children, parents sometimes turn to elementary teachers, who have had training in how to teach the reading process, to tutor their children. These tutors may or may not be effective with students whose reading problems are a result of social promotion policies in our educational system. Children who cannot read should not be passed from elementary to junior high school.

This book reflects the concern for the myriad problems resulting from the presence of poor readers in secondary schools today. Reading is required for educational success. Secondary teachers have to modify textbooks, content, and testing and motivational strategies in order to teach these students. This book shows those teachers why they must and how they can improve students' reading deficiencies. It also gives them lessons to use with students who are unable to cope in the classroom. Likewise, the same material can be used by parents as well as the children themselves. *Reading in the Content Areas for Junior High and High School* will provide the following:

1. The explanation of reading skills and learning difficulties are presented in a quick and easy format with visual organizers and frequent topic headings.
2. Activities can be taken directly from the book and used in the classroom to develop reading skills and remedy learning difficulties.
3. Teachers, parents, and students who want to read more effectively can do so by reading the content explanation in the first part of the chapters and then selecting activities from the Teaching Activities section to address their needs.
4. Each chapter has Application Exercises taken from classroom situations. Teachers can use these for discussion, as examples

in the application of information learned in the text, or for homework practice.
5. The Application Exercises also have questions that require students to apply, synthesize, and analyze information presented in the preceding chapter.

Multiple literacy is the skill of being able to read adequately in all content fields. In order to acquire multiple literacy, key reading comprehension and vocabulary skills must be mastered (Chapters Three and Four) and then modified for each subject area. Reading in the content area, in this book, is defined as the selective use of basic reading skills for different subjects. The knowledge of how the teacher, student, content, and textbook should interact in this selection process is the focus of this book.

Each chapter addresses areas of reading difficulty for all abilities of readers found in junior high and high school. The emphasis is on teachers, parents, and students becoming more self-directed. A parent whose child is having difficulty scoring well on national or state tests will want to read the chapters on testing and study skills (Chapters Three and Seven) and select some practice exercises included in those chapters. A teacher might want to know how to organize his or her classes in order to teach reading more effectively. Chapter Ten, which presents an overview on the organization of reading programs, will help teachers decide how to teach and administer reading instruction. Key reading skills are described and demonstrated for students trying to help themselves. Practice exercises on these skills are also provided. Chapter Nine will help teachers with ESL, special education, and talented and gifted readers.

Practical flexibility is the most important aspect of this book. It will help teachers and parents who want to prevent reading problems with their students and children. It can also become an in-service or self-instructional book for teachers who have neither the time nor money to take courses. The exercises and procedures presented in the Teaching Activities sections may be used as presented or modified for different subject areas, and the vocabulary games can be used in the classroom or at home.

This book has been used in a university course called Reading in the Content Areas, in district-sponsored teacher in-services, for parent tutoring, and as a workbook for junior high, high school, and college students. Practical flexibility is one of this book's most valuable contributions to secondary readers of all ability levels.

## Acknowledgments

I wrote this book for use with content teachers and university students taking courses on reading in the content areas. I have recently taught in public schools as a content teacher and in universities as a professor. As I have taught this university course over the years and in different states, its student composition has changed. Initially, it was required for elementary teachers as well as reading and speech master's and doctoral candidates, and served as an elective for secondary education majors from all fields. Today, it is required for secondary and elementary majors. The majority of students in my classes are parents as well as teachers who have two needs: to help their own children be more successful in school and to help their present and future students. My interaction with the needs of such diverse populations of university students has shaped my perspective of what is needed in this book on content area reading. I used the book in mimeographed form for my classes from 1990 to 1992. My students helped me improve the style and coverage of the book by their comments and criticisms, and by what they showed, in their written or oral tests and in classroom discussions, to be understandable or abstruse. Pike McCasland was notably generous with his time, research, and advice. Some of the other students who helped provide specific material are listed below.

I also wish to acknowledge the influence of the teachers and administrators during my most recent year of teaching in a public high school. I was a regular classroom teacher—not a supervisor of student teachers, coordinator of interns, or director of special programs as I had been in the past. I taught six new classes with no classroom of my own in a high school of over 600 students. I was treated as any first-year teacher in teaching assignments; before, during, and after-school responsibilities; and in lack of direction. I consider this experience a reality check on my 10 years of university-level teacher training experience. Many of my ideas changed as to what teachers really need in order to survive in negative teaching situations caused by student reading difficulties (which, in my experience, had not been addressed for most since sixth grade). Classrooms of poor readers with mainstreamed special education students are realistic expectations for many prospective teachers and actualities for content teachers such as myself.

Special emphasis in this book is placed on a student development perspective in order to help teachers with the reading problems caused by the phenomenon known as *mainstreaming* special education and bilingual students. Mainstreaming in my classes meant having more emotionally disturbed, bilingual, and learning-disabled students randomly placed in my classes of 35 "regular" students than both special education teachers were allowed to have by law. I am indebted to the faculty and students at that high school for being themselves with me, as they were with every other new teacher there. Most specifically, I appreciate the insight, courage, and expertise of the mathematics department and Charlotte Henderson, a wonderful student and faculty advocate.

I also drew on the experience of many experts in their fields— Science: Dennis Ball, Janice Baker, and Carol Mangan; Music: Ted Grille and Francine Owens; English: Sharon Kemmer Ponder, Kristi Findley, Shelly Frietag, Sonia Belcher, Sharon Hollingshead, Garry

Phillips, Dale Harper, and Johnnie Spurgin; Art: Cynthia Stevens and Gerome Black; Mathematics: Rosa Angelica Brito, Boyd Brawley, Lisa Hale, James Epley, and Russell Winkler; Social Studies: Sylvia Bernal, Joy Eyer, Robert Bankston, Jolene Thomas, Ken Kennemer, and Leesa Grando; Physical Education: Chan and Becky Langley; Reading Masters' and Doctoral Students: Dottie Adams, Gayle Boyea, Jodi Baugh, Pat Basden, Darla Fuller, Britt Leach, Susan Peery, Robin Ruppanier, Karen Tetrick, Nan Bowen, Sharon Salloway, Lisa Dixon, Pam Prewitt, and Claudia Baker. I thank each of these individuals, as well as others that I may have inadvertently omitted from this list.

The editorial staff at Allyn and Bacon has been of great assistance. I am especially grateful to Mylan Jaixen. The reviewers Allyn and Bacon selected were as diverse as those who will use this book. I was encouraged by their positive comments and I carefully considered their criticisms. Thank you to Sandra P. Baker (Indiana School District) and Patricia L. Roberts (California State University, Sacramento). Also, I wish to thank Nancy Plane for her morning, evening, and weekend typing assistance as the manuscript was revised. She and many other persons I have not named contributed significantly to this work. And finally, this book could not have been written without the support and free babysitting provided by my parents, Joseph and Dorothy Cochran.

# Reading in the Content Areas
## for Junior High
## and High School

# CHAPTER ONE

# *Reading in the Content Areas: Multiple Literacy*

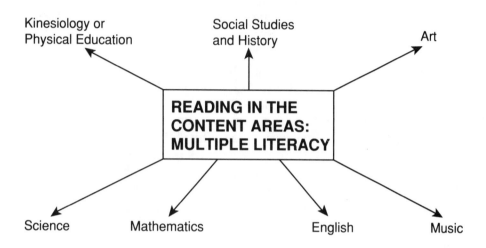

Junior and senior high school teachers have the right to assume that their students arrive with adequate skills that will enable teachers to begin instruction. Likewise, students who have been promoted have the right to assume that they have the skills necessary for success in that grade level. Unfortunately, neither assumption is valid in U.S. schools today. Students who cannot read are passed from first to second to third grade. By fourth grade, the school system has promoted a large number of students who cannot read adequately, and the curriculum focuses more on content obtained from reading than mastering the reading process itself. Upper-elementary teachers begin to emphasize content mastery and those students who have never been able to read adequately fall further and further behind. These students now must learn basic reading processes and the procedures of reading that are needed in different content areas, or multiple literacy.

Procedural reading instruction is just as necessary when one learns more difficult mathematics, science, and social studies as it is when children begin formal education. Thus, it becomes more and more the responsibility of upper-level elementary and secondary teachers to show students the procedure for reading comprehension in each subject area. Obtaining meaning in different content classes is possessing multiple literacy. No one else but the content teacher is available to help students learn the language and thinking processes that need to be developed for success in each specific field. Upper-elementary teachers should begin the instruction in multiple literacy when their students are capable of reading the textbook. Those who cannot read the textbook—remedial readers—need to spend much of their time mastering basic reading skills before receiving instruction in reading in the content areas.

Because of the continued promotion of incompetent students, negative attitudes toward reading often exist for middle-school or junior high students. Refusal to read is a system-caused rather than a student-caused problem. The educational system presents new information in textbooks with language, organization, and values that the students cannot understand. Students' lack of interest or inability to understand the textbook develops negative feelings toward reading. One needs only to attend conferences or be surrounded by people trained in a different discipline to begin to feel overwhelmed by the verbal shorthand they use and the apparent value differences. Students feel the same. There seems to be an attitude shared by those in specific fields that isolates those who did not receive the same training or do not initially hold the same perspective. Teachers are no different—and the higher the grades they teach, the more strongly they identify with the subject area. This identification isolates teachers from the gaps in their students' thinking and language. After all, teachers spend thousands of dollars to get their education and acquire the technical language they use so easily. Unfortunately, their students have not yet been to college and need help in reading and understanding the subject.

The approach of this chapter is not to go directly to the components of reading, textbook organization and assessment, vocabulary differences, or teaching strategies. In this book, reading is identified as an interactive process through which meaning is obtained. The interaction occurs between the students who bring various backgrounds with them for understanding, the content and its objectives, and the textbook, which supports the teacher's instruction. With this approach, the teacher has to understand the requirements of the subject, the reading demands of the textbook, and the needs of the students. The organization of this book follows the content, textbook, and student sequence. Improving student reading skills in different content fields helps the teacher and text provide a clearer picture of the meaning in the subject.

Unfortunately, although many content teachers see the need for reading skills in their classes, they would like to teach as though students already have the necessary reading ability. Even when they are given courses on how to teach reading in their subject area, many teachers do not see how they can add reading to the subject material they must teach. If teachers see themselves as the sole source of information, then their students will not need to read. But if they want students who can continue to learn about their subject beyond what the teacher presents, then teachers will want students who can read effectively in their subject field. An integrative approach to reading, then, considers reading as a means of supporting a teacher's content instruction. However, as demonstrated by the teachers' responses to the following questions, content teachers do not emphasize the same thinking strategies, value similar student behavior, or grade in the same manner. They expect multiple literacy reading skills from their students.

This chapter begins with the content and its objectives as perceived by preservice and employed teachers cited in the References. Although important, it will not present the content as it should be as debated by academicians in each field. It is important to understand how teachers who identify with a content field interpret their instructional mission. Their interpretation will demonstrate how the content is delivered. This chapter will transcribe responses of teachers and prospective teachers in answer to questions that junior high and high school students should ask themselves as they change classes. As other teachers and prospective teachers read the teachers' opinions, they can understand the demands made on the students who must, every hour, change subjects, teachers, and classrooms.

1. How do experts in your field think?
2. What are frequent mistakes in thinking made by students and teachers in your field?
3. What are the criteria for excellence in your field?
4. What strategies can you use to teach multiple literacy in your subject?

## Reading in Social Studies and History

The type of comprehension emphasized in social studies and history is interpretation, synthesis, and analysis. Students should master facts and then think about how these facts contributed to the events of the past as well as how they can be used to predict future events. Historians are concerned with the human context of the past and the present, which emphasizes thinking in a chronological continuum. Possessing historical literacy would include the ability of taking trips into the past and throughout the world, and meeting people, unknown countries, and alternate interpretations of how life could be lived. Historical literacy would be the ability to obtain meaning from foreign cultures and contexts. In the United States, the importance of learning about different countries and cultures is more critical as the schools reflect multicultural community composition. Understanding how or how not to live with Muslims, Mormons, and Jews is part of the meaning of social studies instruction. Even if such individuals do not live in the local neighborhood, television and efficient travel have reduced the isolation of people in the United States. History, social studies, and political science should provide the basis for comprehending and interpreting the splinters of information obtained on TV and through contact with foreigners.

In most history or social studies classes, obtaining meaning requires the ability to read written material, maps, and time lines on a literal level and then reorganize the information in the form of reports, speeches, and critiques. The language of social studies and history encompasses terms specific to the period or area of instruction. For example, when studying the revolutionary period in America, terms such as *colonialism* must be understood before conceptual meaning of the period is obtained. As a result, the language of social studies and history includes names, locations, and terms for political conditions that cannot be expected to be in the students' vocabularies. The language of history and social studies introduces students to foreign languages as well as foreign influences (Hafner & Stakenas, 1990).

### Social Studies Reading Skills

Understanding the organization of content

Reading for main ideas

Careful reading to retain facts

Understanding a great range of vocabulary in government, politics, economics, law, and sociology

Discriminating between fact and opinion

Understanding abstract terms such as *democracy, civilization,* and so on

Dealing with many references about one topic

Making comparisons

Reading maps and globes

### How do social studies teachers and historians think?

People interested in social studies are inquisitive and in-depth thinkers. They are inclined to be global in their thinking, as they are trying to make the parts fit into the bigger picture. Social studies teachers are interested in the human element of historical situations, which makes them concerned with community applications of their content. History is considered the foundation for making projections about the future. Political science and social studies are interpretations of present conditions.

### What are frequent mistakes in thinking made by students and teachers about history?

The first mistake is to have a strictly literal orientation about history. Teachers can compound this problem by going strictly by the textbook and failing to bring in interesting supplementary materials.

Some teachers have a closed mind about conflicting opinions and demonstrate a lack of creativity. A lack of teacher enthusiasm for history also affects student interest in the field.

## *What are the criteria for evaluating performance in history?*

Excellent students in history are able to read facts and interpret them. They must be able to take information and predict future outcomes from what they have read. Reports are evaluated for accuracy in historical facts and logical organization.

## *What strategies can be employed to teach reading in social studies and history?*

**1.** Construct a reading center in the classroom where supplementary materials are kept that relate to the period being studied.

**2.** Relate the past to the present by having students read daily newspapers, magazines, maps, time lines, and graphs.

**3.** Have students write out their interpretations of historical events and dramatize them.

**4.** Teach students to predict and interpret by doing in-depth projects like examining historical buildings in different towns.

**5.** Increase student awareness by discussing the interpretations of historical facts made on TV documentaries and by inviting speakers to present their interpretations on subjects studied in class.

# Reading in Art

Teaching reading in an art class is not often considered necessary. Although art textbooks do exist, they are seldom dusted off and used. However, as students progress in the subject, art history books are assigned to give a reference to the past. There are other types of art books, such as those that deal with technical approaches within the medium or books of criticism that identify what makes a painting or sculpture endure. There are also biographies of great artists and books that detail concepts of modern art or principles behind movements. Art books alone are never enough, but neither are textbooks in other courses the sole source of information. But the resulting artwork can demonstrate the application of the understanding or reaction to what has been read. Although art is viewed as emphasizing individualistic perceptions, there are some commonalities in thinking.

Art has a special language, much of which is ambiguous. In art, students can formulate their own problems that interpret their emotions. They develop a degree of literacy in a medium different from the written language to communicate their feelings. Art evaluators pay attention to subtleties, whereas students must always think in terms of editing their experiences. For both the teacher and the student, art evokes different realms of thinking.

**Art Reading Skills**

Comprehending technical terms and language
Following directions
Reading about the lives of artists
Reading the history of art
Comprehending art criticism, technical approaches, and so on

### How do artists think?

Artists are rational, systematic, intellectual persons who are seeking a meaningful expression of their emotion. They speak in languages of tone, intensity, color, and what might be called visual literacy. An artist must have literal recall in the technicality and mechanics of his or her craft, be able to interpret reasons and motivations during the application process, and be able to synthesize his or her ideas from imagination or inner vision to reality. An artist must successfully analyze the parts and evaluate the whole, but most importantly, he or she must be able to turn off analysis and allow the creative, intuitive, and emotional side to take over when the time is right. An artist will go back and forth between intellect and creativity until he or she is satisfied with the expression. During the process, a successful artist will find many more ideas and problems for visual expression. This creates a circular thinking process that will continue throughout the artist's life.

Artists observe life. They must be open minded because inspiration can come from the most unlikely places. Artists are also risk takers. For example, Picasso went from successful realistic portraits to Cubism—this is risk taking. Also, due to the nature of the work, artists are usually isolated from people while working. They may appear to be standoffish when not working because their minds are always problem solving the visual expression of emotion that will become the next creation.

### What are frequent mistakes in thinking made by students and teachers about art?

The most frequent mistake made in teaching art is allowing art class to become a play period and neglecting the aspects in art that make it a serious subject. Playing with the various media offers students the opportunity to become familiar with what the media will do and how the media can be used, but more substantive criteria must be included in the art classroom if the arts are to survive in public schools. Playing is a part of art, but so are thinking skills, and reading about art history, techniques, other artists, and learning application in visual expression.

Some art teachers feel that helping students find good ideas to express themselves will inhibit creativity. This would mean that problem solving is a component of art. Students must learn to define the problem and develop solutions and symbols of expression.

The intrinsic value of art is that art does more than make you feel something, it increases the awareness students have about themselves and the world around them. Art teachers understand that knowledge and feeling are united. One divorced from the other is emptiness. In all subjects taught in school, students can learn how to think, and the integration of thought in different subjects must be made in order to give students the essentials of education.

## What are the criteria for evaluating performance in art?

In addition to those listed below, other criteria consist of motivation to try new ideas, creativity as measured by something being either original or copied, curiosity, thoughtfulness in work, completion of assignments on time, and interest in class.

**1.** *Composition and overall design.* How well does the composition work and is the design effective?

**2.** *Technical abilities.* Has the artist used his or her control of the medium to the best of his or her abilities? How much improvement has been made?

**3.** *Presentation.* Has the work been addressed in the most enhancing way? Is the work sloppy? Does it appear that the student does not care about the subject or is lost?

**4.** *Expression.* Has the artist clearly shown his or her expression? Is the meaning of the work clear?

## What strategies can be employed to teach reading in art?

**1.** Allow students to make a visual narrative into the form of a comic book. This may help students in their attempts to communicate and encourage them to read other sources of literature, as well as help them learn visual expression (Hoff, 1982).

**2.** Encourage students to study artists in history as well as contemporary artists. By reading about artists and showing their works, the students gain knowledge about different ways of expressing themselves and different reasons the artists in history had for expressing themselves. It will teach them good ideas and open-mindedness (Costanzo, 1981).

**3.** Incorporate reading into the classroom by doing exercises in imaginative visualization. Read literature filled with imagery to the class, and encourage the students to find literature to increase their reading ability and imagination (Wilder, 1981; Hubbard, 1989).

**4.** The best way to teach the arts is to think of them as language. Find out how languages are taught and proceed to teach art in that way (Engle, 1981).

**5.** Help students learn about themselves by having them make "maps." These maps consist of experiences that were positive in the students' lives, skills in which they feel interested and proficient. A third map can consist of the media that could apply to the other two maps (Jefferson, 1981).

**6.** Many students are intimidated by the thought of expressing themselves visually. They are afraid to try to draw because they lack the experience. A helpful strategy for a beginning student is to use handwriting as a tool for expression (Hess, 1981).

**7.** Post instructions with visual illustrations, use vocabulary games and puzzles, give explanations about what the students are to see and how the visual image relates to a current project, and give reading assignments that require research (Peragallo, 1981).

**8.** Incorporate all areas of the curriculum into the art classroom. Use these other areas to help make a connection for the student between art and other life experiences. This will help art become a serious subject worthy of study. Make connections between art and literature, social studies, math, and science, with help from the other teachers.

## Reading in Music

Music, like mathematics, requires the reading of a new set of symbols and technical terms related to the speed, intensity, and duration of music. Reading music also involves thinking about interpretation and the ability to hear sounds—both literal and imagined. The instrument studied also influences the difficulty of reading music. In essence, music introduces a new language, a new sequence of punctuation and syntax, and symbols of dynamics. Although a few musicians cannot read music, almost all are able to read the language and meaning of scores.

Music requires thinking directed toward the part to the whole and the whole to the part. There are obvious parallels between beginning reading instruction and beginning music instruction methodologies. Learning to make meaning from reading words or notes would seem to be a similar process. The difference would be that music asks for interpretation on an instrument and a result in the form of a pattern of sound called music. Reading asks for interpretation in speaking, listening, or writing and a result in the form of a pattern of words called stories, reports, tests, or interpretations.

Students who learn music would be helped by knowing that they are transferring one process to another medium. They would still need to learn the language of music, which includes Italian, and other terms that are usually foreign to students. Reading music is making sense of aural sentences written in treble and base clef and jazz charts.

### Music Reading Skills

Reading words or songs correctly
Knowing meaning of musical terms
Reading biographies of composers and great musicians
Reading stories of operas
Comprehending critical evaluations of concerts
Comprehending descriptive articles about music
Following directions in musical textbooks

## How do musicians think?

Music educators have an enormous responsibility to encourage exploration of life-time musical skills by all students, including high-risk students who do not have advantages at home and label themselves as untalented.

Musicians have to be both global and analytical thinkers. The global thinking comprises the emotional, creative, and expressive aspects of music. The musician examines the mathematical, physical, and analytical aspects of music.

## What are frequent mistakes in thinking made by students and teachers about music?

The most frequent teaching mistake is not taking the student beyond mere rote learning. Rote learning initially is fast and produces an impressive result but then leaves the students unable to help themselves without the teacher.

A frequent student mistake is to build only on aptitudes. Students who have a "good ear" avoid learning how to read music. Likewise, the students who have good technical and mathematical skills do not develop a sense of musical emotion or interpretation.

And finally, there is the failure to relate conceptual development to music performance. Sadly, little conscious effort is spent in developing students conceptually. Instead of viewing difficulties as signals to do something a different way, teachers encourage using the same old concepts. The great music everyone plays originated from some of the greatest minds of our civilization. To try to understand how they felt is surely a most elevating experience. To understand the musical language that they used (harmony, rhythm, form, color) in our concept of a piece makes students and teachers better able to communicate their interpretation of the composer's idea. Musicians then make the mistake of not valuing the imagining or conceptualization of a performance.

*What are the criteria for evaluating performance in music?*

Effective elementary music teachers produce students who enjoy many varied types of music, sing or play with correct production, and want further group participation. Evaluation would be individualized through a baseline developed for each student by an audition procedure designed to assess reading (music) skills, technical ability, and emotional expression. Periodic follow-up auditions would determine the rate and amount of improvement.

Improvement is the primary criterion for excellence because the thinking required for music is multifaceted and aptitudes vary widely.

*What strategies can be employed to teach reading in music?*

1. Studying the biographies of composers is a current strategy for grades 4 through 6. This strategy has limitless possibilities for students to do research, read and write original compositions, and make time lines about a composer's life. Visual and display areas for the school media center can make a composer "come to life" for the entire school. The teacher must go beyond the literal facts and help the students interpret the composer's style and technique.

2. Listening and writing maps are part of current music curriculum. These maps are included in supplemental oversized books and in copy master form for students to complete and take home. These ditto maps are completed while students listen to a musical recording or while the teacher is singing or playing an instrument. A writing map is much like a time line of events and allows students to see sequence and then paraphrase for discussion or a classroom chart.

3. Writing new lyrics to existing music is a motivating strategy to encourage the beginning student to be a "composer." Study of rhyming patterns, narrative style, and matching desired text to expressive music gives the student a background for understanding the parts of a composition. Prewriting, writing, and rewriting techniques are employed as students work to make their lyrics fit the chosen melody.

4. The Orff ensemble is a strategy for teaching improvisation that eventually moves students to note reading. Improvising on wooden instruments, students are gradually weaned to teacher-directed rhythmic commands. Body percussion improvisation and commands teach melodic concepts, theme, and variation. These written or oral commands also give practice in following directions and understanding sequence.

5. Theory practice as a game or rehearsal technique is another reading strategy. Students are taught without using drills and memorization. This practice declares that isolated theory drills, apart from a

whole musical experience, is dull and devoid of retention that will last. This concept promotes teaching music theory by incorporating games, puzzles, worksheets, and the playing of pitched instruments to reinforce theory by doing a related activity. A theory question or an obvious error would be studied as it occurs in a rehearsal at the teachable moment.

**6.** The Kodaly method is a combination strategy that moves from rote learning to rote/note to independent reading of notes on a printed staff. This strategy allows students to explore every aspect of a song by approaching the song rhythmically, melodically, and then finally textually. Reading is taught through the text approach. Guided thinking questions about the text of a song are limited only by the experiences of the teacher and students. A student's written interpretation of a song is an effective method of extending his or her comprehension.

## Reading in English

Obtaining meaning in English requires reading for detail and subtlety. The details in a piece of literature enable students to interpret motive, characterization, and reasoning. Analyzing details provides the basis for comprehending and interpreting the main idea or theme of a piece of literature. The themes of most works are meant to be personally instructional to the readers. Themes are guideposts to help others analyze, interpret, and appreciate their own experiences. Thinking in English begins with details of reading or analyzing a sentence and then moves to more global personal meaning.

English teachers consider themselves artists with words, and their objective is frequently to teach students how to express their emo-

*"You barbeque your way and I'll barbeque my way!"*

tions and thoughts through words. As a result, student papers are marked with questions about clarity, awkwardness, and redundancy. Every child, from second grade on, learns how to analyze the logic of language by identifying grammatical parts of speech used in his or her writing as well as the writing of other authors. Although most students in second grade can recite specific English terminology like verb, noun, adjective, and adverb, they often are unable to apply that knowledge to their own writing or identify parts of speech on a test.

### English Reading Skills

*Vocabulary*

Learning terms unique to English (e.g., *apostrophe, adjective*)

Learning English (literary or grammatical) meanings for common words (e.g., *romantic, subject, feel, act*)

Learning word connotations and understanding figurative language and allusions (e.g., *lemon, two peas in a pod, Narcissus, Pygmalion*)

Understanding words change in meaning and pronunciation (e.g., *edelweiss, croissant*)

Understanding how new words are coined or how they enter our language (e.g., *snafu, morpheme*)

*Comprehension*

Selecting significant details, classifying convergently, formulating main ideas

Following directions

Recognizing sequence

Inferring time, place, mood, motive of characters

Making comparisons

Responding to imagery

Recognizing semantic and literary devices

Distinguishing between fact and opinion

Detecting fallacies of reasoning

### How do English/literature teachers and students think?

Individuals in this field are usually global in their thinking. They synthesize many experiences and ideas that are contained in the literary works they have read. Often the thinking process involves the imagination as well as thinking in terms of pictures and words. They are also analytical in their thinking, as they must examine syntactical structures of sentences in the English language and analyze the author's meaning, motivation, and reasoning in literary works.

## *What are frequent mistakes in thinking made by students and teachers about the English/literature field?*

One of the biggest mistakes made by others is thinking in a superficial manner, which, in turn, often leads them to take information at an emotional level and avoid analyzing details. Another mistake is the assumption that all literature is written purely for pleasure instead of for specific purposes, meanings, and effects. Another flaw is when teachers are biased in the presentation of literary works to the extent that the students' creativity is suppressed or the author's meaning is lost. Additional flaws in the teaching of English/literature are not allowing students to express their opinions, not relating the literature to contemporary experience, not explaining the purpose of reading the work, and not using interesting materials and methods. Also, many teachers think that they must cover too much material in too little time. And finally, the failure to accommodate a wide variety of student interests is also a mistake made by some teachers.

## *What are the criteria for evaluating performance in English/literature?*

1.  Participation
2.  Creativity
3.  Originality
4.  Critical thinking
5.  Open-mindedness
6.  Acceptance and application of constructive criticism
7.  Organized thinking

## *What strategies can be employed to teach reading in English/literature?*

1.  Analyze sentence structures by writing out reasons for various syntactical categories within sentences rather than using diagrams.

2.  Analyze the style and techniques of authors' works, as opposed to reading literature for face value of the plot.

3.  Search for reasons behind the style and techniques used in the works. For example, are the styles and techniques a result of reacting to the immediate environment or are they a reaction to a previously accepted style or technique?

4.  Convey meaning in English/literature by utilizing peer grouping and tutoring.

5.  Teach vocabulary through word origins, phonology, and word evolution.

6.  Relate reading material to the students' prior experiences and current environments.

7.  Require students to use higher-order thinking skills through questions that require skills such as evaluation, synthesis, and analysis.

8.  Avoid prejudice in thinking.

# Reading in Mathematics

The most obvious difficulty in reading mathematics is learning the language of math symbols and terms. *Parabola* is a math term; + is a math symbol. Plus can be read as *plus, sum,* or *add* to name a few different vocabulary words that mean "to put together." Equations can be considered sentences in math that students must learn to read. Furthermore, mathematicians then take math word problems and add meanings to common words. For example, *and* in a math word problem usually means *add*. When the word problem is written, sometimes necessary information is not included. Students must then solve the word problem but they are actually solving for two unknowns when information is deleted from the problem. Word problems require students to read on both the literal and interpretive levels, which is often not a part of content instruction in math classes.

As students take geometry and calculus classes, the math language gets more specialized and technical. The language of math contains both visual and written symbols organized into visual and written sentences. When word problems are read from a mathematical perspective, common words frequently have different meanings.

### Mathematics Reading Skills

Engaging in slow, detailed reading

Reading nonverbal types of material (e.g., alphabetical symbols, formulas, equations, graphs, etc.)

Reading without the aid of running content

Understanding technical vocabulary

Comprehending financial pages in newspapers

Understanding statistical reports

Following directions on tax blanks

*How do mathematicians think?*

1.  A logical mind is considered the most common denominator of mathematics teachers. The act of working any math problem in-

volves taking certain known factors to a logical conclusion (i.e., a desired method or a correct answer).

**2.** The ability to deal with and originate abstract ideas is another quality that a mathematician needs. Many fields of math deal with abstract ideas. To understand, relate, or initiate ideas that do not conform to "the usual" of anything takes the ability to conceptualize the abstract.

**3.** Perseverance to complete any project that has been stated is another common factor. An incomplete project or math problem causes mathematics teachers distress.

**4.** Mathematicians think in a neat and orderly manner. A certain amount of organizational ability is important to the mathematician, as the lack of it will make working a problem difficult.

## What are frequent mistakes in thinking made by students and teachers?

The most frequent thinking mistakes made by students and teachers of mathematics are as follows:

**1.** The student assumes that the problem has been done correctly the first time, without double-checking his or her work.

**2.** The student thinks that homework is a form of "busy work" and not the most important learning exercise available.

**3.** The student does not take notes of examples used in class. This makes it impossible to double-check procedures and methods, particularly with their relationship to specific problems.

**4.** The teacher assumes that the entire class is familiar with a given procedure, regardless of the simplicity of the process.

**5.** The teacher uses buzz words common to the profession without defining them.

**6.** The teacher does not think it is necessary to collect daily homework or give a daily quiz made up of one problem from the homework. The reasoning behind this checking of understanding is that one must *work* math in order to *learn* math.

**7.** The teacher thinks that putting incorrect problem solutions on the board is not damaging to students.

**8.** The teacher works out easier problems during class but assigns homework consisting of much more complex problems. To the uninitiated, the more complex problems often appear unrelated to the ones demonstrated in class.

**9.** The teacher believes that the student will learn math without being motivated.

*What are the criteria for evaluating performance in mathematics?*

**1.** Deriving the correct answer is one of the most important criteria; however, it is not considered the single-most important criterion.

**2.** The use of the proper method, or procedure, in solving a problem is considered to be of almost the same importance as the correct answer.

**3.** Neatness in the presentation of homework or projects is also important.

**4.** Completeness of assignments and showing the work are important criteria.

**5.** The teacher should be correct in all aspects of the grading process. Mistakes will happen, but incorrectly grading work as a standard practice is not acceptable.

*What strategies can be employed to teach reading in math?*

**1.** Use the chalkboard and the overhead projector in classroom presentations to help students in their reading. Discussion of math symbols and technical terms will occur simultaneously with the visual representation.

**2.** Introduce mental exercises into the classroom. Students will begin at the first of the semester with relatively easy problems to solve without the benefit of paper or pencil, and progress to more complex problems. Teaching mental dexterity is of enormous benefit to anyone who is having trouble retaining information.

**3.** Daily homework assignments to familiarize the students with formulas and equations, which would reduce the necessity of memorizing countless formulas, will help students who are having trouble understanding problems. The homework does not have to be time consuming; it should just be sufficient to allow students to go over what has been learned in class, which is in short-term memory.

## Reading in Science

A high school chemistry and physics teacher encouraged her ninth-grade son to excel in math and English. When asked why, she said, "If he can read and figure mathematics effectively, he can teach himself any other subject in any field." Whether one agrees or disagrees with this science teacher and mother, the same statement coming from an art teacher would not carry the same weight. Science is perceived as a difficult, elitist subject in which successful students are viewed as much greater thinkers than those in "soft" subjects. Thinking of science as elitist has resulted in school counselors placing only successful students in science (which reduces the numbers of students who can enjoy science) and teachers avoiding science (because they feel incompetent to teach it adequately).

Aside from the values attached to science, the thinking processes needed to make meaning from the field are varied. Background or factual knowledge must be obtained from reading textbooks and scientific journals. This knowledge must then be tested, explored, and demonstrated in laboratories or experiments. The criteria for excellence in science does not seem to come from one right answer but from the growing process of applying procedures to understand the known and the unknown. Science also has a language of its own in flowcharts, textbooks, and laboratory books. For example, try to make meaning from this science textbook statement:

> Measures of laterality do not correlate perfectly with invasive measures of cerebral asymmetry. For example, dichotic-listening studies show a right-ear bias for words in about 80% of right-handed subjects, but sodium Amytal testing and brain stimulation show language to be represented in the left hemisphere in over 95% of right-handers.

The course is human physiology, and, like astronomy, biology, botany, chemistry, physics, earth science, and geology, obtaining meaning is not necessarily a process of reading the words.

**Science Reading Skills**

Understanding technical vocabulary

Reading symbols and formulas

Following directions

Reading books on scientific research, biographies of scientists, advances in field, and so on

Recognizing pseudoscientific claims in advertisements (e.g., "Doctors everywhere recommend Chippo Cookies")

Drawing conclusions

## How do scientists think?

Many science teachers think science is reserved for the gifted students since gifted and talented classes are oriented toward this field. They also think that science is hard, even for science teachers. Scientists and science-oriented people think differently from people in other disciplines in several ways. The scientist wants to know why and how a particular thing works the way it does and, if possible, to improve on it. If a scientist or science-oriented person is faced with an unpleasant or intolerable situation, she or he works to change it. We saw this with Pasteur's cure for rabies and Salk's polio vaccine, and we are seeing it again with AIDS research and environmental sciences. Scientists have an insatiable curiosity. They are also logical, orderly, and systematic as they investigate, extend, and advance thinking and knowledge. The dedicated scientist is also very persistent, sacrificing for knowledge. How do scientists think? They view themselves as thinking analytically, empirically, and logically with divergent formal strategies. They want to see data, processes, definitions, and progressions.

### What are frequent mistakes in thinking made by students and teachers about science?

Scientists try to figure out the "why" to everything. This analytical thinking bleeds over into the teaching profession. Many teachers feel exploration is the only way to go and may neglect important reading, or feel the exploration is too difficult for young students and don't encourage it.

Frequent thinking differences or mistakes that cause problems in the science disciplines are easily rectified if we adjust our thinking to science, as opposed to social studies or language arts. Many daily happenings fall into the area of science, although we do not always realize that. How much coffee goes in the 30-cup coffee pot? How do we revive a yard in the spring that we think has grub worms or too much shade? Science is everyday problems as well as those beyond our comprehension. Many times, especially in lab work, students do not follow directions or settle too quickly on a solution. Science is also always changing, advancing, and updating itself.

Other mistakes in thinking include the following:

1. The perception is that science is too hard and is not applicable to daily life.

2. The elitist notion is that science is only for those who are superior either in scholarship or professional interests.

3. Failure to link vocational aspects of science to classroom experiences is a frequent mistake.

### What are the criteria for evaluating performance in science?

In science, it doesn't matter if it doesn't work. What is important is whether the scientific method of discovery is followed. Teachers need to be open-minded and allow their students to learn through an inquiry-based approach. An important criterion for excellence as a science teacher is to expect a lot and facilitate success. No one will continue at something where he or she fails continually.

### What strategies can be employed to teach reading in science?

1. Find a balance between exploration science and book science. Predictive reading and webbing for comprehension are two strategies that will help keep that balance.

2.   Reading in science means defining the problem, looking at the problem thoroughly, then organizing a plan of attack for solving it. Explore all possibilities—wrong, right, and multiple conclusions—so that comprehensive solutions can be reached. Do not be afraid to be inventive and creative. Do not be afraid to revise, update, or totally discard findings with advances in knowledge and technology. Becoming an organized thinker will also improve thinking skills, allowing students to proceed from the problem to the solution faster and more completely.

3.   Teach students to read for objectives.

4.   Read current events for enthusiasm and relativity of science.

5.   Look at lab reports to encourage the reading and synthesizing of information that has been read and observed.

6.   Teach students to be risk takers—to not be afraid to be wrong and to consider more than one answer.

# Reading in Kinesiology or Physical Education

Physical education or kinesiology teachers can enhance their instruction by teaching reading skills. Frequently, teachers in this field feel they have little need for reading material unless they are teaching health. However, they do expect students to read play and rule books and use analytical thinking skills as they watch physical activities.

### Reading Skills in Kinesiology or Physical Education

Developing a technical vocabulary

Locating information

Reading charts, diagrams, play books, and so on

Reading to remember details

Reading to follow directions

Reading for the central thought of a passage

Reading orally

## *How do teachers in physical education or kinesiology think?*

1.   They are able to transfer the procedural knowledge of a skill into the correct action of a skill.

2.   They are able to transform procedural memory of how to perform a skill into a cognitive, visual picture in which students can actually visualize themselves performing the skill correctly.

**3.** They have a developed kinesthetic awareness in which students must be able to judge space in relationship to their bodies.

**4.** They can predict where an opponent is going to move.

**5.** They are able to interpret the purpose of a particular activity or an opposing team (e.g., zone or man-to-man defense).

### What are frequent mistakes in thinking made by students and teachers about physical education?

A common mistake made by many students is they think PE is easy. Some teachers try to teach students to think alike when performing basic skills because they believe there is only one truly correct way to perform each skill in order to achieve the best possible outcomes. There are also environmental factors, such as youth sports programs, which often make a child think he or she is learning many of the basic skills correctly when, in fact, the player is receiving improper instruction from a coach or parent.

### What are the criteria for evaluating performance in physical education?

PE should be graded by using what is known as the Body Component model of assessing skill development. That is, each child is evaluated as he or she performs a specific skill (e.g., running). The skill itself is divided into its component parts, which are further broken down into beginner stage, intermediate stage, and advanced stage. As the child performs the skill, the teacher positions herself or himself appropriately in order to concentrate on each one of the components mentioned above. After the performance test is completed, the teacher adds up the scores from each component and looks the score up on a preassigned chart that determines what percentile the child is in (ranging from 100 to 5 percent). Another 20 percent may be added if the child shows exceptional effort, which allows some consideration for those who simply cannot perform the skill correctly.

### What strategies can be employed to teach reading in kinesiology or physical education?

**1.** Technical vocabulary can be easily taught by playing games like basketball, football, and baseball using word definitions. For example, in order to get to first base in Vocabulary Baseball, the student must be able to give three definitions of *foul*, as used in football, basketball, or baseball.

**2.** Physical education terms can be written down when watching professional games on TV. Class discussion of the terms can follow the viewing of an assigned game.

**3.** Biographies of sports heroes can be assigned to students for reading. Development of comprehension skills is easier when students are familiar with the sports figure.

4. Remedial readers can be given baseball cards or articles from sports magazines, such as *Sports Illustrated,* in order to find words they do not know.

5. PE students can write their own scripts and read them for a local sportscast to be presented over the intercom, before a game, or at a pep rally.

# Summary

Each content area supposedly focuses on a different area of human experience. A student's background information in that subject and the ability to listen, speak, read, and write in a specific subject determines how well meaning is obtained. An educated individual is one who can obtain meaning or read in different subject areas. Such reading is called *multiple literacy* or reading in the content areas. Students do not naturally begin upper-elementary school with such skills. Furthermore, the usual procedure of teaching them to read by using fiction rather than information books does not adequately prepare them to learn from reading in nonfictional content textbooks. The different values, objectives, and interests reflected in the answers of various teachers and prospective teachers in this section should indicate some of the demands placed on students as they read in different content areas.

# Application Exercises and Teaching Activities

## Application Exercises

1. You have a seventh-grade son who just started junior high. His course schedule is as follows: English, Math, PE, Biology, History, Band, and Computers. What different reading skills will he need?

2. Take one of the questions about thinking strategies required in your subject field and agree or disagree with what was written.

3. Make a grid of specific thinking skills required in each subject area. These thinking skills are called *outputs.* Based on your grid, determine which subjects are most alike and which are most alien to each other in thinking objectives.

4. Identify the technical language required for comprehending the reading material in your subject.

5. Give your opinion as to whether schools should educate students toward similar thinking strategies or encourage different thinking strengths.

**6.** What should be the criteria for excellence in your subject field?

**7.** Read the following discription of a junior high developmental reading improvement laboratory. Provide several reasons why 60 percent of U.S. high schools have no such reading programs.

*Student Interview with Mrs. Rolfe*

Mrs. Rolfe teaches classes in developmental reading and reading approvement at Lake Highlands Junior High. Lake Highlands is located in the Richardson Independent School District, which has been known as the pioneer in the reading lab classes of Texas. The program has been in operation for 10 years. Mrs. Rolfe's main problem is lack of space and facilities for her large classes. A solution to this problem is to group the classes according to remedial and advancement reading levels. A screening process could be implemented, which could be done through a series of reading tests. Once the initial classes are formed according to reading levels and reading specialties, each class could have its own grouping program. The groups may be constructed so that three or four daily activities could go on at one time. These activities would rotate daily. With this type of grouping, a large class could be handled easily and fairly efficiently.

This reading class is an elective in the school's curriculum, so most students are in the classes because of their own interests. But there are some students enrolled because of parental pressure and concern to improve their child's reading ability. Problems often arise with these students. The lack of motivation is a problem. These students should first be placed into the receiving and attending matrixes. Second, teachers should become more receptive to the students' needs and try to point out all the advantages to better reading. Hopefully the barriers and fears will be removed, resulting in reading levels advancement.

The labs are well equipped. Mrs. Rolfe utilizes five to six machines in her program. The mechanical reading resources are fantastic but the teacher should not forget the personal side of teaching. The students must see the teacher's personality. Her interest and excitement can flow into her class and be revealed through the progress of her students.

Last, I asked Mrs. Rolfe, "What do you enjoy the most in your reading classes?" She answered, "The results!" She said that about 98 percent of her students advance in their reading levels. But she pointed out that patience is very important. I agree. This virtue needs to be stressed. A little patience and hard work will get results. To see students excel in their reading levels must be a fulfilling moment.

**8.** Develop assignments where the following reading skills could be taught.

**Industrial Arts**

Reading explanations and instructions

Understanding safety rules in shops and factories

Comprehending instructions for the care of tools, equipment, and so on

Reading about current affairs, labor problems, industrial relations, seeing both sides of an issue, and so on

### Homemaking

Reading bills, statements, and so on, accurately

Interpreting charts and graphs

Following directions in recipes and clothes patterns

Understanding instructions for using mechanical appliances

Reading labels

Reading household pages in newspapers and magazines

Reading books on dietetics, fashion, and so on

Critical reading of advertising claims (i.e., understanding how words are chosen for their evocative value to flatter, to entice, and to stimulate buying)

### Commercial Subjects

Reading to follow directions

Developing a technical vocabulary

Locating information

Reading graphs, charts, diagrams, and so on

Reading to remember details

Comprehending sentences and paragraphs

Reading for the central thought of a passage

Reading orally

## Teaching Activities:
## A Scale to Measure Teacher Attitudes toward Teaching Reading in Content Classrooms

Directions: Indicate on the left your feeling toward each of the following items using the following scale:

7 = strongly agree    3 = tend to disagree
6 = agree    2 = disagree
5 = tend to agree    1 = strongly disagree
4 = neutral

___ 1. A content area teacher is obliged to help students improve their reading ability.

___ 2. Technical vocabulary should be introduced to students in content classes before they meet those terms in a reading passage.

___ 3. The primary responsibility of a content teacher should be to impart subject knowledge.

___ 4. Few students can learn all they need to know about how to read in six years of schooling.

___ 5. The sole responsibility for teaching students how to study should be with reading teachers.

___ 6. Knowing how to teach reading in content areas should be required for secondary teaching certification.

___ 7. Only English teachers should be responsible for teaching reading in secondary schools.

___ 8. A teacher who wants to improve students' interest in reading should show them that he or she likes to read.

___ 9. Content teachers should teach content and leave reading instruction to reading teachers.

___ 10. A content area teacher should be responsible for helping students think on an interpretive level as well as on a literal level when they read.

___ 11. Content area teachers should feel a greater responsibility to the content they teach than to any reading instruction they may be able to provide.

___ 12. Content area teachers should help students to learn to set purposes for reading.

___ 13. Every content area teacher should teach students how to read material in his or her content specialty.

___ 14. Reading instruction in secondary schools is a waste of time.

___ 15. Content area teachers should be familiar with theoretical concepts of the reading process.

# Teacher's Classroom Checklist

*Procedures Related to Reading in the Content Areas*

— 1. I know the reading ability of my students from standardized tests or other evaluative materials and/or cumulative records.

— 2. I know the reading level of the textbooks being used.

— 3. The materials used are suited in difficulty to the reading levels of my students.

— 4. Students are sometimes grouped within my classroom for differentiated instruction.

— 5. The course content is broader in scope than a single textbook.

— 6. Adequate reference materials are available.

— 7. Students are taught to use appropriate reference materials.

— 8. An adequate quantity of related informational books and other materials are available for students who read below grade level, at grade level, and above grade level.

— 9. I take advantage of opportunities that may arise to encourage students to read recreational as well as informational materials.

— 10. I encourage students through assignments to read widely in related materials.

— 11. At the beginning of the year, adequate time is taken to introduce the text and to discuss how it may be read effectively.

— 12. I am aware of the special vocabulary and concepts introduced in the various units.

— 13. Adequate time is given to vocabulary and concept development.

— 14. I know the special reading skills involved in my subject.

— 15. I adequately teach the special reading skills in my subject.

— 16. Provisions are made for checking the extent to which vocabulary, concepts, and other skills are learned, and reteaching is done when needed.

— 17. Time is allowed in class for reading pleasurable materials and for the informal sharing of ideas from those materials.

Adapted from Burmeister, 1978.

# CHAPTER TWO

# *Using Textbooks Effectively*

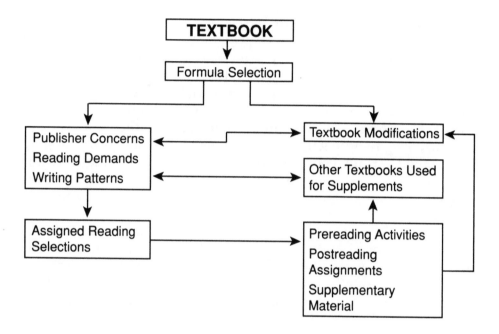

Every teacher in middle, junior, and senior high school has several state-adopted textbooks to select from for instructing in each class. Whether the district has *purchased* all state-adopted textbooks is another matter. In general, however, teachers may go to the book room in the school or district office and select the text that seems most appropriate. The teacher makes selections based on personal values and content emphasis, such as those presented in Chapter One. After experiencing at least four years of instruction in college subject textbooks, most secondary texts seem attractive and simple. What is not readily apparent is that textbooks for the different subjects are as varied from each other as the teachers' values, attitudes, and objectives.

No teacher wants to select a textbook that will sabotage his or her instruction. However, without knowledge of readability formulas and other subjective and objective factors to consider in textbook content, a textbook may make the teacher's job more difficult, rather than easier. In an informal survey of all science books adopted for high school in one state, the author found the range of reading difficulty going from seventh-grade level to graduate college level. And yet, it has been estimated that between 50 to 80 percent of learning in science takes place due to reading the text (Cairns, 1987). In English, no one needs to conduct a readability formula on Shakespeare to know that it is more difficult than the ninth-grade level where it is sometimes a part of the literature curriculum. It would be interesting to learn how many English teachers have found Shakespeare too difficult to read on any level and have dropped it from their curriculum. Textbook reading levels do not necessarily match the reading abilities of the students. In those classes where there is a mismatch, teachers cannot rely on their textbook for help in teaching.

Sometimes the reading difficulties of a textbook are a result of the organization of the content. In spite of the lack of prose, mathematics textbooks must be read. They have four areas that require reading skills: (1) understanding symbols and specialized devices, (2) understanding the general organization of material, (3) developing arithmetic vocabulary, and (4) reading to solve verbal problems. Teachers should also consider in what direction to read a mathematics book—up and down, right to left, or, when solving for an unknown, possibly left to right. Art textbooks also require a visual literacy that does not necessarily follow a left-to-right sequence. As with mathematics books, some art textbooks can be understood without even reading the prose.

And finally, textbooks have influenced the content field itself. Think about social studies textbooks and how they have changed over the years. The curriculum and sequence of courses has remained amazingly uniform, according to the 1982 study of academicians at the Social Science Consortium in Boulder, Colorado. The elementary curriculum has followed Hanna's 1963 proposals, and secondary curriculum has not changed from the pattern of courses recommended by the 1916 NEA Commission on the Reorganization of Secondary Schools. So, while the United States has been in two world wars, fought on three foreign continents, and experienced economic, political, and cultural explosions, social studies content has been maintained in part by conventional textbooks from the major publishing houses (Gross & Dynneson, 1983). Publishers of social studies textbooks have become more pluralistic, global, and considered some ideas that originated with "new social studies," which took place between 1957–1975 and tended to emphasize the role of the social sciences. In contrast, during the same period, social studies educators considered ethnic studies, values education, law-related education, global studies, women's studies, free-enterprise schooling, citizenship education, and career preparation. Clearly, social studies textbooks have been a major factor in defining the content of social studies instruction.

This chapter will help teachers learn how to use their textbook more effectively through answering the following questions:

1. How do you select a textbook and make assignments?
2. How do you select a readability formula?
3. Why don't publishers write texts on levels appropriate for the targeted students?

4. What other reading and writing factors need to be considered in content textbook selection?
5. What can you do if your text is impossible for you and your students?

### *How do you select a textbook and make assignments?*

Discipline problems and poor lessons result from assigning textbook chapters that are too difficult for students to read. Many useful strategies are available for teachers to assist them in using textbooks effectively; readability formulas are one strategy. Using a readability formula is an objective means of deciding how difficult a text is for students. Teachers can then make adjustments in the sequence of instructional material and teaching strategies to aid in student comprehension. There are many types of formulas but most base their assessment on the number of difficult words and the length of sentences. Although these are not the only factors to consider in text difficulty, they are beginning places for teachers to determine whether or not they want to make certain assignments.

## Readability Formulas

It seems natural to assume that if a text has been adopted for a particular grade level, the reading level of that book will be the same as the adoption level. If this were true, then there would be no need for teachers to learn how to use readability formulas to determine the reading level of their basal and content textbooks. Unfortunately, adopted texts are not always written on grade level of reading difficulty. Thus, readability formulas are necessary tools for all teachers. The first step is knowing which chapters may be problem areas. For many reasons, publishers cannot be depended on to develop material that is consistently on grade level in readability and content. If teachers want to make their textbooks a support for their instruction and a resource for learning content skills, they must begin instruction by considering the reading level of their texts, which means using a readability formula.

### *How do you select a readability formula?*

There are over 56 different readability formulas used by educators, government officials, and businesses. In education today, readability formulas are used to match children's reading ability to the difficulty level of classroom books and other reading material. In business, readability formulas are used by manufacturers concerned with safety, product liability, and proper use; by companies and banks concerned with difficulty of their consumer publications; and by companies concerned with advertising effectiveness. Governmental concerns with readability involve "Plain Language Laws" that affect consumer-oriented contracts, federal government publications, military publications, and drivers' license manuals. Readability formulas are also used by publishers of elementary and high school textbooks as well as newspapers (Fry, 1986).

Some of the most popular readability formulas are discussed below.

**Fry Graph.**   This procedure assesses material from grade 1 to college graduate level. It is easy to learn and requires no use of mathematical formulas. The number of words and sentences per 100 words is plotted on a graph containing lines that indicate grade levels. Devised by Edward Fry when he was at Rutgers University Reading Center, the graph provides an approximate grade-level score considered reliable within a year. (See Teaching Activities at the end of this chapter.)

**Flesch Reading Ease Formula.**   Used for material in grades 5–12, the Flesch needs no mathematical skill other than counting syllables and number of words in sentences. The raw score obtained is matched against a reading-ease score that also provides the level of magazine or outside reading material (pulp magazines, comics, etc.) that would be appropriate for that reading score. The formula was first published by Rudolf Flesch in 1943. He was interested in assessing adult reading matter in terms of reading ease and human interest. As a result, the Flesch does not calculate readability for material below fifth grade.

The Powers readability formula is a recalculation of the original Flesch formula. It gives a score in grade levels rather than reading-ease range. The Flesch-Kincaid is a modification of the original Flesch formula for use with Navy-enlisted personnel receiving technical training. The Flesch-Kincaid will calculate reading levels below fourth grade. It has become a military standard to use when assessing technical manuals.

**The McLaughlin SMOG Index.**   This is a popular formula because of its simplicity in application and consistency of results. It counts the number of polysyllabic words in 10 sentences. Knowledge of square roots is necessary.

**The Spache Formula.**   This formula is used with elementary-level reading materials. It uses both a mathematical formula and a list of vocabulary words that must be identified in the passage.

**The Dale-Chall Formula.**   This formula uses an extensive list of 3,000 words known to 80 percent of a sample of fourth-graders. The list is used in conjunction with sentence length and other factors in an equation that yields grade ranges. The list of 3,000 words was developed in the 1940s and is difficult to apply manually. The Holmquist is a recalculation of the Dale-Chall formula. Dale and Chall have recently updated their formula and the list of 3,000 words.

Teachers select a readability formula according to the level they are teaching and their need for exacting data. For example, if a teacher thinks the elementary text should have little variability of range, she or he would want an exacting formula such as the Spache or Dale-Chall to give a more precise evaluation of reading level. If the teacher is trying to select some supplementary material that might have a wide range, the SMOG, Fry, or Flesch would be good choices. And finally, one might want to refigure publisher data using the same formula as the publisher used. Grade level, type of material, and ease of use are factors that should be considered when selecting a readability formula.

# Publisher Considerations of Textbooks

*Why don't publishers write texts on levels appropriate for the targeted students?*

Textbook adoption committees are composed of faculty members who are considering the content of textbooks. Publishers state the reading level, but many factors can contribute to a book having one chapter written on third-grade level, another on sixth-grade level, and yet another on eighth-grade level. When the three paragraphs are averaged, the average may turn out to be on the appropriate level. Furthermore, publishers can select formulas that show their math, science, or history textbooks to be on the appropriate grade level. For example, the following ratings were conducted on two passages using different readability formulas (Noe & Standal, 1984):

| Readability Formula | Assessed Reading Level |
|---|---|
| *Passage One* | |
| Estimated Dale | 3.7 |
| Flesch | 6.3 |
| FOG Index | 6.3 |
| SMOG | 6.0 |
| *Passage Two* | |
| FOG Index | 13.5 |
| SMOG | 10.1 |

The publishing company that wanted its books adopted on the fourth-grade level would most certainly use the Estimated Dale formula for assessing reading difficulty and the resulting reading level.

Occasionally, textbook publishers have not been accurate with their use of readability formulas. When the Fry readability formula was used to determine the readability levels of 12 first- and second-grade basal texts, 4 of the 12 books tested did not correspond closely to the publisher's stated readability levels. Only one basal series showed an exact correspondence between the publisher's data and the Fry readability formula data (Langan, 1980). Samples from 20 selected reading materials for second-grade reading adolescents were checked using the Spache readability formula and the Fry readability formula. Results using the Spache formula corresponded to the publisher's stated readability levels, with no significant variability within books. But the results from the Fry formula were inconsistent with the publisher's stated readability levels. Since the Fry graph is not as rigorous at the lower-elementary and upper-secondary levels as in the middle, the results of this study could be a product of using the wrong formula for the material. A second factor was that there was intrabook variability, which wasn't identified in the passages selected by the publisher (Hilgendorf, 1980). In another study, fourth-, fifth-, and sixth-grade basals were analyzed using the Fry readability graph. The majority of the basals investigated had an average readability level commensurate with the publisher's recommended grade level, but there were widespread variabilities in reading levels within each basal text (Sloan, 1980). Research indicates the need for teachers to be concerned about textbook variabilities and to be aware of publishers' marketing interests.

## Textbook Reading Considerations

Not only is it to the publishers' advantage to selectively report readability data for marketing purposes but the publisher does not have a perfect instrument in many of the readability formulas. Four readability formulas (Dale-Chall, Gunning FOG, Flesch, and McLaughlin SMOG) were analyzed to determine the reading grade equivalence of middle and secondary school and two formulas were evaluated for primary grade materials. The following problems emerged:

1. The formulas ignored much of the current knowledge and theoretical bases of the reading process.
2. The formulas rest on a shaky statistical base.
3. There is considerable variation in grade-level designation for the reading selections. (Olson, 1984)

Knowledge of these potential problems with publishing companies and the formulas themselves should make the teacher wary of placing complete confidence in readability formulas or publisher-identified reading levels (O'Hear & Ramsey, 1990).

Another critical factor in assessing reading difficulty for one text is that the variability in textbook readability differs within the books and basals, as demonstrated by the following books evaluated using the Fry readability formula. Passages 1, 2, and 3 are taken from the beginning, middle, and end of the book.

Early, Canfield, Karlin, & Schottman (1979). *Moving Forward, Skills Reader.* New York: Harcourt Brace and Jovanovich. (6th-grade text)

| Selection Area | Sentences | Syllables | Readability |
|---|---|---|---|
| Passage 1 | 7.2 sentences | 147 syllables | 7th grade |
| Passage 2 | 8.2 sentences | 148 syllables | 7th grade |
| Passage 3 | 11.9 sentences | 132 syllables | 4th grade |
| Average | | | 6th grade |

Loftin, R. (1988). *Our Country's Communities.* Morristown, NJ: Silver Burdett & Ginn. (3rd-grade text)

| Selection Area | Sentences | Syllables | Readability |
|---|---|---|---|
| Passage 1 | 8.3 sentences | 151 syllables | 7th grade |
| Passage 2 | 6.1 sentences | 156 syllables | 9th grade |
| Passage 3 | 7.9 sentences | 149 syllables | 7th grade |
| Average | | | 8th grade |

Wright, D. F., & New, B. (1978). *Introductory Algebra.* Boston: Prindle, Weber & Schmidt. (used in grades 7–10)

| Selection Area | Sentences | Syllables | Readability |
|---|---|---|---|
| Passage 1 | 4.9 sentences | 121 syllables | 6th/7th |
| Passage 2 | 4.7 sentences | 148 syllables | 9th grade |
| Passage 3 | 4.8 sentences | 24 syllables | 7th grade |
| Average | | | 8th grade |

The obvious conclusion from the formula application data and research is that teacher judgments must be a component in assessing reading difficulties of passages. The reading-level scores are no more helpful than are scores from reading tests; in both cases, interpretation of particular conditions is required (Chall, 1981). Teacher judgments must consider the use of general and technical vocabulary and student familiarity with the words. For example, the passages in the third-grade social studies text cited above contained many multisyllable proper nouns of Mexico and United States, which raised the readability level; but most third-graders were familiar with the words.

## Textbook Writing Considerations

Sometimes stated readability may be higher than the comprehension level because of the nature of the textual organization. For example, mathematics texts might be easier to understand because terms are supported by examples, context, and progressive sequence. On the other hand, technical vocabulary in science textbooks might be clearly demonstrated but the concept density is so great that the reader must understand each word in order to comprehend the content. Comprehension is also influenced by the simplification of difficult concepts to the point that the ideas are not clearly presented even though the readability level is low (Crandall, 1990). In simplified science books, the simple vocabulary encourages students to read assignments quickly. Because it is not challenging to decode the language, students do not concentrate on the concepts behind the words (Knight, 1989). Sometimes, the concepts are simplified to the point that comprehension is difficult. The following passage from a sixth-grade social studies text demonstrates how easy readability is sometimes damaging to meaning.

> Most Muslim countries claim that Israelis are foreigners on Arab land. They believe the Palestinian Arabs should have their own country. The Muslim countries also want Israel to give back the land won in wars with Arab countries. In 1979, Israel gave back some territory it won but it is unwilling to give back the fertile West Bank of the Jordan River. Many Jewish settlers have moved into this area.
>
> Meanwhile, the Palestinian Arabs are widely scattered. The majority live in refugee camps or work in cities of Jordan and Lebanon. Some have formed armed groups which hope to drive Israel out of the Middle East. (Drummond & Kraig, 1988, p. 415)

A brief sequencing of the concepts in these two paragraphs can show how logically confusing this material would be to sixth-graders. Israelis are foreigners in a Muslim Arab land. Israelis, the foreigners, don't want to give back their land. Palestinians, who are all Arabs, are scattered, live in refugee camps, work in different countries, and are terrorists. In order to make the material comprehensible, the teacher may have to provide contextual information about the influence of colonialism, the Arab/Israeli wars of 1956, 1967, and 1973, the conflict in the West Bank, and the location of the region of Palestine.

Finally, the writing style of a textbook can be very difficult for students. Those who learned to read from basals are familiar with what is called *narrative* or *story organizational patterns*. When they encounter expository writing, they frequently approach it with narrative comprehensional patterns. The elementary or content teacher needs to help students develop a different framework for approaching nonfiction. Narrative and expository differences are summarized in Table 2–1.

The expository writing of most content textbooks explains some of the reading skills necessary for reading specific content fields. Generally, the following organizational patterns are found in the expository writing of content textbooks: cause and effect, explanation, chronological, classification, demonstration, problem/solution, and spatial organization. These are not organizational patterns used in narrative or story writing found frequently in beginning reading books called *basals*. The basals use fiction with a carefully sequenced introduction of reading skill instruction and vocabulary in a controlled sequence of books. First, the student starts reading in a preprimer book and then moves through all the books in the reading series in a

**Table 2–1**  *Narrative and Expository Differences*

| Narrative | Expository |
|---|---|
| 1. Tells story with plot, theme | 1. Provides information |
| 2. Description provides context for frequent vocabulary replay | 2. Repeats specialized and technical vocabulary more frequently |
| 3. Character identification of motives and empathy | 3. Conceptual organization of subject matter |
| 4. Holds attention by plot description | 4. Holds attention by content presentation and format |
| 5. Refers to reader's background | 5. Has unfamiliar abstract concepts presented concisely |
| 6. Descriptive writing | 6. Factual writing |
| 7. Aims to entertain | 7. Aims to inform |
| 8. Can be quickly read | 8. Must vary reading rate |

*Source:* Adapted from Roe, Stodt, and Burns, 1987, pp. 205–206.

page-by-page progression. That progression is lost when the student leaves the basal readers and reads content textbooks.

A second reading problem in the content textbooks is learning to integrate material from maps, graphs, charts, and pictures with written prose. These features are frequently most important in science books but are often overlooked by students. They generally make things clear and they always contain essential information on a topic (Livingston, 1989). In mathematics, art, and music textbooks, students also need to understand special symbols, signs, formulas, and specialized technical vocabulary.

Other problems in reading may result from an author's writing style that uses abstractions to the point of confusion, material that is poorly organized, and content that is not interesting. The best way to determine interest is to ask the students if they like their textbook. Another option is to use the checklist in the Teaching Activities section at the end of this chapter to examine other readability factors that are not accounted for in formulas.

Despite all of these considerations, readability formulas give teachers reasonable but not absolute security that the reading assignments they make are on a student's reading level. Because they can be a useful tool, applying readability formulas to the textbook should be the first activity of the student teacher or content teacher. Once the appropriate formula has been selected for the supposed grade level of the textbook, teachers then select at least three passages of approximately 100 words from different chapters in the book. Each of the formulas uses a different application procedure. Some use graphs (Fry, Raygor), others use mathematical formulas (SMOG, FOG), and others use combinations of word lists and computation procedures (Dale-Chall, Spache). The selection of a formula is usually made because it is easy to use, readily available, or addresses the possible reading range of the textbook. Some schools have purchased a readability check on computer disk. In this case, teachers may assess readability without having to compute by hand. Teacher judgment, however, still needs to be a part of the equation. Content teachers should select formulas that give the most consistent results when combined with their own judgment. After the reading levels are found, teachers begin to know how to sequence their content and textbook assignments. However, if the textbook is impossible for the students to read, there are strategies that the teacher can adopt.

### What can a content teacher do with an impossible book?

When the author returned to the public school classroom after teaching in a university for 10 years, the textbooks she was given promised to be her major problem. A class of honors seniors could not read the textbook assigned. The same series had an easier textbook but that was assigned to the "regular" senior classes. The honors sophomores had only enough books for half of the class to have "honors" books and other half to have "regular" books. Although the covers of the sophomore books were the same, the activities were quite different. And finally, the regular sophomore classes were actually remedial classes with average reading levels of seventh grade, with some students reading as low as second- and third-grade levels. One third of each "regular" class were special education students with learning disabilities or emotional disturbances who had been mainstreamed into the regular classes. At any one time, the author had more special

*"With a few little refinements he's got in mind,*
*he says it could well be the car of the future."*

education students in her regular classes than the two special education teachers had together in their class. In short, the textbooks for the regular classes were impossible for most students to read. To make the situation worse, none of the textbooks had teacher's manuals. Student teachers, new teachers, and experienced new teachers had no support from the adopted textbooks or hope of purchasing others, as the school was due to have a new adoption next year. The following list of survival approaches for teachers to use when their textbooks are impossible or missing was compiled by the author, by experienced new teachers, and by student teachers at this hopefully not typical school.

### How to Live with a Poor Textbook

**1.**   Go to other faculty members to see if they have old textbooks or teacher's manuals in their rooms. Although they may not exactly match the adopted textbook, the activities in them might be duplicated or modified for your classes.

**2.**   Ask the department head to unlock the cabinets in the department office to examine films, videos, and other media that the department might have to supplement the textbooks.

**3.**   Go to the local federally funded educational service center and ask for kits, media, and support from their resource persons.

**4.**   Contact friends in other schools to see if they have someone teaching the same class you are teaching. Ask if they can send you some material to help you survive.

**5.**   Go to the local post office and ask for donations of tradebooks, weekly readers, newspapers, and journals that are written on a variety of reading levels. To determine frustrational level in these materials, use the "fist-full" technique. Have the student read a 100-word selection from the material. Count on both hands the number of words the student is unable to read. A fist-full (or 10 words) means that the material is on the student's frustrational level and should not be used.

**6.**   Use prereading activities to clarify new concepts, form relationships to what students are already familiar with, and introduce new vocabulary. (DRA, DRTA, semantic mapping, scaffolding, and story structuring are described in Chapters Five and Six.)

**7.**   State purposes for reading. Vary the purpose with different levels. Discuss all purposes in the whole group. Write purposes so that students can refer to them as they read.

**8.**   Control the amount of material to be read and the number of questions to be answered.

**9.**   Match assignments to text organization. Give specific page numbers, subheadings, or paragraph numbers for locating information.

**10.** Help students determine which thinking/comprehension strategy to use in answering a question.

**11.** Encourage student questions and predictions before and during reading.

**12.** Read the chapter aloud with students. Give them their reading assignments the day before so they can practice.

**13.** Assign pairs of students to read the assignment together. Make sure each pair has an adequate reader in it if possible.

**14.** Develop outlines of chapters or units to give overviews of key concepts and facts.

**15.** Use multiple senses as support for textbook information. Use overhead projectors, TV, videos, movies, demonstrations, laboratories, writing, speeches, and drama to deliver information.

**16.** Vary the amount of time needed to complete work, and consider that the length of time needs to be doubled for slower readers.

**17.** Do not abandon the book entirely. Even students who cannot read the book at all like to carry it around so that they are not identified as remedial.

**18.** Gather all the textbooks in your content area that you can find. Let the students select their own textbook.

## Summary

Selecting appropriate textbooks can be done before classroom instruction starts. Having the best textbook possible is part of improving the interaction among content, student, and teacher. Specific content experts have written numerous articles on strategies to make textbooks more interesting. At this point, we have attempted to look only at structural and language difficulties that contribute to student boredom and teacher frustration.

The purpose of a readability formula is to make teachers aware that their textbooks are not always (or even frequently) written appropriately for the grade level they are teaching. Whereas basal readers used in elementary school place more emphasis on appropriate reading level, secondary texts suffer more from publishers' interest in marketability, making it to their advantage to average readability assessments and, in some cases, disguise reading range variability. Furthermore, students who learn to read by reading stories in basal readers or whole language literature programs know how to comprehend narrative story organization patterns but not nonfiction content textbook organizational patterns. It then becomes important for both elementary and content area teachers to use questionnaires, familiarity with concepts and terms, and concept density and clarity to assess their textbooks and supplementary material. In other words, discern how "user friendly" the text is for both the teacher and the students. And finally, teachers should use their own judgment regarding the difficulty of the organization, vocabulary, and writing style. The readability assessment at least allows teachers to determine whether their students will find the material they are assigning within students' reading competency range. Teachers have many formulas to use and some have been put on computer programs. If this is the case, teachers need only type in paragraphs from various parts of the text and the program will test readability for them.

Inconsistency of reading level within books and between formulas can be expected. The reasons for some of these factors are related to the formulas themselves, content organization, writing style, and appropriate selection of formulas. Nevertheless, readability formulas are useful for matching reading material difficulty with student reading level, or at least being aware that such a mismatch could result in discipline and motivational problems in the classroom. When the available textbooks are the only choices, there are strategies for survival.

## Application Exercises and Teaching Activities

### Application Exercises

**1.** Assess the reading levels of the following sample textbook passages taken from basal readers and content textbooks. See if your answers agree with those of your classmates.

**2.** Discuss writing style factors that might make the sample textbook passages easy or difficult for students to read and comprehend.

**3.** Identify technical vocabulary in the sample passages that might contribute to comprehension difficulties.

**4.** What organization patterns do the sample textbook passages use?

**5.** Which of the sample textbooks would you select for your class?

**6.** Get some old and new textbooks in your subject area. What statements can you make about the changes in textbooks in the last 20 years in your subject field?

**7.** Ms. Leach is a first-year teacher who is expected to use a science book with sections that are three years beyond grade level of the students. What can she do to alter the sections that are too difficult?

**8.** Mr. Harmon is a seventh-grade history teacher whose students read independently on the following levels:

grade 2 (1 student)      grade  8 (2 students)
grade 3 (2 students)     grade  9 (3 students)
grade 4 (4 students)     grade 10 (2 students)
grade 5 (2 students)     grade 11 (1 student)
grade 6 (4 students)     grade 12 (1 student)
grade 7 (3 students)

His textbook averages on the seventh-grade level. How can he group them for reading instruction?

**9.** Using the student reading levels in #8, what behavior could you expect from students when the teacher assigns a text chapter to be read during class period?

**10.** What does the Textbook Readability Checklist at the end of this chapter show you about the reading difficulties of an adopted content book in your area?

**11.** What advice could teacher textbook selection committees give to publishers to help them address readability problems in their textbooks?

## Sample Textbook Passages

*Mathematics*

Franklin, D. (1978). *Introductory Algebra*. Boston: Prindle, Weber & Schmidt. (Adoption level: 9th or 10th grade)

*Passage 1, p. 205:*

First-degree equations were discussed in Section 2.6 and used to solve problems in Sections 2.7 and 6.6. Equations are first degree when they can be written in the formula $ax + b = c$, where $x$ is a variable, and $a$, $b$, and $c$ are known constants, and $a = 0$. Both sides of the equation contain only the sums and differences of first-degree polynomials in one variable, or one side contains constants and the other contains sums and differences of first-degree polynomials in one variable. As a review, the equation $3x + 14 = x + 1$) is solved here.

There is only one number in the solution set because the equation is first degree in the variable $x$. There can be at most one solution to a first-degree equation in one variable. This statement can be proved by the method of contradiction and is not given here.

Equations discussed in Chapter 8 will have more than one solution, and inequalities discussed in the next section of this chapter will have an infinite number of solutions. The following are examples of equations with more or less than one solution. Unless otherwise stated, the replacement set for all variables in this chapter will be Q, the set of rational numbers.

*Passage 2, p. 12:*

On a horizontal number line, smaller numbers are always to the left of larger numbers. Thus, 5 is less than 8, 0 is less than 3, $-2$ is less than 1, and $-7$ is less than $-4$. The symbol $<$ is read "less than," and we write $5 < 8$, $0 < 3$, $-2 < 1$, and $-7 < -4$. We can also use the symbol $>$, read "greater than," and write $8 > 5$, $3 > 0$, $1 > -2$, and $-4 > 7$. Each number is smaller than any number to its right and larger than any number to its left.

For the set $A = \{x,y,z,\}$, we have $x$ for $A$. For the set $B = \{-1,0,1,2\}$, do we have $X$ for $B$? The answer is no. In algebra, however, we do write $X = \{-1,0,1,2\}$ not to mean that the symbol $x$ is an element of the set, but to mean that $x$ can represent any element of the set. When a symbol is used this way, it is called a variable.

## Literature

*Discoveries in Literature* (1989). Glenview IL: Scott, Foresman. (Adoption level: 9th grade)

*Passage 1:*

Year in and year out she had spent the summer evenings like this on the dike. The first time she was seventeen and a bride, and her husband had shouted to her to come out of the house and up the dike, and she had come, blushing and twisting her hands together, to hide among the women while the men roared at her and made jokes about her. All the same, they had liked her. "A pretty piece of meat in your bowl," they had said to her husband. "Feet a trifle big," he had answered depreciatingly. But she could see he was pleased, and so gradually her shyness went away.

*Passage 2:*

You could almost hate Rollie Tremain. In the first place, he was the only son of Auguste Tremaine, who operated the Uptown Dry Goods Store, and he did not live in a tenement but in a big white birthday cake of a house on Laurel Street. He was too fat to be effective in the football games between the Frenchtown Tigers and the North Side Knights, and he made us constantly aware of the jingle of coins in his pockets. He was able to stroll into Lemire's and casually select a quarter's worth of cowboy cards while the rest of us watched, aching with envy.

## Science

Bishop, Sutherland, & Lewis (1981). *Focus on Earth Science.* Columbus, OH: Merrill. (Adoption level: 8th grade)

*Passage 1, page 43:*

Earth is the third planet outward from the sun. Its origin has been debated for a long time. Many questions still are unanswered. Probably the most widely accepted theory for the origin of the solar system is the dust cloud theory. According to this idea, a dust cloud began to rotate. Movement grew faster and faster until the dust and gas flattened into a disk-shaped cloud which separated into eddies. These eddies were similar to the ones seen in swiftly moving water. At the center of the cloud, the largest eddy formed the sun. In the smaller eddies, grains became the rings around the planets.

*Passage 2, p. 288:*

Most of what we know about the interior of the earth comes from studies of earthquakes. The trembling of the earth that we call an earthquake accompanies a sudden break or movement of rocks somewhere below the surface. We may feel these tremblings, or vibrations, only near the earthquake. Instruments called seismographs can record the trembling from the opposite side of the earth. Seismographs measure the speed of Earth waves that travel outward from the fault. Seismograph records are clues to the density and physical states of materials within the earth. Most earthquakes occur along well known belts of activity.

*Passage 3, p. 513:*

Space stations in orbit need a craft to transport astronauts to and from the station, carry supplies to the station and bring products back to Earth. The space shuttle is the craft designed and built for this use. The shuttle system has four major elements. These are the orbiter, its liquid fuel rocket engines, an external liquid fuel tank and two solid fuel rocket booster engines. When launched, all four elements are joined. All engines are fired at once, sending the shuttle to an altitude of 40 kilometers in about two minutes. Then the solid fuel rockets will drop off.

*Music*

*World of Music* (1988). Morristown, NJ: Silver, Burdett and Ginn. (Adoption level: 8th grade)

*Passage 1, p. 52:*

"I'm an individual, and I'm going to do my own thing."
"I need to express myself in my own way and for myself alone."
"When I compose, I want to use more instruments and write for the largest orchestra ever!"
"The piano is my instrument of choice. I'll write piano music of technical brilliance."
These are not the sentiments of young twentieth-century composers. These were the sentiments of composers who lived in the nineteenth century, a period we know as the Romantic period. The composers in the Romantic period were interested in expanding the whole musical vocabulary. Harmony became thick with notes, and dissonance began to play a more expressive part. Long melodies were written to provoke a strong emotional response.

*Passage 2, p. 37:*

Many feel that Shostakovich, a Soviet composer, is perhaps the finest symphony composer of the mid-twentieth century. His fifteen symphonies show not only a great deal of depth, but a struggle to be fresh and original without overstepping the bounds laid down by the government for a Soviet composer. The Soviet government insists that composers write within the style of "socialist realism," a style that demands folk or folk-like elements, little dissonance, straight-forward rhythms, simple harmonies, a patriotic element and so forth.

*Passage 3, p. 163:*

Igor Stravinsky's colorful ballet tells the story of an old Russian folk tale. Prince Ivan, lost in a forest, finds a marvelous bird with flaming red feathers. He captures her, then, seeing that she is frightened, releases her. In gratitude the firebird gives the prince one of her feathers to protect him against evil, and she pledges her help should she ever be in trouble. Ivan meets a princess who, with her twelve sisters, is held prisoner by the evil King Katschei (Kaht'shay) Katschei tries to cast a spell on Ivan, but Ivan overcomes the wicked sorcerer with his firebird feather. The firebird appears and, placing Katschei in a trance, tells Ivan that Katschei's power lies in a monstrous egg, which she reveals to Ivan. The egg is broken, Katschei perishes, the princess and all of Katschei's prisoners are freed. Ivan and his princess are married in a sumptuous finale. The finale begins with a simple melodic phrase played slowly and quietly.

## Computer Science

Boillot, M. (1984). *BASIC Concepts and Structured Problem Solving.* St. Paul: West Publishing. (Adoption level: 11th and 12th grades)

*Passage 1, p. 18:*

To many users, the operating system (OS) is more important than the particular chip their computer uses. It is the operating system that gives a computer its personality. The operating system takes care of the internal housekeeping of the computer (saving, copying, editing files, etc.); it also allows the user to interact with various software such as application programs, computer games, word processing systems, and languages, all of which are dependent in one way or another on the particulary operating system used.

Most computer manufacturers sell their computers with their own operating systems and with their own assortment of operating system-dependent software. For example, Radio Shack has its own TRS Disk Operating System (TRS-DOS) and myriads of business, educational, and text processing programs. Apple uses DOS or SOS operating systems. Atari uses Atari OS. There are, however, software companies that specialize in designing extremely "user-friendly" operating systems that can be used on different types of computers. One well-known company, Microsoft, develops operating systems MS/DOS and a related library of programs that can be used on 16 bit machines such as IBM PC, WANG, NEC and DEC computers. Another equally well-known company, Digital Research, has been very successful with its CP/M operating systems and related software, which have been used by thousands of small business computing systems over the last decade. This CP/M software, due to sharp price reductions, has filtered through to home computer owners and can be used on such machines as the TRS-80, the Commodore 64, and the Xerox and others.

# Teaching Activities:
# Recognize Text Cues

**Definition:** Showing students how to make use of within-the-text features such as illustrations, graphics, headings and other devices.

**Background:** Many students do not use the features in their textbooks which are designed to help them comprehend what they read. Often, students have no real strategies for reading informational text other than simply rereading difficult sections of a chapter. Even good readers may not realize that they can do things prior to reading to enhance their comprehension and learning from a text.

**Strategy:** Generally known as *Previewing,* this strategy is based on work of Aukerman (1972) and Robinson (1961). Robinson is the author of the famous SQ3R method of study, and Aukerman outlined a six-step procedure to guide students through the first step of SQ3R (the Survey step).

Steps in Previewing:
1.) Analysis of chapter title
2.) Analysis of subtitles
3.) Analysis of visuals
4.) Introductory paragraph(s)
5.) Concluding paragraph(s)
6.) Deriving the main idea

**Advantages:** Previewing helps students establish a structure for reading. It can be thought of as building a "tree": putting down roots and establishing the trunk and branches. Later, during their actual reading of the chapter, students will be putting leaves on the basic tree structure. It is important to demonstrate this strategy and model it several times before students can do it independently.

*Source:* Aukerman, R. C. (1972). *Reading in the secondary school classroom.* New York: McGraw-Hill. Reproduced with permission of McGraw Hill, Inc.

# Textbook Readability Checklist

This checklist is designed to help you evaluate the readability of your classroom texts. It can be best used if you rate your text while you are thinking of a specific class. Be sure to compare the textbook to a fictional ideal rather than another text. Your goal is to find out what aspects of the text are or are not less than ideal. Finally, consider supplementary workbooks as part of the textbook and rate them together. Have fun!

Rate the questions below using the following rating system:
5—Excellent
4—Good
3—Adequate
2—Poor
1—Unacceptable
NA—Not Applicable

Further comments may be written in the space provided.
Textbook title: _____
Publisher: _____
Copyright date: _____

## Understandability

— A. Are the assumptions about students' vocabulary knowledge appropriate?

— B. Are the assumptions about students' prior knowledge of this content area appropriate?

— C. Are the assumptions about students' general experiential backgrounds appropriate?

— D. Does the teacher's manual provide the teacher with ways to develop and review the students' conceptual and experiential backgrounds?

— E. Are new concepts explicitly linked to the students' prior knowledge or to their experiential backgrounds?

— F. Does the text introduce abstract concepts by accompanying them with many concrete examples?

— G. Does the text introduce new concepts one at a time with a sufficient number of examples for each one?

— H. Are definitions understandable and at a lower level of abstraction than the concept being defined?

— I. Is the level of sentence complexity appropriate for the students?

— J. Are the main ideas of paragraphs, chapters, and subsections clearly stated?

— K. Does the text avoid irrelevant details?

— L. Does the text explicitly state important complex relationships (e.g., causality, conditionality, etc.) rather than always expecting the reader to infer them from the context?

_\_\_ M. Does the teacher's manual provide lists of accessible resources containing alternative readings for the very poor or very advanced readers?

## Learnability

*Organization*

_\_\_ A. Is an introduction provided for each chapter?
_\_\_ B. Is there a clear and simple organizational pattern relating the chapters to each other?
_\_\_ C. Does each chapter have a clear, explicit, and simple organizational structure?
_\_\_ D. Does the text include resources such as index, glossary, and table of contents?
_\_\_ E. Do questions and activities draw attention to the organizational pattern of the material (e.g., chronological, cause and effect, spacial, topical, etc.)?
_\_\_ F. Do consumable materials interrelate well with the textbook?

*Reinforcement*

_\_\_ A. Does the text provide opportunities for students to practice using new concepts?
_\_\_ B. Are there summaries at appropriate intervals in the text?
_\_\_ C. Does the text provide adequate iconic aids such as maps, graphs, illustrations, etc., to reinforce concepts?
_\_\_ D. Are there adequate suggestions for usable supplementary activities?
_\_\_ E. Do these activities provide for a broad range of ability levels?
_\_\_ F. Are there literal recall questions provided for the students' self-review?
_\_\_ G. Do some of the questions encourage the students to draw inferences?
_\_\_ H. Are there discussion questions which encourage creative thinking?
_\_\_ I. Are questions clearly worded?

*Motivation*

_\_\_ A. Does the teacher's manual provide introductory activities that will capture students' interest?
_\_\_ B. Are chapter titles and subheadings concrete, meaningful, or interesting?
_\_\_ C. Is the writing style of the text appealing to the students?
_\_\_ D. Are the activities motivating? Will they make the student want to pursue the topic further?
_\_\_ E. Does the book clearly show how the knowledge being learned might be used by the learner in the future?
_\_\_ F. Are the cover, format, print size, and pictures appealing to the students?

___ G.  Does the text provide positive and motivating models for both sexes as well as for other racial, ethnic, and socio-economic groups?

## Readability Analysis

*Weaknesses*

1.  On which items was the book rated the lowest?
2.  Did these items tend to fall in certain categories?
3.  Summarize the weaknesses of this text.
4.  What can you do in class to compensate for the weaknesses of this text?

*Assets*

1.  On which items was the book rated the highest?
2.  Did these items fall in certain categories?
3.  Summarize the assets of this text.
4.  What can you do in class to take advantage of the assets of this text?

# Graph for Estimating Readibility

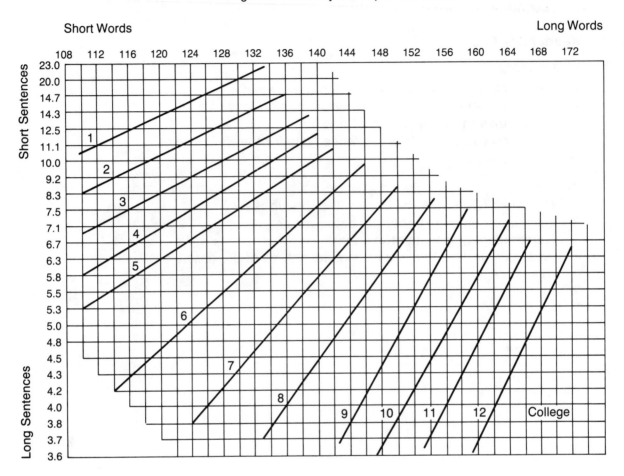

Average Number of Syllables per 100 Words

Randomly select three 100-word passages from a book or article. Plot the average number of syllables and the average number of sentences per 100 words on the graph to determine the grade level of the material. Choose more passages per book if greater variability is observed, and conclude that the book has uneven readability. Few books will fall in the gray area, but when they do, grade-level scores are invalid.

*Source:* Edward Fry, Burgess University Reading Center, New Brunswick, NJ.

# CHAPTER THREE

# *Testing*

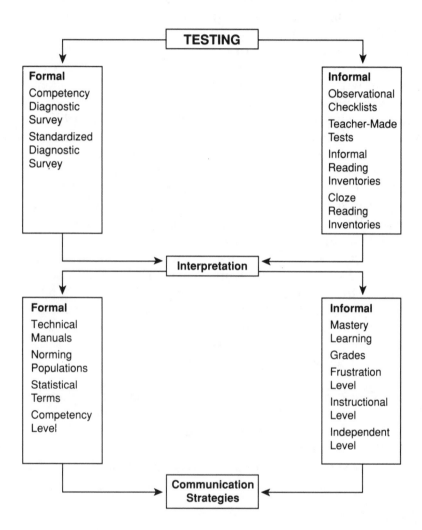

Testing and the resulting scores can become the basis for elitist education. Those with the highest scores generally go to the best schools and colleges, receive the most honors, and are placed in talented and gifted programs. For school administrators, test scores demonstrate the comparative excellence of their school and provide data support for budgetary items. For teachers, test scores can either be the basis of instruction or be ignored. But for students, test scores are always important, regardless of whether they are accurate or not.

Unlike most secondary content courses, instruction in remedial and regular reading classes begins with a test. The test may be found in the reading series textbook, in the reading resource room, in central administration offices where standardized tests are dispersed, or ordered from a test publisher.

Depending on the importance of the test to the school administrators, teachers may find themselves teaching to the test. Or they may find their teaching interrupted by frequent testing. Regardless of new assessment models used in Michigan, Illinois, or Vermont, most content and reading teachers are linked to skill-based testing. Reading educators such as Valencia and Pearson (1987; Pearson, 1985) advocate portfolio assessment of reading, but if most content teachers looked at a remedial reader's records, they would find test score documentation with the recommended portfolio assessments kept informally in the remedial reading teacher's mind.

Reading educators like Thelen (1990) and Pearson (1985) feel that reading tests must reflect advances in the understanding of the reading process. They find that instructional decisions are too often made from assessments and tests that define reading as a sequence of discrete skills that students must master to become readers. Testing reading as an interactive process is not as easily accomplished.

Hopefully, there are no great discrepancies between how reading is tested and taught. But with testing so much in control of instructional and administrative decisions, discrepancies may not be as infrequent as reading educators would want. When instructional decisions are made based on inappropriate testing, excellent reading programs can be misinterpreted. Testing is an important measure of student growth in reading. When either the test and/or the interpretation of the test results are inappropriate, students suffer.

This chapter will answer the following questions:

1. What types of tests are available to content teachers?
2. How do I write better informal reading tests?
3. How do I select a standardized test for my class?
4. What do I interpret test results?
5. How should I communicate test results to my students?

## Tests and Measurement

*What types of tests are available to content teachers?*

There are two types of tests used to measure reading growth: formal tests (which are competency, standardized, diagnostic, and survey) and informal tests (which are teacher-made tests, observation checklists, informal reading inventories, and cloze tests). The differences between the two major categories are the construction of the test and information obtained from the scores.

Informal tests are written by teachers and constructed by using information that the teacher thinks is important. If he or she takes the test from the teacher's manual, the test is still informal because it has not been developed in any other manner than the composition of questions that the author of the text, rather than the teacher, thought important to check reading mastery of the textbook. Informal tests are developed by the teacher to measure knowledge presented in the classroom, and most are called achievement tests. Informal tests developed by the teacher to measure reading are called Informal Reading Tests (IRI) or cloze tests. Observation checklists can examine either mastery of facts or reading skills such as identifying main ideas.

Formal standardized tests are published by an agency outside the school system. The tests are developed by individuals hired to construct items that will measure ability in areas considered nationally important. Once the test is developed, it is administered to random samples of students of appropriate ages in different geographic areas and in different types of educational institutions. The responses from this procedure, called *norming,* are then used to determine the score information and technical data available when the test is administered. The administration of formal tests is decided on a regional or statewide basis. For example, first-graders in one town are tested at the beginning of the school year on the test taken from the front of their basal reader (informal). They are then tested by the reading specialist using an IRI (informal). At the end of the year, they are given a statewide test, such as the California Test of Basic Skills (standardized).

Formal tests can be made for different purposes—to measure content understanding in a large area (survey) or to measure skill deficiency (diagnostic). The Nelson Denny Adult Reading Test is an example of a survey test. The Nelson Denny measures comprehension, vocabulary, and speed of reading. In contrast, the Botel Phonics Mastery Test only measures ability in phonics. When a student is finished with that test, the teacher has a diagnosis that tells where to begin with instruction in skill-deficit areas of phonics such as blends.

Another type of formal testing is called *competency testing.* Important skill areas are identified, then the student is required to pass the test with a score that surpasses the competency level established before the test. For example, if the skill area is word recognition and the competency level is 80 percent, the student must get more than 80 percent of the answers correct in order to demonstrate mastery in that area. However, if the same student transfers to another school and takes the test where the competency level is set at 75 percent, he or she would not have to do as well to demonstrate mastery. Mastery levels can be moved up and down in order to make programs and schools look effective. The following excerpt taken from a newspaper article discusses the results from the statewide administration of a competency test and demonstrates administrators attempting to maintain the image of the school district.

"Since the 1985–86 school year, we have seen steady progress here as well as in the state," said Larry Lusby, executive director of computer and special services. "Our teachers have made a lot of effort to improve those scores.

"For example, the number of third-graders passing all three sections—math, reading and writing—went from 48 percent in 1986 to 75 percent in 1988, then fell to 68 percent this year. Improvements generally parallel statewide performance. For example, the percentage of third-graders statewide who mastered all three tests went from 52 percent in 1986 to 74 percent this year."

Superintendent Joe Baressi said improvements are in spite of progressively difficult tests each year. "Statewide [improvements are] because many districts are focusing on that test, and it's basically all they're teaching," Baressi said. "We've certainly not attempted to do that in any official way. [This] is a long-term plan and effort and it's hard to compare one year to the next. Groups of students do differ in ability from year to year." (*Midland Reporter Telegram*, 1990)

Nowhere in the article does it state what the competency level was for each year. In 1991, the competency test name was changed and data to begin standardization were collected. It remained a competency test whose levels of competency were not made progressively more difficult, as demonstrated by the required mastery level shown in Table 3–1.

Teachers must not be confused by the name of the test, which may have words like *competency* in the title but be constructed like a standardized test. Or the test may be called a *diagnostic* test (e.g., Stanford Diagnostic Test) and be written as a survey test. The important step is to determine how the test was constructed. This can be done by obtaining a technical manual, which should be available in school libraries or come with the test. That manual will describe how competency levels were determine or how standardization was conducted.

Tests are necessary, but many teachers are uncomfortable with them and there are a number of problems in using them. The questions and comments on the next pages will help the content teacher assess reading on both the elementary and secondary reading levels.

**Table 3–1**  *Required Competency Levels for First-Graders, 1986–89\**

|      | Reading | | Writing | | Mathematics | |
|------|---------|---------|---------|---------|-------------|---------|
|      | *English* | *Spanish* | *English* | *Spanish* | *English* | *Spanish* |
| 1986 | 24/36 |       | 10/16 |      | 26/32 |       |
| 1987 | 24/36 |       | 10/16 |      | 26/32 |       |
| 1988 | 23/36 | 21/32 | 10/16 | 8/12 | 26/32 | 25/32 |
| 1989 | 22/36 | 21/32 | 9/16  | 8/12 | 25/32 | 25/32 |

\* Mastery levels set by State Board of Education. First-graders were no longer tested statewide after 1989.
*Source:* Data collected from Texas Education Agency Memos by Shannon Housson, Research Specialist, Texas Education Agency.

**Content Classes**

*How do I write better informal reading tests?*

The informal reading test is most useful for content teachers because it can be constructed from their textbook. The construction is as follows:

**1.**  Have a particular class in mind for which you wish to construct the informal reading inventory. If you are teaching now or know what grade level you will be teaching, aim your inventory for that grade. If you have no idea, imagine a fourth-grade class with children whose standardized test scores show a range from 2.5 to 7.0. (Remember that these scores are often commensurate with frustration level, rather than instructional level.)

**2.**  Choose a set of reading material to use as a basis for your informal reading inventory (IRI). The series that is in your classroom has the advantages of being available and being constructed from the books that the children use, thus making the instructional level more meaningful. If the children are very familiar with these materials, or have had instruction in them, try to choose another series of comparable difficulty level.

**3.**  From each grade-level book, choose at least six selections from the beginning through the end of the book: passages for silent reading, oral reading, and listening comprehension. The listening passages may be chosen from books beyond the expected reading levels, because listening comprehension usually exceeds reading comprehension. Having passages from all parts of the books will allow for a more precise estimate of the children's reading levels. The length of the passages will vary according to the grade level. The amount of time spent reading should be typical—neither longer than the children's attention span nor so short that not enough information is obtained. The examples of the Missouri Child Study Clinic's IRIs run from 125 words at preprimer level to over 900 words for the eighth-grade selection. These are quite lengthy; Johnson (1987) suggest 30 to 40 words at the preprimer level and end up to 300 words in the upper grades. When you have chosen the passages, make a copy of them so that you will have somewhere to mark the students' errors.

**4.**  Comprehension questions must be developed for each passage. The Missouri IRI divides the silent reading comprehension section into five parts: main idea, noting details, inferred meaning, organization, and vocabulary. Points are given for the questions within each area. Johnson (1987) suggests that for each group of five questions, two should be factual, two inference, and one vocabulary. Samples of these kinds of questions are given, but basically you as the teacher will have to decide what comprehension skills you expect your students to have and what information about their comprehension abilities will be helpful to you in planning their reading programs. Then develop questions to get at this information.

**5.** If possible, try out your informal reading inventory on a child to familiarize yourself with the story and to develop a system of recording errors.

**Cloze Informal Reading Test.** The second form of informal reading test, which is called the cloze, is easier to construct. Ranking (1970) describes the cloze as a deletion method in which underlined blanks are substituted for certain words that have been taken out of reading material. The reader simply tries to guess the words that were taken out and then writes them in the proper blank spaces. For example, if a student taking the test finds the statement, "The professor assigned a _____ of readings to his students," he may form a complete structure by writing the word *book* in the blank space. Provided that the original message contained the word *book*, the student will receive credit for the correct answer only if the exact word *book* is filled in. Why does the respondent have to fill in the precise word that was deleted? Because the ability to make correct word predictions of the precise words deleted in a cloze test is indicative of the student's grasp of "meaning" contained in the message.

Construction of the cloze is as follows:

**1.** Select passages from the textbook that have differing levels of difficulty. Each passage should begin at the normal beginning of a paragraph and should be at least 250 words in length. Delete every fifth word. Each test should have 50 deletions. The passages should be selected by some random process and a range of readability found in the textbook should be included. If the text you are using happens to have reading difficulty on a narrow range, find other paragraphs from other texts in the same subject field that will give you the range of reading levels necessary. Anywhere from 12 to 60 passages from a book can be selected.

**2.** Duplicate the tests and distribute them to a class of 25 to 30 students. Students should not have read the passages from which the tests were made. No time limit is given to the students.

**3.** Instruct the students to write on each blank the word they think was deleted. Responses are scored correct when they exactly match, but disregard minor misspellings.

Both the IRI and the cloze are useful informal tests for content teachers. Teachers simply select passages from their textbooks on different levels of reading difficulty. They then either write 10 comprehension questions (Burns & Roe, 1988) or delete every fifth word. Student answers will tell the teachers which students can read their content textbook. Teachers can also determine which portions of the book students can't read and adjust assignments accordingly. And finally, when materials are being considered for adoption by a school, these informal tests are valuable to use in testing the materials with different groups of students who might possibly be assigned these materials.

Checklists are easily constructed. First, the teacher decides on a format. Sample formats are used in the checklists provided in the Teaching Activities on pages 77 and 86–88. Sometimes scoring systems can be developed like the one provided on page 76. Otherwise, the teacher simply checks the skill or behavior when it is mastered or observed. Checklists provide documentation and structure for procedures the teacher regularly evaluates but does not need to formally test.

After constructing an IRI, cloze, or observation checklist to start the year, teachers spend the rest of the year writing informal achievement tests. Some teachers construct excellent exams; others could use some instruction in basic test development. For example, in writing clear tests, one should begin by writing explicit directions. Teachers need to watch sentence structure as well as the use of prepositional phrases and complex sentences that make tests difficult to read. The easiest conjunctions to use are *and, for,* and *as.* Directions are easier to understand if they are presented in small steps. Avoid using abstract terms like *determine, hypothesize,* and *observe.* Instead, use *find out* for *determine, guess* for *hypothesize,* and *look at* for *observe.* On the other hand, the word *show* is too broad—be more specific by using examples and illustrations or models of what you want. Here are some questions to consider when writing directions:

1. Is the purpose clear?
2. Is the sentence structure appropriate?
3. Are direction-related words appropriate in difficulty?
4. Can pictures, illustrations, or models make directions easier?
5. Is the sequence of directions clear?
6. Is the physical arrangement of the directions such that no one will miss them?
7. Can color or underlining help the student focus on key words?

After writing the directions, the teacher should decide what learning results he or she wants to measure. Retention of facts, procedures, chapter readings, relationships between concepts, and analysis of situations outside the classroom are a few of the accomplishments that are important learning. Once the end result is identified, the teacher then needs to determine how much time to spend on each area. The percentage of class and homework time spent on a topic should aid in determining how much weight each section should receive. And finally, the teacher should decide the format of the test: multiple choice, true or false, essay, fill in the blank, or problem solving. Once these decisions have been made, the teacher can begin to write the tests. Of course, if time is critical, the teacher may take questions and answers from the teacher's guides that accompany the textbooks. Text tests are expedient, simple to administer and score, and encourage mostly literal or lowest level of student thinking.

If the teacher is measuring reading development, he or she may want to consider Pearson's (1987) chart of contrasts between differing views of reading and practices in assessing reading (Table 3–2).

**Table 3–2**   *A Set of Contrasts between New Views of Reading and Current Practices in Assessing Reading*

| New views of the reading process tell us that . . . | Yet when we assess reading comprehension, we . . . |
| --- | --- |
| Prior knowledge is an important determinant of reading comprehension. | Mask any relationship between prior knowledge and reading comprehension by using lots of short passages on lots of topics. |
| A complete story or text has structural and topical integrity. | Use short texts that seldom approximate the structural and topical integrity of an authentic text. |
| Inference is an essential part of the process of comprehending units as small as sentences. | Rely on literal comprehension test items. |
| The diversity in prior knowledge across individuals as well as the varied causal relations in human experiences invite many possible inferences to fit a text or question. | Use multiple choice items with only one correct answer, even when many of the responses might, under certain conditions, be plausible. |
| The ability to vary reading strategies to fit the text and the situation is one hallmark of an expert reader. | Seldom assess how and when students vary the strategies they use during normal reading, studying, or when the going gets tough. |
| The ability to synthesize information from various parts of the text and different texts is hallmark of an expert reader. | Rarely go beyond finding the main idea of a paragraph or passage. |
| The ability to ask good questions of text, as well as to answer them, is hallmark of an expert reader. | Seldom ask students to create or select questions about a selection they may have just read. |
| All aspects of a reader's experience, including habits that arise from school and home, influence reading comprehension. | Rarely view information on reading habits and attitudes as being as important information about performance. |
| Reading involves the orchestration of many skills that complement one another in a variety of ways. | Use tests that fragment reading into isolated skills and report performance on each. |

| New views of the reading process tell us that . . . | Yet when we assess reading comprehension, we . . . |
| --- | --- |
| Skilled readers are fluent; their word identification is sufficiently automatic to allow most cognitive resources to be used for comprehension. | Rarely consider fluency as an index of skilled reading. |
| Learning from text involves the restructuring, application, and flexible use of knowledge in new situations. | Often ask readers to respond to the text's declarative knowledge rather than to apply it to near and far transfer tasks. |

*Source:* Pearson, P. D. (1987, April). Reading assessment: Time for a change. *The Reading Teacher.* Reprinted with permission of P. David Pearson and the International Reading Association.

While taking a graduate class with the author, Jodie Baugh and Darla Fullen, kindergarten and first-grade teachers, developed the following developmental checklist of drawing and writing competencies compared to reading level. The model has been subsequently verified with other elementary and ESL secondary students.

### Drawing and Writing Stages Demonstrated by Five- and Six-Year-Old Children Reading Below Preprimer to Seventh Grade

*Stage I*
Preprimer
Readers

Drawings rich in detail but lack attempt of child to write words

*Stage II*
Primer
Readers

Drawings increased in size and detail with random letters added; letters stood for words because child had begun to notice letters in print

*Stage III*
First-Grade
Readers

Drawings with few words and random string letters

*Stage IV*
Second-Grade
Readers

Drawing and adding a sentence using invented spelling

DRAWING WITH SENTENCES

*Stage V*
Third-Grade
Readers

Gave up drawings and concentrated on writing; spaces between words began to appear and periods at ends of sentences

*Stage VI*
Fourth-Grade
Readers

Sentences descriptive and longer stories with drawings that illustrate story

*Stage VII*          Variety of writing modes including cartoons,
  Seventh-Grade    plays, and poems
  Readers

Comparing writing and reading development can be a means of determining reading readiness, reading level, and reading growth. When the student has reached stage III in drawing/writing, Baugh and Fullen found that students were ready for reading instruction to begin. If content teachers have ESL students, it is possible that they had little or no education in their native countries. Having the students write/ draw and use this writing stage checklist is a good diagnostic tool for identifying levels of reading placement. (See Figure 3–1.)

**Figure 3–1**   *Diagnostic Writing Sample of First-Grader Reading on Fourth-Grade Level: Stage VII*

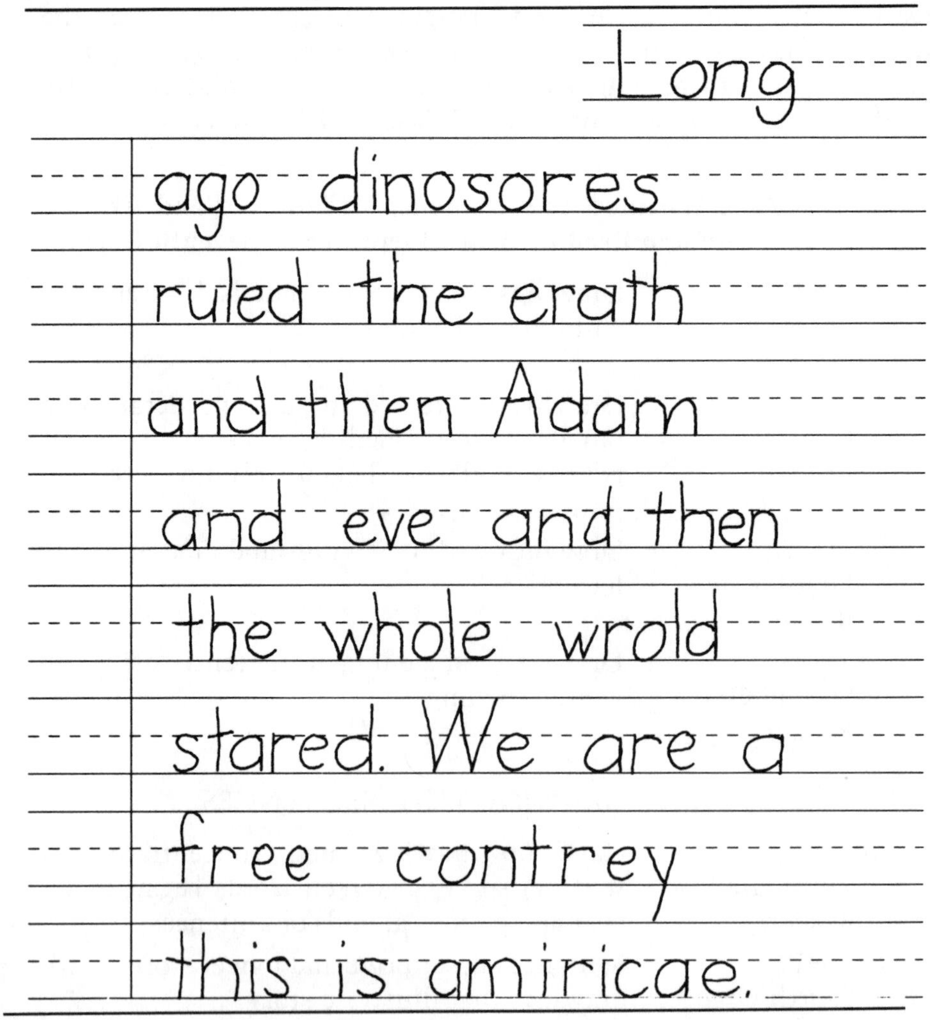

Long
ago dinosores
ruled the erath
and then Adam
and eve and then
the whole wrold
stared. We are a
free contrey
this is amiricae.

For a reading program to be effective, it must have its objectives measured by some means. Teachers and administrators tend to think in terms of administering one test to measure program effectiveness. However, it would make more sense to measure student improvement by examining reading in other content areas rather than increasing the importance of comparison testing among students on a single test. One of the more effective means of measuring reading growth is through examining students' reading and writing abilities. Karen Trammell, a junior high English teacher, investigated the correlation between regular and accelerated high school English students' reading and writing abilities. She found no correlation between the two in all of her classes. One explanation for her findings is that writing skills develop after reading skills. She took a writing sample from her students and conducted a readability on it to find out if students read and write on the same level of difficulty. It is apparent from examining the scatter diagrams (Figures 3–2 through 3–5 for each grade level that writing skills are lower than reading skills in average and above-average students.

**Figure 3–2**   *Scatter Diagram for Writing Level and Reading Level for Ninth-Grade Students*

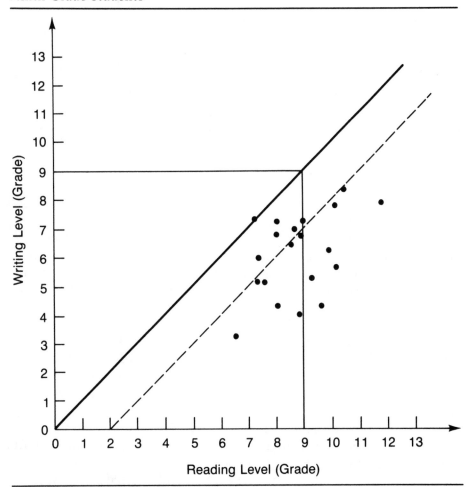

**Figure 3–3**   *Scatter Diagram for Writing Level and Reading Level for Tenth-Grade Students*

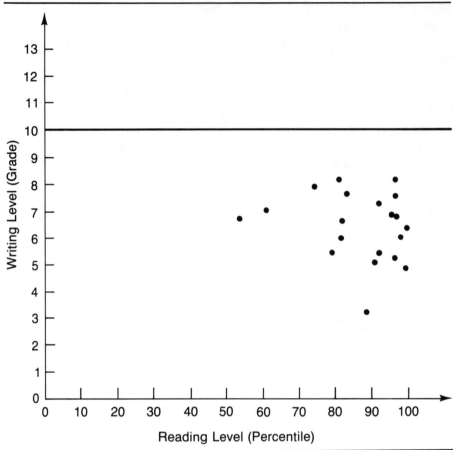

*Summary*

The purpose of testing is to determine student competencies and growth in reading. To do this, there are formal and informal instruments that differ according to construction. Informal instruments are teacher constructed or published, but not standardized. Formal tests have been standardized or, as with competency tests, skill areas and competency levels have been established. Standardized tests are considered the most critical measures when making decisions for grouping children into programs, granting admission to schools and colleges, and placing students in talented and gifted or special education projects. When used for such purposes, standardized tests become a means for comparison among students and schools rather than a method for determining whether reading improvement has taken place.

Competency tests are formal tests that are usually constructed to accompany mastery learning materials. The concept is that students must master a certain area with a level of predetermined mastery. Unlike standardized tests, mastery level can be raised and lowered to make a school district or program look more successful than it has

**Figure 3–4** *Scatter Diagram for Writing Level and Reading Level for Eleventh-Grade Students*

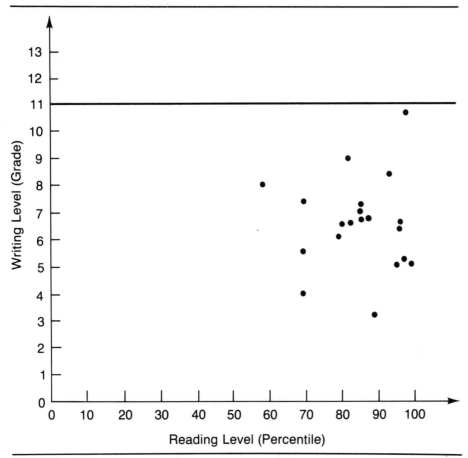

actually been. If the teacher has ESL or remedial students, competency tests or taking writing and drawing samples and applying either a readability formula or the reading/writing comparison chart will give the teacher beginning reading diagnosis. In conclusion, all types of tests are alive and well in students' experiences and are a source of anxiety, no matter how appropriately or inappropriately the tests are constructed or how poorly or well a student does when scores are interpreted.

## Selection and Interpretation

*How do I select a standardized test for my class?*

First, students should be given either an IRI or a cloze to determine if they can read the textbook. If they cannot read the textbook or if the IRI does not measure their level of reading, a survey test should be given. You should use tests to help you come to decisions, but don't expect tests to make the decisions for you. Also use observations, rating scales, checklists, anecdotal records, interviews, and data collected by other teachers. For example, the author had a student in

**Figure 3–5** *Scatter Diagram for Writing Level and Reading Level for Twelfth-Grade Students*

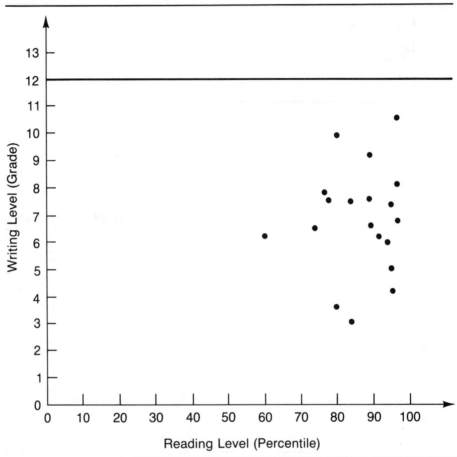

honors English who failed the first three tests. Before giving this girl another test, the author went to other teachers. From them, it was learned that the student's parents consistently demanded that the girl be put into honors classes. Each year she was placed in honors math, science, social studies, and English. Each year she was removed from those classes because she could not do the work. New teachers are frequently unaware of what is common knowledge to the other teachers. In the same class were twins, one who passed the first three tests and one who failed the first three tests. Again, it was known in the school that these twins should not be placed in the same class, but the counselor favored these two girls and they wanted to be in the honors English where "all their friends were." Since the counselor honored student requests over faculty requests (which was also common knowledge), the twins were not moved even though test results in all classes indicated that the work would be too difficult for one of them. These two situations demonstrate that teachers should not rely on test information alone. Test results should be interpreted in light of all other information the teacher has about a child and school procedures.

If there is a need for further testing beyond the survey test, a standardized diagnostic test should be given. Do not assume that all tests are "good" just because they are published. Even the technical manuals that accompany tests are written by publishers who want to sell tests. The best source for selecting a good reading test is to find the test in the Oscar Burro's Institute's *Mental Measurement Yearbooks*. These books and the one written specifically on reading tests review all formal and informal published tests. The reviewers are experts in the fields being measured and can accurately evaluate the tests. Also, they do not have an interest in selling the tests.

When selecting a test for classes, keep in mind the purpose of testing. Test results can help a teacher group pupils, show growth or progress of a class, determine what teaching methods to use, and help individualize instruction. They can point out individual differences and help teachers decide whether a child is working up to his or her capacity. They can also help teachers accept a child's limitations. And finally, they can identify deficiencies that can be changed and help identify students' strong points.

### How do I interpret test results?

Interpreting test results on teacher-made tests can be individually or district determined. For example, an "A" can range from 90, 95, or 96 to 100 percent. The interpretation of these results is fairly straightforward if the test is a good one. To determine if a test is good or not, construct an item analysis. Student responses to each question or activity are recorded. Those questions missed by most students can be assumed to be poor indicators of what the student knows, poor measures of what was covered in class, poorly written, too hard, or ambiguous. Likewise, the questions that every student gets correct may indicate excellent teaching, cheating, or too easy a question. Item analysis can be very instructional for teachers as they continue to prepare tests.

The interpretation of teacher-made test results should be clear to the teacher who constructed the test. Informal reading tests and cloze tests have predetermined interpretation scales.

When finished testing, the teacher will have an independent, instructional, and frustration reading level on the informal reading and cloze tests. The *independent* reading level is the highest level of reading at which a student can read fluently and with relative ease and where he or she can comprehend what is read. At the independent reading level, the student can pronounce at least 98 percent of the words and can correctly respond to 90 percent of the questions asked about what has been read.

The *instructional* reading level is the highest level at which a person can pronounce 95 percent of the words in a selection and accurately respond to 75 percent of the comprehension questions. The independent level is named that because the student can be handed material on that reading level and operate with no help from the teacher. The instructional level is the reading level where the teacher begins instruction and can help students progress.

The *frustration* level is the level where the student shows signs that he or she is having difficulty reading the material. Visible signs of tension or frustration often become obvious. The frustration level is reached when the student does not pronounce correctly at least 95 percent of the words in a selection or when he or she cannot answer at least 75 percent of the questions asked.

These percentage levels may differ on published informal reading inventories such as the Sivoroli or Burns and Roe. For example, the criteria for Burns and Roe's instructional level is 85 percent or higher for grades 1 and 2 and 95 percent or higher for grades 3–12 in word recognition and 75 percent or higher in comprehension. Below 50 percent is considered frustration level in comprehension measurement on Burns and Roe.

The cloze test also gives the same three score interpretations. Below 44 percent is considered frustration level. When the score is between 44–58 percent, the text is considered appropriate for instruction, but the teacher will need to assist the student in its use. Scores above 58 percent are considered independent level. A score of 50 percent on the cloze equals 90 percent on conventional testing, while 44 percent is the equivalent of 75 percent. The correlations between the cloze and conventional tests range from .73 to .84. The cloze test has a very high correlation as a measure of the ability to recognize an author's style. It also provides an accurate measure of the levels of difficulty of passages. A correlation ranging from .90 to .95 was found in the measuring of word recognition and comprehension difficulties of paragraphs.

There are also quick ways of determining students' reading levels, such as the 1 out of 20 rule. Ask the student to read aloud from a book. If he or she makes about 1 mistake out of every 20 words, the book is on instructional level. If he or she misses more than 1 out of 20 words, the book is on his or her frustration level. If he or she makes fewer errors than 1 out of 20 words, the book is on independent level. Standardized test scores do not give teachers the independent or instructional levels. Scores from standardized tests are assumed to be on frustration reading level.

Before interpreting any standardized test to a student, the teacher should make sure that the test is valid or measures what it is supposed to measure. Description of tests in the Teaching Activities section of this chapter shows the variety of standardized tests available.

Interpretation of test results on standardized tests is completed for teachers, providing they can read complicated charts and graphs and understand statistical measures of content, construct, and predictive validity and measures of central tendency. The major criticism of most standardized tests is that they are not easy to interpret. The first step the teacher must take is to determine the size of the norming population. The larger the number of people the test was piloted on, the better the basis for making statistical interpretations. If the reliability is above 75 percent and the validity is above 85 percent, the test is considered good. However, the best way to interpret standardized scores is to read about the test in the *Mental Measurements Yearbook* and then find professional journal articles on the test. The difficulty in interpreting raw and percentile scores can be seen in the chart for teachers from the Nelson Denny Adult Reading Test seen in Figure 3–6.

## Summary

Test scores have little meaning without interpretation. If the interpretation is not supplied by the test administrator, the students will invent their own meaning. For example, a retired military officer became terribly depressed and showed it in class. When asked why he was so sad, the man said that he had wanted to go on to graduate school and he had only gotten a 600 in math and a 600 in the verbal on the Graduate Record Exam. He needed 1,000 for graduate school. No one had told him that two sections of the test were added together for graduate school admission requirements. His score was higher than needed for the school he wanted but he did not know how to interpret the scores and so made up his own interpretation.

Informal reading tests and cloze tests provide information regarding the relationship that should exist between the student, textbook, and teacher. Instructional decisions are more easily made from informal tests than from standardized test data. Standardized tests are useful for comparisons between schools, districts, and states. They can become decision-making factors in college, program, and school admissions. No teacher should develop a reading program based on standardized survey test data because the reading level obtained is frustrational. Diagnostic tests aside, most formal reading tests function better for administrative purposes than they do for instructional purposes. If a 15-year-old student reads on the fourth-grade level according to a standardized reading test, the teacher still has no indication what reading deficits are causing the low reading level. Informal reading tests tell the teacher what reading level to begin on to find instructional material.

**Figure 3–6**   *Percentile Norms for Cut-Time Administration*

| VOCAB-ULARY (11 min) | COMPRE-HENSION (15 min) | TOTAL (V + 2C) | READING RATE | %-ILE RANK | VOCAB-ULARY (11 min) | COMPRE-HENSION (15 min) | TOTAL (V + 2C) | READING RATE |
|---|---|---|---|---|---|---|---|---|
| | RAW SCORE FORM E | | | | | RAW SCORE FORM F | | |
| 98-99 | 68 | 162 | 633 | 99 | 97 | 70 | 168-171 | — |
| 97 | — | 161 | 619 | 98 | 95-96 | — | 162-167 | — |
| 96 | 66 | 159-160 | 609 | 97 | 94 | — | 158-161 | 610-622 |
| — | — | 158 | 593 | 96 | 93 | 68 | 155-157 | 587-598 |
| 95 | — | 157 | — | 95 | 92 | — | 153-154 | 563-575 |
| — | 64 | 156 | 578 | 94 | 91 | 66 | 152 | 549 |
| 94 | — | 154-155 | 566 | 93 | 90 | — | 150-151 | 541 |
| — | — | 153 | — | 92 | 89 | 64 | 149 | 530 |
| 93 | — | 152 | 553 | 91 | 88 | — | 148 | 518 |
| — | 62 | 151 | 542 | 90 | 87 | — | 147 | — |
| 92 | — | 150 | — | 89 | — | 62 | 146 | 502-506 |
| — | — | 149 | 529 | 88 | 86 | — | 145 | 496 |
| 91 | 60 | 148 | — | 87 | 85 | — | 144 | — |
| — | — | 147 | — | 86 | 84 | — | 143 | — |
| 90 | — | 146 | 514 | 85 | — | 60 | 142 | 482 |
| 89 | — | 145 | — | 84 | 83 | — | 141 | 472 |
| — | — | — | 501 | 83 | 82 | — | 140 | — |
| 88 | — | 144 | 490 | 82 | — | — | 139 | 461 |
| 87 | 58 | 143 | — | 81 | 81 | — | 138 | — |
| — | — | 142 | 483 | 80 | — | 58 | 137 | — |
| 86 | — | 141 | 479 | 79 | 80 | — | — | 450 |
| 85 | — | 140 | — | 78 | — | — | 136 | — |
| — | — | 139 | — | 77 | — | — | 135 | — |
| 84 | — | 138 | 465 | 76 | 79 | — | 134 | 438 |
| 83 | 56 | 137 | — | 75 | — | — | 133 | — |
| — | — | 136 | 451 | 74 | 78 | — | 132 | — |
| 82 | — | 135 | — | 73 | — | 56 | 131 | — |
| 81 | — | 134 | — | 72 | 77 | — | 130 | — |
| — | — | 133 | 442 | 71 | — | — | — | 424 |
| 80 | 54 | 132 | — | 70 | 76 | — | 129 | — |
| — | — | 131 | — | 69 | — | — | 128 | — |
| 79 | — | 130 | — | 68 | 75 | — | 127 | — |
| 78 | — | 129 | 429 | 67 | — | 54 | — | — |
| — | — | 128 | — | 66 | 74 | — | 126 | 413 |
| 77 | 52 | 127 | — | 65 | — | — | 125 | — |
| — | — | 126 | — | 64 | 73 | — | 124 | — |
| 76 | — | 125 | 423 | 63 | 72 | — | 123 | — |
| — | — | 124 | — | 62 | — | 52 | 122 | — |
| 75 | — | — | — | 61 | 71 | — | 121 | — |
| 74 | — | 123 | — | 60 | — | — | 120 | 400 |
| — | 50 | 122 | — | 59 | 70 | — | — | — |
| 73 | — | 121 | 411 | 58 | — | — | 119 | — |
| 72 | — | 120 | — | 57 | 69 | — | 118 | — |
| — | — | 119 | — | 56 | — | — | 117 | — |
| 71 | — | — | — | 55 | 68 | — | 116 | — |
| — | — | 118 | — | 54 | 67 | 50 | — | 390 |
| 70 | — | 117 | 402 | 53 | — | — | 115 | — |
| — | 48 | 116 | — | 52 | 66 | — | 114 | — |
| 69 | — | — | — | 51 | 65 | — | 113 | — |
| 68 | — | 115 | — | 50 | — | — | 112 | — |
| — | — | 114 | — | 49 | 64 | — | 111 | — |
| 67 | — | — | — | 48 | 63 | 48 | — | 378 |
| 66 | — | 113 | 391 | 47 | — | — | 110 | — |
| — | — | 112 | — | 46 | 62 | — | 109 | — |
| 64-65 | 46 | 111 | — | | — | — | 108 | — |

# Communication Strategies

*How should I communicate test results to my students?*

Teacher-constructed test results should be given to students with some commentary as to how the test was constructed, what the correct answers are, and how to prepare for future tests. Standardized test results are given to students usually in a computerized form with some explanation. The teacher or school administrator should provide a cover letter if test results are sent home to parents. And finally, there is the problem of access to results. In some schools, only teachers have access to standardized test data. With open access laws, students also can see any files or testing documents. Standardized test results may be deprecated but it is good to remind students that if they want to go elsewhere to school, standardized test results indicate how well they would do when compared to other students their age on comparable questions. Standardized test results, however, do not necessarily reflect teaching effectiveness. For example, if the test measures specific skills and the student has been taught "holistically," test results may not reflect what was learned.

# Summary

Constructing, administering, scoring, and interpreting test data are very important tasks for teachers. However, test scores do not provide instructions as to how to communicate the information to students. To many students, the score is not merely a number but a public demonstration of how incompetent they are in reading. Students' reactions after getting tests returned indicate how important it is for this information to be correctly and carefully communicated.

# Application Excercises and Teaching Activities

## Application Excercises

**1.** Your son has just come home with his test results. What additional information do you as a parent need to have from the teacher or test administrators?

**2.** Critique poor examples of informal tests on pages 72 and 78–85.

**3.** Your daughter has received miserable grades on the teacher-made tests in history. She has never before had such low grades in history. What do you say to her in order to interpret her scores to her?

**4.** Which of the following standardized tests would you use in your content classroom? What are your reasons for your selection?

### Test 1

The purpose of this test is to measure the pupil's ability to understand the overall theme of the story, identify the main idea in paragraphs, infer logical ideas, retain significant details, and understand the meaning of words in context.

*Strengths*

**1.** The comprehension subtests at all levels are good. The passages are interesting and the multiple-choice questions require a broad range of skills such as recall, inference, and identification of central themes.

2. No vocabulary items are in the comprehension subtest.
3. The usability is good. No special training is necessary for teachers or administrators to administer or interpret the test.
4. The instructions are clear and everything is color coded.

*Weaknesses*

1. The total reading score of the level for grades 1–2 test is weighted too heavily with the language perception subtest.
2. The vocabulary at all levels requires recognition in context, but the words and context are the same as the ones in the comprehension section administered immediately before the vocabulary section.
3. Standardization procedures are not clear. More information concerning intelligence and socioeconomic status of norming population is needed.
4. Separate norms for boys and girls are not provided.

## Test 2

The items of this test can be classified into four areas: identification of explicit facts, details, and relationships; comprehension of information that has been identified; application of information in drawing conclusions and forming inferences; and evaluation of the theme or purpose of the writer.

*Strengths*

1. Paragraphs for the comprehension questions are long enough to provide an opportunity for testing more than superficial comprehension.
2. The test is arranged in a multilevel format, which permits a student in any grade to respond only to those items at his or her level.
3. The comprehension questions require reading skills far beyond the literal level.

*Weaknesses*

1. The comprehension skills are not sampled extensively.
2. There is no measure of reading rate or rate of comprehension.

## Test 3

This test is a group survey test yielding conventional scores for vocabulary, comprehension, and total reading.

*Strengths*

1. It is good for evaluating total groups with respect to general level of reading skill and in selecting cases of reading disability that are in need of more intensive diagnosis.
2. The intellectual processes measured are recognition and/or application, translation, interpretation, and analysis.

3. Each test item is classified according to intellectual processes.
4. It provides a developmental sequence from the first grade through secondary school.
5. The use of overlapping levels at grades 4, 6, and 8 allows a choice of levels for the measurement of reading at these grades.
6. A variety of derived scores are provided for interpreting test results.
7. Norms are based on a large standardization sample of representative students.

*Weaknesses*

1. The process by which items were classified was loose and simple, and the number of test items designed as measuring one particular intellectual process may be as few as only three or four in the test as a whole.
2. An in-service program is necessary to enable the average user to be able to use the manuals competently.

## Teaching Activities:
## Sample Informal Reading Test in English

*English Around the World*

English came from Britain. That is a small corner of Europe. How did English go around the world? There are many ways.

The British traveled around the world, then they settled. English would be spoken there.

There is another way. It was trade. England made many kinds of goods. The ships would carry them all over the world.

There is another way. It was war. The English soldiers went to many other countries.

There is another reason. It is TV. Movies send English around the world, too.

*Jazz* and *football* are English words.

English is around the world.

1. Who took English around the world?
2. Where is England?
3. How did English go around the world? (Tell one way.)
4. What is another way?
5. Did war or TV take English around the globe first?

# Sample of Informal Reading Test in Social Studies

*The Consumer in the Economy*

A man's income is a valuable indicator of his tastes, political views, education, and even his age. The income of a family determines its role as a consumer—the amount of goods and services it receives, and thus its degree of economic health. Consumers set the guidelines for production by their dollar choices in markets. These choices are called consumer patterns of expenditures. To measure the incomes of families, officials consider living units. They look at the characteristics of a living unit—the number of people in it, whether it is urban or rural, and the specific needs of the unit. Location can be a factor in income differences. It is true that American families do not receive equal incomes in each of the 50 states. Although it is also true that each American belongs to some minority, the economic impact of minority status, class consciousness, and inequality of opportunities falls the heaviest on blacks, working women, and the elderly. The black unemployment rate is higher than the white race in every occupational group. The median income of employed females is only half those of employed males. When an older worker tries to find a new job, it is much harder for him than for a younger man to locate new employment. The onus of practicing discrimination does not fall on any one group alone. Unions, industry, government, and the general public all have participated.

Comprehension questions:

1. What are the characteristics of a living unit?
2. What types of people are discriminated against in jobs?
3. Why do American families not receive equal income in all of the 50 states?
4. Why do you think that blacks do not receive as much income as whites?
5. Give me a sentence using the word *inequality.*

## Sample Cloze Test in History

The 17th and 18th _____ unlocked the door to _____. The 19th century opened _____ door. That century witnessed _____ changes in political, social, _____ economic matters that would _____ shocked a man living _____ century earlier. We who _____ in the 20th century _____ still feeling the effects _____ these changes; in fact _____ has been often noted _____ the most important characteristic _____ modern man is his _____ that change will continue _____ go on all around _____. This point of view _____ its origins in the _____ changes in outlook concerning _____, society, nature, and the _____ provided us by men _____ lived during the Age _____ Reason and the Enlightenment _____ followed. The 17th and _____ centuries set us on _____ of the courses that _____ now pursue.

How had _____ ideas concerning his fellow _____ changed in the 17th _____ 18th centuries? Fundamentally, man _____ viewed as a rational _____ who was, to a _____ degree, a product of _____ political, social, and economic _____ in which he was _____. Man had the unique _____ to reason. With this _____ he did not need _____ live in poverty and _____. Instead of waiting for _____ life in another world, _____ had only to use _____ reason to determine _____ best ways to improve _____ and his society. There _____ hope for man; in _____, a new idea was _____ beginning to emerge. Progress! _____ would not only be _____, it would be improved _____ applying reason to the _____ that plagued society.

72

# Sample of a Cloze Test in Physics

An object moves on _____ curved path because the _____ that pushes it has _____ component perpendicular to the _____ of motion. The component _____ force along the path _____ the speed. The force _____ not change the direction. _____ the other hand, a _____ perpendicular to the motion _____ the object side-wise so _____ the path curves. If _____ total force is perpendicular _____ the velocity, it leads _____ a perpendicular acceleration which _____ the direction but not _____ magnitude of the velocity _____.

While a projectile is _____ on its parabolic path, _____ force of gravity acting _____ it has components both _____ the path and perpendicular _____ it. The direction of _____ velocity changes because the _____ component of force produces _____ perpendicular acceleration. The magnitude _____ the velocity changes because _____ component of the force _____ the path produces an _____ along the path.

We _____ now concentrate on change _____ direction alone, that is, _____ motion at constant speed. _____ is such uniform rotation _____? Suppose we push steadily _____ a body, always pushing _____ right angles to its _____. As there is never _____ component of force in _____ direction of motion, there _____ no acceleration along the _____. The speed of the _____ stays constant while the _____ of motion changes. Now _____ we keep the magnitude _____ the force constant, the _____ of the path will _____ the same amount in _____ equal time interval, and _____ path must be a _____.

Level:  11th grade
Subject:  Physics
Text:  *Physics*
Authors:  U. Haber-Scham, J. B. Cross, J. H. Dodge, & J. A. Walter
Passage:  Chapter 12, section 5, page 252
This text is currently used in Texas for ninth-grade physics. Passages from different sections placed reading difficulty from sixth grade through college level. The passage selected for this cloze was modified to an eleventh-grade level using the Fry readability graph.

*Words Removed from Cloze*

| | | | |
|---|---|---|---|
| 1. | a | 26. | of |
| 2. | force | 27. | the |
| 3. | a | 28. | along |
| 4. | direction | 29. | acceleration |
| 5. | of | 30. | shall |
| 6. | changes | 31. | in |
| 7. | does | 32. | circular |
| 8. | On | 33. | How |
| 9. | force | 34. | produced |
| 10. | shoves | 35. | on |
| 11. | that | 36. | at |
| 12. | the | 37. | motion |
| 13. | to | 38. | a |
| 14. | to | 39. | the |
| 15. | changes | 40. | is |
| 16. | the | 41. | path |
| 17. | vector | 42. | body |
| 18. | moving | 43. | direction |
| 19. | the | 44. | if |
| 20. | on | 45. | of |
| 21. | along | 46. | direction |
| 22. | to | 47. | change |
| 23. | the | 48. | every |
| 24. | perpendicular | 49. | the |
| 25. | a | 50. | circle |

# Sample of Informal Reading Test in Science

*What Is "Hot"?*

You know that kinetic energy is the energy of motion and that everything that moves has kinetic energy. All matter is composed of very tiny particles, and these particles are in constant movement. The kinetic energy of movement inside things is called internal kinetic energy. The total internal kinetic energy of a body is called heat. The temperature of a body is a measure of the average internal kinetic energy of all the tiny particles within it. A thermometer is one of the many instruments which is used to measure temperature. Most thermometers are glass tubes which contain mercury which rises and falls. The temperature is read from a scale which is placed on or near the thermometer. The marks on the thermometer are called its scale, and its divisions are called degrees. A thermometer can have a Celsius temperature scale or a Fahrenheit scale. It can also have the Kelvin or absolute scale. The zero point on the Kelvin scale is called absolute zero. Much work has been done in the field of low-temperature study, which is called cryogenics.

Comprehension questions:

1. What is all matter composed of?
2. What is the temperature of a body?
3. How are all thermometers alike?
4. How are thermometers different?
5. Give me a sentence using the word <u>kinetic</u>.

Number of words <u>179</u>                     Accuracy:   90% <u>161</u>
Number of words correctly pronounced _____          99% <u>177</u>

# Summary Sheet for Results—Informal Reading Inventory

Name _____  Grade _____
Administrator _____  Date _____

| Oral Reading Passages: | Level: | Word Recognition # Errors: | Miscues %: | Comprehension # Errors: | Errors %: | Instructional Level: |
|---|---|---|---|---|---|---|
| | _____ | _____ | _____ | _____ | _____ | _____ |
| | _____ | _____ | _____ | _____ | _____ | |
| | _____ | _____ | _____ | _____ | _____ | |
| | _____ | _____ | _____ | _____ | _____ | |

| Silent Reading Passages: | Level: | Comprehension # Errors: | Errors %: | Instructional Level: |
|---|---|---|---|---|
| | _____ | _____ | _____ | _____ |
| | _____ | _____ | _____ | |
| | _____ | _____ | _____ | |
| | _____ | _____ | _____ | |

Summary:

Begin overall instruction at ___ level because _____.

The major problem is in word recognition ___ ; comprehension ___ ; other ___ (please explain) _____

_____

Recommendations for instruction: _____

_____

# Analysis of IRI Errors Checklist

NAME _____  TEACHER _____

GRADE _____  SCHOOL _____

| # | 1st Check | 2nd Check | 3rd Check | Item | Category |
|---|---|---|---|---|---|
| 1 | | | | Word-by-word reading | Oral Reading |
| 2 | | | | Incorrect phrasing | |
| 3 | | | | Poor pronunciation | |
| 4 | | | | Omissions | |
| 5 | | | | Repetitions | |
| 6 | | | | Inversions or reversals | |
| 7 | | | | Insertions | |
| 8 | | | | Substitutions | |
| 9 | | | | Basic sight words not known | |
| 10 | | | | Sight vocabulary not up to grade level | |
| 11 | | | | Guesses at words | |
| 12 | | | | Consonant sounds not known | |
| 13 | | | | Vowel sounds not known | |
| 14 | | | | Vowel pairs and/or consonant clusters not known (digraphs, diphthongs, blends) | |
| 15 | | | | Lacks desirable structural analysis (Morphology) | |
| 16 | | | | Unable to use context clues | |
| 17 | | | | Contractions not known | |
| 18 | | | | Comprehension inadequate | Oral Silent |
| 19 | | | | Vocabulary inadequate | |
| 20 | | | | Unaided recall scanty | Study Skills |
| 21 | | | | Response poorly organized | |
| 22 | | | | Unable to locate information | |
| 23 | | | | Inability to skim | |
| 24 | | | | Inability to adjust rate to difficulty of material | |
| 25 | | | | Low rate of speed | |
| 26 | | | | High rate at expense of accuracy | |
| 27 | | | | Voicing-lip movement | Other Abilities |
| 28 | | | | Lacks knowledge of the alphabet | |
| 29 | | | | Written recall limited by spelling ability | |
| 30 | | | | Undeveloped dictionary skills | |

D—Difficulty recognized
P—Pupil progressing
N—No longer has difficulty

The items listed above represent the most common difficulties encountered by pupils in the reading program. Following each numbered item are spaces for notation of that specific difficulty. This may be done at intervals of several months. One might use a check to indicate difficulty recognized or the following letters to represent an even more accurate appraisal:

# Example of Informal Teacher-Made Reading Test

*Death Be Not Proud*

I. *Vocabulary:* Place the correct letter from the column on the right which defines the word in the left column.

| | | | |
|---|---|---|---|
| __ | 1. placid | A. | turning point |
| __ | 2. abscess | B. | unyielding |
| __ | 3. indomitable | C. | system of rule or government |
| __ | 4. modicum | D. | a powerful poison |
| __ | 5. cyanide | E. | stir up; make busy |
| __ | 6. eminence | F. | undisturbed; calm |
| __ | 7. utmost | G. | endure; suffer through |
| __ | 8. regime | H. | extreme; farthest |
| __ | 9. criteria | I. | minimum amount |
| __ | 10. undergo | J. | fame; high rank |
| | | K. | something unusual |
| | | L. | rule for making a decision |
| | | M. | infection; painful sore |

II. *Multiple Choice:* Place the correct letter in the blank which best completes each statement.

__ 1. The year *Death Be Not Proud* was published was (a) 1929, (b) 1949, (c) 1960, (d) none of these.

__ 2. One of Johnny's bad habits, especially at Deerfield, was his ability (a) to lose his temper, (b) to never call his girlfriend, (c) to never write his parents, (d) to misplace his belongings.

__ 3. Which of the following best describes Johnny? (a) witty and eager, (b) a reluctant student, (c) athletic and active in sports, (d) none of these.

__ 4. The subject that Johnny and Francis discussed most frequently was (a) art, (b) death, (c) his girlfriend, (d) science.

__ 5. One of the many effects the tumor had on Johnny was (a) all of the following, (b) his loss of hearing, (c) his loss of feeling, (d) the loss of the use of his left hand.

__ 6. The Gerson diet had the following effects on Johnny: (a) gain in weight, (b) spectacular improvement, (c) the tumor stopped growing, (d) all of these.

__ 7. Johnny graduated from Deerfield in (a) June, (b) September, (c) December, (d) none of these.

__ 8. When Johnny died, who was at his bedside? (a) Doctors Traeger and Mount, (b) the nurses, (c) Francis and John, (d) all of these.

__ 9. Which statement best describes the day of the funeral? (a) peaceful and warm, (b) snowing, (c) cloudy and dreary, (d) stormy and gray.

__ 10. The *second* form of treatment which Johnny received was (a) X-ray, (b) mustard gas, (c) Gerson diet, (d) operation.

— 11. On Johnny's seventeenth birthday, he (a) was too ill to enjoy it, (b) had ice cream and recorded people's laughter, (c) took a trip to the country, (d) none of these.

— 12. Throughout his long ordeal, Johnny was always (a) complaining about the nurses, (b) too tired to care, (c) sad and made everyone else sad, (d) none of these.

— 13. When Johnny could no longer see the chess board, he (a) worked on his chemistry, (b) began playing the bassoon, (c) memorized the plays, (d) listened to his records.

— 14. Which of the following were included in Johnny's special diet? (a) soup, fruit, oatmeal, (b) ice cream, sausages, spices, (c) only vegetables, (d) meat, eggs, fish.

— 15. One of Johnny's goals in life, which he never was able to accomplish was (a) complete all his schoolwork, (b) write a textbook for teenagers, (c) graduate from his academy, (d) meet Professor Einstein.

III. *Essay* (worth 50 points):   Write a 1–1½ page essay about three or more qualities of Johnny's personality. Give at least four examples that occur in the novel which prove each of these qualities. These examples must come from the last half of the book.

Your essay will be graded on neatness as well content, organization, spelling, and grammar.

# Teacher-Made Sight Word Test in Science

1. absolute zero
2. alternates
3. aromatic compounds
4. beta particle
5. chain reaction
6. covalent bond
7. diode
8. electric effect
9. energetic particle
10. fossil fuels
11. galvanometer
12. halogens
13. inert
14. isotopes
15. liquid
16. molecules
17. north-seeking pole
18. pentane
19. plasma
20. prism
21. ray
22. scientific notation
23. spectrum
24. temperature
25. transverse wave

Instructional level:   23 words correct

# Informal Structural Analysis Test

Underline the base or root word in each word:

| | | | |
|---|---|---|---|
| scornfully | distraught | hydroplane | disdainful |
| unfamiliar | loneliness | offhandedly | formality |
| attachment | companions | immediately | disappearance |

Underline the prefix in each word:

| | | | |
|---|---|---|---|
| submarine | deport | dismantle | enfold |
| translate | tricycle | nonsense | abnormal |
| binocular | deport | improbable | promote |

Underline the suffix in each word:

| | | | |
|---|---|---|---|
| disturbance | gracious | pleasantly | credible |
| baggage | vicinity | egotism | instinctively |
| proximity | acquaintance | occurrences | curiosity |

Divide these compound words by placing a / between each of the two syllables:

| | | | |
|---|---|---|---|
| chairman | foreman | bricklayer | moonlight |
| highlight | parlormaid | nineteen | overshoe |
| overlook | thundershower | clergyman | grandchildren |

Divide each of these words into syllables by placing a / between each syllable:

| | | | |
|---|---|---|---|
| superintendent | describe | doctor | remedial |
| obstinate | impulse | desolation | convenience |
| distraught | insolent | grossly | ardent |
| remnant | safety | currency | certainty |
| translation | distance | reflection | admission |
| parchment | application | experiment | phantom |
| leafy | tempest | impending | azure |

Why did you divide impulse as you did?

Why did you divide application as you did?

# Teacher-Made Inventory in Context Clue Usage

Underline the word that makes the best sense in the sentence:

1. Mrs. Short shouted triumphantly after him as she watched his figure with _____ as it disappeared into the hall.

   container
   contempt
   courageous

2. She was no more than the servant, but a very _____ old lady wearing her spectacles on the end of her nose.

   independent
   impunity
   irrelevant

3. Dr. Peterson came out of the corridor looking distraught and _____ .

   haranguing
   haggard
   hypocrisy

4. The swing of his nature took him from extreme _____ to devouring energy.

   languid
   languor
   labyrinth

5. The _____ sand slope allowed no escape from a spot which I had visited most involuntarily.

   terminate
   transgress
   treacherous

6. We had reached the same crowded _____ in which we had found ourselves in the morning.

   thoroughness
   thoroughfare
   thoroughly

7. I know that you share my love of all that is _____ and outside the conventions and humdrum routine of everyday life.

   bizarre
   billion
   bigot

**8.** The little house was hidden among the dense _____ on the island.

faint
foliage
foundation

**9.** It was a region of _____, emptiness, truth, and dignity.

loneliness
lonelier
lonesome

**10.** He never said that he would be glad to listen to an _____.

hypochondriac
hysteria
hydrogen

# Teacher-Made Test on Dictionary Usage

1. On what page are the two guide words mounted and movement located?
2. Look up the word gopher. What are the two guide words on this page?
3. What does the word defensive mean?
4. On what page are the two guide words postpone and pottery?
5. According to this dictionary, what is the sound of the e in the word lead, which means to guide or to conduct?
6. According to the pronunciation key of this dictionary, how is the long o sound such as in the word flow marked?
7. On what page are the two guide words nationalism and nature located?
8. According to this dictionary, what is the meaning of the word plateau?
9. What are the two guide words on the page upon which the word situation is located?
10. According to this dictionary, what word is a synonym of the word skillful?

## Preinstructional Technical Vocabulary Test in Social Studies

1. absolute advantage
2. capital
3. collective bargaining
4. competition
5. demand curve
6. derived demand
7. economic growth
8. equation of exchange
9. goods and services
10. indirect tax
11. interfactor substitution
12. land
13. macroeconomics
14. mixed economy
15. national income
16. opportunity cost
17. price index
18. productive resources
19. real capital
20. scarcity
21. specialization
22. law of supply and demand
23. technology
24. velocity of circulation
25. workable competition

Instructional level:   23 words correct

# Checklists of Teacher Observations for Secondary Student's Reading

I. Word Recognition Techniques
- A. Sight Word Recognition
  1. Has a good stock of general vocabulary terms that can be recognized at sight _____
  2. Has a good stock of specialized vocabulary terms in a content area that can be recognized at sight _____
- B. Phonetic Analysis
  1. Is able to use phonetic analysis to determine the pronunciation and meaning of unknown general vocabulary terms _____
  2. Is able to use phonetic analysis to determine the pronunciation and meaning of specialized vocabulary terms in a content area _____
- C. Structural Analysis
  1. Is able to use a base or root word to determine the pronunciation and meaning of an unknown general or specialized vocabulary term _____
  2. Knows the meaning of the following prefixes and can use them in determining the pronunciation and meaning of unknown general or specialized vocabulary terms: a, ante, anti, bi, circum, con, de, dis, ex, in, non, post, pre, pro, re, sub, trans, un _____
  3. Knows the meaning of the following suffixes and can use them in determining the pronunciation and meaning of unknown general or specialized vocabulary terms: able, en, hood, less, ness, er, ment, ward _____
  4. Can correctly divide general and specialized vocabulary terms into syllables _____
  5. Can understand and apply accent in general and specialized vocabulary terms _____
- D. Picture Clue Usage
  1. Is able to use a picture in a tradebook or a content textbook to determine the meaning of an unknown word on the same or a nearby page _____
- E. Context Clue Usage
  1. Is able to apply context clue usage effectively in determining the meaning of an unknown word in a tradebook or a content textbook _____
- F. Dictionary and Glossary Usage
  1. Can use the dictionary or the glossary in a textbook effectively in locating the pronunciation and meaning of unknown words that are met in a content textbook or a tradebook _____
  2. Is able to apply alphabetical sequence _____
  3. Is able to use guide words _____

4. Is able to use the pronunciation key    ————

5. Is able to choose the correct dictionary definition for use in the context of the unknown word ————

II. Comprehension Skills
   A. Literal Comprehension
      1. Is able to answer literal or factual questions that have been posed from content textbooks (Example: What is the duodenum?)    ————
   B. Interpretive Comprehension
      1. Is able to answer interpretive questions that are posed from content textbooks. These questions call for inferring, drawing conclusions, drawing generalizations, summarizing, and reading between the lines. (Example: Why do you think the deciduous teeth sometimes are called "milk teeth"?)    ————
   C. Critical Reading
      1. Is able to answer critical or evaluative questions that have been posed from content textbooks (Example: Do you believe that a teenager who has crooked teeth should see an orthodontist? Why or why not?)    ————
      2. Is able to evaluate such propaganda techniques as the halo effect, the bandwagon effect, glittering generalities, testimonials, and emotionally toned words    ————
   D. Creative Reading
      1. Is able to follow up content reading in a problem-solving situation such as an oral book report, a written book report, an experiment, creative dramatics, roleplaying, or creative writing    ————

III. Study Skills
   A. Finding the Main Idea
      1. Is able to locate a topic sentence in a paragraph    ————
      2. Is able to state a directly stated main idea in a paragraph in his or her own words    ————
      3. Is able to state an implied main idea of a paragraph in his or her own words    ————
      4. Is able to locate the main idea of a longer passage    ————
   B. Significant Details
      1. Is able to locate the significant details in a paragraph    ————
      2. Is able to locate the irrelevant details in a paragraph    ————
   C. Organizational Skills
      1. Is able to outline a single paragraph of a content textbook using main headings and subheadings    ————

        2. Is able to outline a section or a chapter of a content textbook using main headings and sub-headings     _____

        3. Is able to take notes from a content text-book     _____

        4. Is able to summarize a paragraph from a content textbook in his or her own words     _____

        5. Is able to summarize an entire selection from a content textbook in his or her own words     _____

  D. Following Directions

        1. Is able to follow directions in sequence     _____

  E. Location of Information

        1. Can use textbook aids effectively such as the table of contents, index, and glossary     _____

        2. Can locate information using reference material     _____

  F. Graphic Aids

        1. Can interpret maps, charts, tables, and diagrams     _____

IV. Silent Reading

  A. Is interested in reading content materials     _____

  B. Enjoys reading content materials silently as determined from facial expression     _____

  C. Is able to read silently in thought units     _____

  D. Has proper posture and book position while reading silently     _____

  E. Does not use lip movements or whispering in silent reading     _____

  F. Does not use head movement in silent reading     _____

V. Oral Reading

  A. Enjoys reading orally in front of an audience     _____

  B. Is able to read orally in phrases or thought units     _____

  C. Has good expression in oral reading     _____

  D. Observes punctuation marks in oral reading     _____

# CHAPTER FOUR

# *Vocabulary Development*

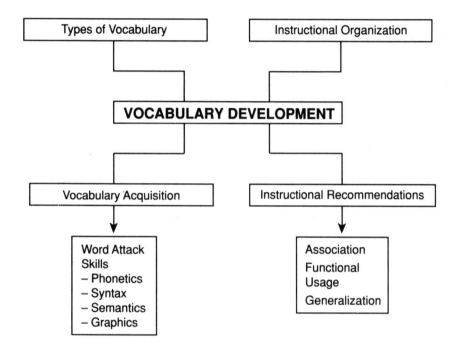

Vocabulary development expands a reader's comprehension by relating known vocabulary to the unknown concepts found in written material. Vocabulary is the bridge that connects the known and the unknown. Unfortunately, vocabulary instruction has historically consisted of abandoning the bridge concept and looking up unfamiliar words in the dictionary, memorizing the definition, and perhaps writing sentences using the new word. When examining this process closely, the unfamiliar word is identified by the teacher, not the student who may or may not need instruction on this word. Then the student is asked to learn the supposed new vocabulary in isolation by reading the word in the dictionary and memorizing the definition. This process does not utilize the background of the student nor does it enable connections to be made between the known and the unknown in the student's background. Despite well-intentioned effort on the part of the students and the teachers, vast amounts of instructional time have been spent on rote learning of vocabulary, with many of the words not retained. The instructional process, not the intention, is limited.

The first problem is that the instructional process has not been related to the student's need to recognize the meaning in the context of reading the textbook, or the need to use the word in speaking or writing situations outside the classroom. Historically, vocabulary instruction has neither considered what the student brings to the instruction (background or schema) or how the student needs to use the word after he or she has demonstrated mastery. This chapter will describe how vocabulary can be taught according to the written, spoken, and reading needs of the student.

Effective vocabulary acquisition is the result of formal vocabulary instruction, which differs from traditional methods. Instructional emphasis should be placed on the following:

1. *Association*—Link the word with prior knowledge or new meaning. In linguistic terms, this is also called *semantics* or the *study of meaning.*

2. *Functional Usage*—Use the word in oral and written activities within classrooms. In linguistic terms, this is also called *syntax.* Saying the word correctly involves the study of *phonetics* and writing the word correctly involves *graphics.*

3. *Generalizability*—Transfer skills to written and oral situations found outside the classroom and on tests constructed by agents other than the teacher.

## Types of Vocabulary

All vocabularies or groups of words are divided into eight different types that differ in size. The usefulness of this distinction is that it keeps teachers from making the mistake of thinking that the student who has a large speaking vocabulary has an equally large reading vocabulary.

1. Nonverbal (by far the largest group; bilingual and remedial readers rely heavily on nonverbal vocabulary of teachers and students)
2. Listening (the second largest group and, like the nonverbal, extremely important means of acquiring information for the culturally deprived student and the slow learner)
3. Reading (limited by the experiences and concepts the reader brings to the material)
4. Speaking (even more limited than the vocabularies previously discussed, with standards of peer group limiting generally to group's accepted means of expressions)
5. Spelling (students think with large vocabularies and then translate their thoughts into limited spelling vocabularies, which results in their thoughts also becoming limited [Olson & Ames, 1972])

6. General (consists of everyday, general vocabulary words which take on specialized meanings when adapted to particular content area.

7. Technical (words which have usage and application only in a particular content field)

The different vocabularies make it apparent that students may have one large vocabulary in listening, for example, and a small vocabulary in reading. Vocabulary size is not uniform in different situations. In addition, teachers cannot assume that the student who reads widely has a large vocabulary. With so many different types of vocabularies, accidental acquisition may or may not occur. If a student reads voraciously in science, he or she may not be considered a competent reader in history. The vocabularies are different in each field and may not reinforce each other. In fact, technical vocabularies like those used with computers often serve to isolate students from communicating with others rather than act as a bridge to already existing vocabularies.

The remainder of this chapter will focus on questions asked by subject specialists or content teachers about vocabulary instruction.

1. What are vocabulary and word attack skills?
2. How should content teachers provide vocabulary instruction?
3. How do content teachers organize their classrooms to provide vocabulary instruction?

Whatever the question or the type of vocabulary the teacher is attempting to expand, the objective remains the same—to enhance the students' abilities to express themselves. The greater the vocabulary mastery students have, the more satisfactorily they will be able to express and receive meaning. Extensive vocabularies enable students to participate more successfully in our overwhelmingly verbal, information-based society.

# Vocabulary Acquisition

*What are vocabulary and word attack skills?*

The place to begin vocabulary instruction is with words that are necessary for understanding each content field, referred to as *key vocabulary*. The teacher must identify key concepts in the specific subject area. Once the concepts are delineated, then the words in those concepts become the key vocabulary vital to the comprehension of the text and the course. Herman (1979) found that both able and less able readers who read text versions in which key vocabulary and the relations among them had been explained thoroughly, learned significantly more word meanings than did other students who read text that used other comprehension aides. Although key vocabulary may be obvious to the teacher, it is not so obvious to students. Earle (1976) stated it well when he said, "The teaching process must always be one of trying to ensure student success in reading and learning; do not expect students to already know what they come to class to learn."

**Semantics.**   Vocabulary, word attack skills, and instruction fall into four general linguistic areas: semantics, syntax, graphics, and phonetics. Semantics is the study of words associated with their meaning. Historically, semantics has been the classification of changes in the significance of words or forms viewed as factors in linguistic development. This means the study of the history of words, sound changes, and meaning changes would be a part of vocabulary development. "Did you know that the word *cot* came from India, and those words ending with "eau," like *bureau* or *beau*, that give you problems in spelling were borrowed from the French during the period when the Normans occupied England?" This might be a question that a history or English grammar teacher would ask related to the study of the history of language. Semantics can also be the simple association of a word with the definition relevant for the particular content classroom. In this manner, semantics activities expand reading vocabularies by taking words in general vocabularies and placing them in special and technical vocabularies. Vocabulary instruction must begin by making associations that provide meaning for the student. The most frequent method of teaching word associations or semantics is having students look the word up in the dictionary, which is appropriate if they can spell it in the first place.

**Syntax.**   The next linguistic area, syntax, is the study of words using the sentence as a means of obtaining meaning. Within this area, the study of context clues has had a great deal of emphasis. Also, the relationship of the word to other words in the sentence, called the study of *grammar*, is a syntactical strategy for associating the word with meaning. For example, the words *vestiges* or *predominate* in the following extract could be understood from placement in the sentence and grammatical relationships:

> While there may remain towns or outposts where even a black family will be something of an oddity, where English and Irish and German surnames will predominate, where a "traditional" America will still be seen on almost every street corner, they will be only the vestiges of an earlier nation. By 2056, the average U.S. resident will trace his or her descent to Africa, Asia, the Hispanic world, the Pacific Islands, Arabia—almost anywhere but white Europe. (*Time*, April 9, 1990)

**Graphics.**   Graphics is the third word attack area. *Graph* means spelling. This area of vocabulary development and word attack looks at graphemes, which are the sum of all written letters that represent one phoneme or morpheme. The phoneme is the smallest unit of recognizable spoken sound, and the morpheme is the smallest unit of written sound. Within this area of study are such strategies as prefix, suffix, and root study; learning to break words into syllables; and recognizing compound words. Graphics has also become associated with graphology, the study of handwriting as a means of determining personality characteristics. Although this is not the primary function of graphology in classroom instruction, the study of handwriting could be a strategy for improving and developing an interest in writing and language. Graphics expands vocabulary by integrating listening and speaking vocabularies with reading and spelling vocabularies.

**Phonetics.** Phonetics is the study of spoken language. Since much of beginning reading instruction begins with the spoken language and then moves to the written language, phonetic instruction is frequently found in lower elementary and ESL classrooms. Phonics rules that have high utility are often memorized by students: "When two vowels go walking, the first one does the talking." For native speakers, phonetics instruction is a means of expanding vocabulary size by integrating sounds of the listening vocabulary into the reading vocabulary.

Whether the instruction focuses on word attack or vocabulary expansion, instructional activities can be identified as semantic, syntactic, graphic, and phonetic. Debates on whether children should learn vocabulary using whole language or the skill-based approaches are questions as to whether associations in semantics or phonetics should be the first step in vocabulary instruction. Thelen (1990) describes the debate as follows:

> Whole language is a philosophy that views reading as a cognitive process where readers use semantics, syntactics, and graphophonics to predict meaning. When readers come to an unknown word, they are asked to think about what word would make sense in the sentence, to think about the meaning of the sentence by using prior knowledge, and to apply what they know about letters and sounds. Merely sounding out an unknown word without reflection on the total meaning only leads to word calling. . . . Intensive phonics teachers and whole language teachers use phonics; the only difference is when and why.

# Instructional Recommendations

*How should content teachers provide vocabulary instruction?*

**Associate Words with Meaning.** Vocabulary instruction should concentrate on what the student is asked to perform rather than what he or she is expected to memorize. Is she asked to work on a math problem that uses unknown symbols or is he asked to write a critique? At the most basic level, the association level, students are asked to have an understanding of new word meanings. In order for a sequence of letters or words to have meaning, they must be associated with a definition or decoded into a word that is recognizable in the listening or speaking vocabulary. The association must be accurate because once made, primary associations are difficult to replace. Everyone who has learned someone's name incorrectly and then attempts to learn the actual name can testify to the difficulty of changing associations once they are made. It is much easier to associate an unknown word with something familiar in the person's background or connect both the word and the meaning to relevant information. In essence, decoding and word association is the process of understanding relationships between the word and its definition or the word and prior knowledge of letters, phonemes, and morphemes or in a listening or speaking vocabulary. Association with prior meaning or new meaning is the first activity.

Initially, all individuals follow a similar sequence in learning words. They make associations of print to graphic to phonemic awareness, which results in word comprehension (Lomas & Shanahan, 1988; Chall, 1989). Students are inclined to learn words that relate to their background knowledge, the attitudes of those using the words toward the subject discussed, and the response of people in the environment to the vocabulary usage. For example, words used in political articles, such as *peristroiyka, glasnost,* and *detente,* are unlikely to be learned even though they are repeated frequently on the television and in the newspaper. Most people will not learn new words that do not have a personal meaning for them.

In order to associate a word with its meaning, several approaches are possible. The word and definition can be given directly in lecture or written form, which follows the traditional pattern. This instructional pattern is introduced first because most students can associate it with their own experience. Disadvantages of using this strategy are introducing the word in isolation and not providing an association of the word to an event, experience, or skill in the students' backgrounds. A second strategy is to have students look for synonyms and antonyms, which is still studying the meaning associations or semantics. Other strategies are to use syntax and have students associate meaning from context, from the word's grammar location or construction, or from graphic and phonetic construction by breaking the word into parts, looking at roots, prefixes, and suffixes.

According to Nicholson and Hill (1984), the ability of students to decode words independent of context seem to separate good readers from poor readers. But again, this is how students are tested in vocabulary sections of reading tests. So, those who can decode well are likely to be identified as good readers. Even high school students have limited skills in determining meaning of unfamiliar words from context. Schatz-Kress and Baldwin (1986) found high school students incompetent in using context clues. An interesting question was not asked of the students in the study, however: How long ago had they had direct instruction in how to find context clues? Wysolki and Jenkins (1987) and Simpson (1986) found that students' success in deriving meanings from unfamiliar words is affected by prior experience with related word-decoding skills they possess before they read a word in context.

Techniques of instruction should begin with word attack skills or key word activities. Examples of such activities are found at the end of this chapter. They demonstrate how to teach reading subskills in a subject matter or content lesson. Much research has been directed toward isolating subskills related to vocabulary and reading. These subskills have been introduced in elementary school reading and language arts programs and could be reinforced in the content classroom. More than likely, the word attack subskills are also taught in remedial reading programs and ESL programs. The content teacher can either pick a subskill to reinforce or provide instruction for key words in the content field. For example, one of the subskills related to vocabulary and reading comprehension is that words may have more than one meaning. Becoming familiar with the multiple meanings of words and word histories would be part of a vocabulary reinforcement program. Other subskills, such as the use of context clues and structural analysis of prefixes, suffixes, roots, morphemes, syllables, could be the focus of an instructional lesson of vocabulary words taken from any subject area. The vocabulary games that follow in the Teaching Activities section demonstrate how vocabulary instruction could be conducted in various content classrooms. Some vocabulary games can be used with any subject, whereas others are specifically developed for one content area.

To reading instructors, word-decoding skills have meant structural analysis of syllables, morphemes, prefixes, suffixes, and roots. Also included is knowledge of specific regular sound-symbol correspondences necessary to decode words and a systematic approach to using context and/or syntax and written-sound correspondences to help in attacking words and deriving word meanings. The selection of skills for instruction and the emphasis or length of time spent on them has been the teacher's decision.

**Functional Usage Level.**   The second expectation is that students can use new words in spoken, written, or reading activities. Everyone has speaking, writing, reading, and listening vocabularies. These vocabularies are not the same in either content or number of words, although there is obviously overlap. For example, a student may be able to use a word in speech but not be able to read the same word, or the student may be able to read the word silently but not know how to pronounce it. When teachers have a student use new vocabulary in sentences, they are providing instruction on this application level of learning. Functional-level activities ensure that the student uses words learned at the association level. If teachers also had the student find the word in the textbook or use the word in classroom discussions, then they would be asking the student to use the word in functional spoken or reading activities. In the functional usage activities, teachers provide opportunities to use new vocabulary in as many different types of vocabularies as possible.

A great deal of word repetition is necessary in order to overlearn or retain vocabulary. Many years ago, Gates (1953) identified the number of repetitions needed for word mastery as related to IQ. Even the most intelligent people require at least 20 repetitions. Gates's findings have not been disproved in the decades that have followed. Multiple encounters with words or applications, then, is the key to mastery learning of vocabulary. Effective reading occurs when almost all the words encountered are firmly fixed in long-term memory. The process of placing words in long-term memory is one of repeated encounter and application.

**Generalize Beyond Classroom.**  One purpose of education is to transfer skills from the classroom to the world beyond the school. To *generalize* means to transfer. Students who have learned the meaning of a word and are able to read it in a written passage are ready for the third step in vocabulary mastery—to demonstrate competence through using the word outside of a textbook-controlled situation. Mastery might be shown by scores on vocabulary portions of the Stanford, PSAT, SAT, ACT, or other standardized tests that are state or district mandated. The words might appear in spoken or written activities, called *extension activities.* Generalizing vocabulary should be the goal of all instruction and testing. More explicit expression of meaning for the student is the purpose of expanding vocabulary.

Additional support for the generalization principle comes from Hafner (1978):

> A major goal of education is the accomplishment of transfer of training in as many situations as possible. If you expect transfer of training, you should teach for transfer. Whether you use an identical elements theory or a generalization theory of transfer it is incumbent upon you to teach concepts, rules, skills and attitudes for transfer to similar concepts rules and the like and for transfer to related life situations.

Hafner's point is that transfer of learning in and from the classroom is not automatic. Failure to teach transfer skills accounts for low standardized test scores when students have already learned the material. How does a teacher help students transfer learning? Here are some discussion questions and activities that promote transfer and thus expand the expertise of the student.

*Sample Transfer Activities*

**1.**  List some things that you recognize visually. How do you recognize them? What, if any, are the similarities between the recognition of the printed word and other things that you recognize?

**2.**  Test several people with a number of difficult words to determine 5 to 10 printed words that they do not recognize. Using word-picture cards, teach the words to mastery level. After one hour, test the people individually to determine how many words they can recognize or recall.

**3.** Have a class discussion to see what kinds of mediating devices students use.

**4.** Make a list of tasks that lend themselves to overlearning. Have students overlearn material in an area in which they are weak; they can note the degree of overlearning. Discuss any change in self-concept and/or attitude toward task and/or subject matter related to the task.

**5.** Consider the quantity and quality of self-instruction and transfer taking place in one of your classes. Devise a set of concrete recommendations for improving self-instruction in the class. (Hafner, 1978, p. 55)

Vocabulary instruction must make certain that students can identify new words in settings that are not textbook controlled. (Sometimes these are called *tests.*) When students' vocabularies are assessed on standardized tests, they must read, recognize, understand, and relate to the word in the format given in the test. The process of demonstrating vocabulary knowledge on standardized tests has little relationship to the skills the students mastered in traditional instruction of using the dictionary, memorizing the definition, and using it in a sentence. Tests also have little relationship to the background of the student. Although there are indications that testing formats are considering changes in what Manzo and Manzo (1990) call emerging trends in testing, word identification in isolation has not disappeared from reading tests.

Students are still expected to recognize a word without the help of context or personal or subject matter background. This means their skills at recognizing a word out of context must be practiced. The traditional spelling lists were good examples of how this testing skill could be practiced. However, most students were assisted by the fact that they had learned the words that week. If the words were scrambled, given from the month before, and listed in a different fashion, students would have been given practice in vocabulary testing as it currently exists. The best way to practice the third level of expanding vocabulary is through the use of practice tests and vocabulary games. Television game shows have helped the classroom teacher motivate students by introducing this process of instruction as entertainment. Vocabulary games can provide entertaining means of expanding students' vocabularies on all three levels.

## Summary

The three major instructional principles of vocabulary acquisition are association, functional, and generalization concepts. These progressively difficult levels of instructional procedures demonstrate how vocabulary will not be retained unless it can be used and recognized in reading, listening, writing, and speaking experiences that may or may not occur inside the classroom. By providing vocabulary instruction that follows this process, learning new words will be integrated into the experiences and backgrounds of the students. And students will have mastered the words in a manner that will ensure they will retain the vocabulary.

## Instructional Organization

*How do content teachers organize their classrooms to provide vocabulary instruction?*

The variety of options for scheduling vocabulary instruction are based on classroom organization. If the classroom is self contained and whole class instruction is used, then the easiest way to expand vocabulary is to follow one of these three patterns.

### Class Organization Patterns

1. Write the vocabulary words on the board. Then provide five minutes at the beginning of class for students to define the words and write a paragraph using the words. On the next day, have them find the words in magazines or in their text. On the third day, have students make tests on the words for other students. These five-minute activities follow the three principles of vocabulary instruction with an additional benefit for the teacher. Five minutes at the beginning of class for vocabulary instruction enables the teacher to take roll, handle individual students, and establish a predictable pattern of student behavior at the beginning of class.

2. When introducing a new chapter, select key words that are represented by pictures or symbols other than letters and integrate them into DRAs (Directed Reading Assignments). Introduce the words on the literal level at the beginning of the chapter, ask questions about the words on the functional level in the middle of the chapter, and use the words in the test at the end of the chapter.

3. One day can be set aside as vocabulary game day. If classes are organized into small groups, the vocabulary games and activities given in the Teaching Activities section can be given to each group following the word meaning, reading, writing, speaking, and listening application and generalization sequence.

A whole-class instructional schedule would look something like this format, which could be given to the students in a handout. This could be any content or subject area class.

### Sample Class Schedule

1. During the first 10 minutes of class, you will do the vocabulary activities written on the board while I take roll.

2. Next, we will correct homework.
3. New material will be explained and questions will be answered.
4. We will have a class activity that demonstrates the new material.
5. You will have time to do homework in class.

When a new vocabulary word is found in context, the context will not be useful unless some of the following questions can be answered:

1. Is the context definition close to the unknown word?
2. Is there a clear connection between the new vocabulary word and the context amplifiers?
3. Is the context information explicit?
4. Is the new word important to the understanding of the vocabulary?
5. Is the passage well written and complete?
6. Will the context be familiar enough to be useful to the student's perception of necessary information? (Konopak & Williams, 1988)

It makes sense that students must be prompted to repeat the word in reading or listening experiences. Teachers might give reading assignments and assume that the students will encounter the word one, two, or three times. But as most content teachers have found, students will not read assignments unless the work is discussed or tested in class. Many beginning content teachers assume that they can give reading homework assignments and that students will complete them with very little teacher help. However, they soon learn that students need classroom instruction before reading can be done outside of class. Although new vocabulary encountered in written material is one way to increase repetition and place words in long-term memory, classroom activities must reinforce the reading of assignments by testing or class discussion. Otherwise, teachers cannot assume that reading the vocabulary taught in class and then read in the content textbook will be an effective manner of increasing the number of repetitions.

Another recommendation is that the repetition of vocabulary not be confused with the repetition of word attack strategies. For example, students can be taught how to break words into syllables by using the vccv rule. (When two consonants are together, like in the word *also*, the syllables are found by dividing the word between the two consonants.) Students are then given lists of words that they are to divide into syllables. This is a repetition of the word attack strategy but not the vocabulary words learned in the association level of instruction. The teacher cannot expect the repetition of the strategy to reinforce the vocabulary retention. Although there is value in both repetition of the strategy and vocabulary words, there is little merit in confusing the two in the levels of instruction.

# Summary

Research recommends that teachers must hold students accountable for textbook reading assignments and the vocabulary found in the reading. The more encounters a student has with a word, the more likely he or she will remember and use it. Teachers should also follow the associative, functional, and generalizable levels of vocabulary instruction in word attack skills as well as in technical and key vocabulary instruction. The important issues are not to confuse word attack skill mastery with vocabulary instruction. Word attack skills address means of dividing words according to phonetic or graphic principles. Vocabulary instruction relates to phonemic, semantic, and syntactic uses. Teachers also should not stop instruction on the association or functional level. And finally, the more students can be exposed to vocabulary both inside and outside of the classroom, the more likely they are to extend their vocabularies. That is why vocabulary games have been provided as both a motivating and instructional method to be used with students at school, on the bus, and at home. One vocabulary game for each subject area is included in the Teaching Activities section.

# Application Exercises and Teaching Activities

## Application Exercises

1.   David gets 100 percent on most of his vocabulary quizzes. He seems to enjoy learning new words. However, his vocabulary scores on the yearly standardized tests are always around 20 percent. What instructional problem is taking place here?

2.   Nancy hears a word and then she recognizes the word in her textbook. The teacher is forced to read the textbook questions aloud to her and then she understands the material. Discuss the vocabulary difficulty that exists for Nancy.

3.   Rod talks all the time but will not read the textbook. What would the teacher suspect in this case?

4.   A teacher has students look up words they do not know in the dictionary. A week later, she is disappointed when the students are unable to recognize the same words in the text. What should she have done in providing vocabulary instruction beyond having the students look up the word in the dictionary?

5.   Dictionary work is considered the first step in word mastery. What instructional steps should follow for a teacher interested in not having to spend a great deal of time providing vocabulary instruction?

**6.** How could verbal vocabulary level be a factor contributing to a teacher's lecture that fails to communicate to students?

**7.** Listen to the language of several secondary students who are the same age. Do you notice any differences in their spoken vocabulary size?

**8.** Schizophrenia is a mental illness. One of the characteristics is being unable to select the appropriate sense of a word. This is both the chief symptom of the disease and a major factor that prevents patients from arriving at an appropriate interpretation of information. What vocabulary subskill is disturbed for these people?

**9.** Your principal has just asked you how you plan to teach the technical vocabulary of your subject. What is your response?

**10.** Identify key vocabulary in a specific chapter of your content textbook.

**11.** What is the difference between key vocabulary and word attack subskills?

**12.** Devise a plan for increasing your own vocabulary.

# Teaching Activities:
# Math Jeopardy Vocabulary Game

*Materials*

1. Algebra book
2. Construction paper or 3 × 5 cards
3. Scissors
4. Rings for cards
5. Black marker (king-sized)
6. 4 dowels and 2 slats or something to hold the cards in place

*Reading Skill*

1. Graphics
2. Semantics

*Level*

This game is intended for secondary math students. Its target area is algebra and trigonometry, therefore it can be used as a review for a midterm or ACT/SAT test, functional and generalization levels.

*Number of Players*

Range from 2–15; preferably 3 columns of 4 or 5 players

*Teacher Instruction*

Organize students into 3 or 4 columns, each column having approximately 4 players. Once the order of play has been set (who goes first, etc.) then the game can begin. After a player selects a category, the teacher reads the answer or explains what the equation is asking. The teacher is basically the host of this game show. Try to be lively and entertaining *(get wild and crazy)*—the students will remember more and enjoy the experience. For more information, read the rules.

*Rules*

*How to Play*

The first person to play will pick a category that the team desires. After selection of the category, the teacher reads the answer or explains what the equation is asking. If the student asks the correct question, the next student in the column is asked the next card. Once the category has been answered, the next team chooses another category and "answers" the question. This continues until all "answers" are given or time expires.

## Incorrect Answers

If a person asks an incorrect question, the next person in the column has a chance to pose a question. If the two members of the team both give wrong questions, then the next person on the next team has a chance to "steal." Stealing a question is the only time that the team can jointly give the answer to their teammate. If the person (with the help of his teammates) gives an incorrect question, it continues down the line until it goes back to the original team. If the original team cannot ask the correct question, it is discarded and the game resumes with the original team. (Of course, all responses must be in the form of question, such as, "What is _____?")

## Categories

A team must choose a category that has not been previously answered. The team cannot jump over unanswered categories to get a category in a higher point bracket.

## Points

A team receives the points for a specific category only after "answering" all the questions in that category. If a team "steals" a question, that team must answer the remaining question in the category correctly to receive the points. Bonus points are given to the team whose member answers the "bonus" question correctly. Bonus questions will have individual point value on them and will be a different color than the particular category.

## Winning

The team with the highest points at the end of the game (without cheating) WINS!

# Vocabulary Games

*Machine Works—Science*

Vocabulary Area:   Semantics, Syntax
Instructional Level:   Association
Materials:   1 gameboard, 2 dice, 2 markers, 1 vocabulary list

Directions:

1. Form two teams with one, two, or three players on each team.
2. Each team needs a game board and 1 marker.
3. Each team throws a die. The team with the highest number plays first.
4. One team member throws both dice. The team must then add, subtract, multiply, or divide the 2 numbers to select the number of the sentence they will complete.
5. If the right answer is given, a check is put in the box to the right of the sentence. The other team should check the key on the back of their gameboard for the right answer.
6. If you give the right answer, take another turn. If you give the wrong answer, it is the other team's turn.
7. Keep playing until all the boxes on the right have been checked. The first team to fill them all is the winner!
8. Use the vocabulary list if you need help with the words.

## Vocabulary List—Set 1

| | | | |
|---|---|---|---|
| work | pulleys | friction | load |
| computer | screw | motion | column |
| magnet | fixed pulley | steep | ramp |
| force | gravity | magnetism | energy |
| movable pulleys | wedge | mass | compound |
| simple machine | machine | gear | machine |
| meter | wheel and axle | inclined plane | lubricant |

**Machine Works**

*Team 1, Set 1*

| | | |
|---|---|---|
| 1 | A doorknob is a simple machine called a _____. | |
| 2 | A snow shovel is a _____. | |
| 3 | _____ is always needed to make something move. | |
| 4 | The incline up the hill was very _____. | |
| 5 | A ball thrown into the air always falls to the ground because of _____. | |
| 6 | _____ is used whenever a force moves something. | |
| 7 | The force of _____ causes metal objects to be attracted. | |
| 8 | A _____ must be turned to move into the wood. | |
| 9 | You are doing _____ if you push a chair across the room. | |
| 10 | A _____ on a flagpole stays in one place. | |
| 11 | Slowing down and stopping are changes in the motion of the shuffleboard disk caused by _____. | |
| 12 | Scissors are made of two levers that work together and are an example of a _____. | |
| 13 | The _____ to be moved was very heavy. | |
| 14 | A _____ is a special kind of machine with teeth. | |

**Key**

*Team 1, Set 1*

| 1 | wheel and axle |
|---|---|
| 2 | simple machine |
| 3 | Force |
| 4 | steep |
| 5 | gravity |
| 6 | Energy |
| 7 | Magnetism |
| 8 | screw |
| 9 | work |
| 10 | fixed pulley |
| 11 | friction |
| 12 | compound machine |
| 13 | load |
| 14 | gear |

**Machine Works**

*Team 2, Set 1*

| | | |
|---|---|---|
| 1 | The iron filings were attracted to the _____. | |
| 2 | A _____ can be used to split things apart. | |
| 3 | Speeding up, slowing down, turning, and stopping are all changes in _____. | |
| 4 | You can use a _____ to move a heavy rock. | |
| 5 | _____ are used to move objects up, down, or sideways. | |
| 6 | A heavy object has more _____ than a light object. | |
| 7 | A steering _____ is a vertical axle you will see in a car. | |
| 8 | _____ are used to lift heavy loads. | |
| 9 | The car uses oil as a _____ in the engine to keep the parts moving freely. | |
| 10 | A _____ is something that helps people do work. | |
| 11 | Moving things into the back of a truck is made easier by using a _____. | |
| 12 | A _____ is a machine that can solve difficult problems in only a few seconds. | |
| 13 | Any slanted surface can be called an _____. | |
| 14 | A _____ is a measure of length equal to 100 centimeters or 39 inches. | |

**Key**

*Team 2, Set 1*

| 1 | magnet |
|---|---|
| 2 | wedge |
| 3 | motion |
| 4 | lever |
| 5 | Pulleys |
| 6 | mass |
| 7 | column |
| 8 | Movable pulleys |
| 9 | lubricant |
| 10 | machine |
| 11 | ramp |
| 12 | computer |
| 13 | inclined plane |
| 14 | meter |

# History/Geography

*Know the U.S.A.*

Objective:   To help students with American history and to provide vocabulary instruction in analogies and semantics.
Level:   Functional
Number of Players:   2 or more
Materials Needed:   playing cards, score sheet, answer sheet

### Rules of Play:

1. Pick a card from the deck.
2. Answer the question.
3. If answered correctly, the student writes his or her name next to each of his or her correct answers on the score pad.
4. If answered incorrectly, it is the next player's chance to try. If answered incorrectly by the second player, the card is passed until a player answers accurately.
5. The game continues until all the cards have been answered correctly and all the answers are circled on the score sheet.
6. The winner of the game is the student with the most correct answers on the score pad.

### Sample Vocabulary Analogies To Be Put On Playing Cards

1. Literature is to novel as _____ is to Little Rock.
2. Circle is to center as _____ is to Hartford.
3. Constitution is to articles as Massachusetts is to _____.
4. Sentence is to subject as North Dakota is to _____.
5. Ranch is to stable as Connecticut is to _____.
6. Tree is to root as Ohio is to _____.
7. House is to yard as New York is to _____.
8. Body is to appendix as _____ is to Salt Lake.
9. School is to class as Ohio is to _____.
10. Language is to sign as Delaware is to _____.
11. Land is to soil as North Carolina is to _____.
12. Play is to ticket as Wisconsin is to _____.
13. Pants are to belt as West Virginia is to _____.
14. Engine is to points as Colorado is to _____.

## Score Sheet

| | |
|---|---|
| Alabama | Albany |
| Alaska | Annapolis |
| Arizona | Atlanta |
| Arkansas | Augusta |
| California | Austin |
| Colorado | Baton Rouge |
| Connecticut | Bismarck |
| Delaware | Boise |

| | |
|---|---|
| Florida | Boston |
| Georgia | Carson City |
| Hawaii | Charleston |
| Idaho | Cheyenne |
| Illinois | Columbia |
| Indiana | Concord |
| Iowa | Denver |
| Kansas | Des Moines |
| Kentucky | Dover |
| Louisiana | Frankfort |
| Maine | Harrisburg |
| Maryland | Hartford |
| Massachusetts | Helena |
| Michigan | Honolulu |
| Minnesota | Indianapolis |
| Missouri | Jackson |

# Inner Circle (Shown for Science)

Vocabulary Skill:   phonetics, graphics
Instructional Level:   associative and functional
Materials:   dice, any gameboard, playing pieces, question cards constructed from textbook vocabulary words at front of chapter or in glossary

Long ago, the inner circle was reserved for only the best: the best athletes, the best thinkers, the best craftsmen. Can you make it to the inner circle?

Rules:

1. The Inner Circle may be played by 2 to 7 players.
2. Choose a gatekeeper. The gatekeeper keeps score and guards the magic words. Since he or she does not move a playing piece around the board, a new gatekeeper must be chosen for each game.
3. Each player rolls the dice. The one with the highest roll goes first, then the person to his or her right, and so on.
4. The game begins at Gate 1.
5. The beginning player rolls the dice and moves her or his playing piece the number of spaces indicated by the dice. If the player lands on a white space, he or she must follow the instructions printed on that space. If the white space contains a question mark, the player must draw the top card from a color-coded stack of question cards. For example, if a player lands on a space with a blue question mark, then he draws a blue question card. If she lands on a red question mark space, she draws a red question card, etc.
6. On the back of the question card is a magic word. The player must give the gatekeeper a definition of the magic word and use the word in a sentence. The gatekeeper refers to his or her list of magic words for the definition. If the player is able to define *and* use the word correctly, the gatekeeper marks a "1" for that player's score.
7. When a player has defined and used 5 magic words correctly, he or she may enter the next circle by placing his or her playing piece on the gate space for that circle. No partial credit is given if the player knows the definition but cannot use the word in a sentence, and vice versa. (When a player goes from the 4th circle to the inner circle, he or she simply places his or her playing piece in the inner circle.)
8. The first one to reach the inner circle wins.

Another Way to Play:
Divide the players into teams. The first team to get all of its members into the inner circle wins.

1. Biology—the study of life
   bi—life; ology—study of
2. Archeology—study of life and culture of ancient people
   arche—beginning; ology—study of
3. Autobiography—the practice of writing one's own life story
   auto—self; bio—life; graphy—write
4. Binomial—a two-word scientific name of a plant or animal
   bi—two; nomial—name
5. Decapitate—behead, or to cut off the head
   de—off or away from; capit—head; ate—act of
6. Carcinogen—any substance that produces cancer
   carcin—relating to cancer; gen—to produce
7. Insecticide—any substance used to kill insects
   insect—insect; icide—to kill
8. Cooperate—to work together
   co—together; operate—operate
9. Leukocyte—a white blood cell
   leuk—white; ocyte—cell
10. Dislocate—to pull out of place
    dis—away from; locate—locate
11. Epidermis—the outer most layer of skin
    epi—upon; dermis—skin
12. Erythrocyte—a red blood cell
    erythro—red; cyte—cell
13. Fission—to split
    fis—to split; sion—the act of
14. Deflect—to turn or to make to go to one side
    de—away from; flect—to bend or divert
15. Function—the normal or characteristic action of anything
    func—perform; tion—the act of
16. Epiglottis—the thin lid-like piece of cartilage that folds back over the opening of the windpipe
    epi—upon; glottis—tongue-like
17. Genetics—the study of heredity and variation in similar or related animals and plants
    gene—to produce; tics—study of
18. Intravenous—directly into a vein or veins
    intra—inside; venous—veins
19. Microscope—an instrument used to magnify small objects for study
    micro—small; scope—to look, observe
20. Morphology—the branch of biology that deals with the form and structure of plants and animals
    morph—form, shape; ology—study of
21. Neurology—the branch of medicine dealing with the brain.
    neuro—nerve; ology—study of

22. Hydrophobia—the fear of water
    hydro—water; phobia—the fear of
23. Zoology—the study of animals
    zo—animals, life; ology—study of
24. Autotroph—an organism capable of making its own food through photosynthesis
    auto—self; troph—grow
25. Photosynthesis—the biological synthesis of chemical compounds in the presence of light
    photo—light; syn—together; the—put or place; sis—act of
26. Pericardium—a thin, membranous sac that surrounds the heart
    peri—around; cardium—heart
27. Chlorophyll—the green pigment found in the leaves of plants
    chloro—green; phyll—leaf

## Speech/ESL

*Recall Game Manual*

Content Area:   Speech
Skill:   To familarize students with definitions of phonetics and articulation, thereby increasing the students' awareness of some
of the processes involved in speech production. The purpose
of this game is to enhance the phonetic and communication
skills of the speaker.
Number of Players:   2–4
Age Appropriateness:   Secondary grade levels.

Game Rules:
Each player begins by spinning the arrow. The player must be
able to:

1. Give a relevant definition of the term the arrow is spun to.
2. Use the term meaningfully in a complete sentence.
3. Choose the correct phoneme, or combination of phonemes,
   from the word located under the phonetic term that the arrow
   had originally been spun to.

Upon the successful completion of all three tasks, the player receives one chip and the game proceeds to the next player. If,
however, the player is unable to complete any of the three tasks, an
opposing player may challenge. If the opposing player is able to
complete the remaining task(s), then that player receives the chip
and the game proceeds to the next player. If the opposing player is
unable to complete the remaining task(s), then the challenger loses
one of his or her chips. A player must have at least one chip previously earned before he or she may challenge. The player who has
earned the most chips wins the game.

*Recall Answer Sheet*

Affricative—A single speech sound that can be analyzed as the
sequence of a plosive followed immediately by a homorganic
fricative.

Back Vowel—The vowel sounds produced as a result of the
action (position) of the back of the tongue.

Bilabial Consonant—The consonants that are produced as a
result of lipclosing action that stops or diverts the flow of breath.

Central Vowel—Vowel sounds produced as a result of the action
(position) of the central portion of the tongue.

Cluster—A group of consonants in the same syllable without a
vowel between them.

Cognate Sound—A term used to indicate a sound that shares manner and place of articulation, but differs in voicing.

Continuant Consonant—A consonant sound having duration and produced with the articulators in a fixed position.

Diphthong—Vocalic glides of two vowels uttered in a single breath impulse within one syllable.

Fricative—A class of consonants in which air is forced through a narrow opening between two articulators.

Front Vowel—The vowels produced as a result of the action (position) of the front of the tongue.

Glide Sound—Sounds produced as a result of the continuous movement of the articulators.

Glottal Sound—Refers to sound produced as a result of laryngeal tension and action, as by a sudden stoppage and release of breath by the vocal folds.

Homorganic—Said of a speech sound having the same place of articulation as another sound.

Labial—A class of speech sounds articulated with the lips.

Labiodental—Consonants produced as a result of the activity of the lower lip and upper teeth.

Lateral—A class of speech sounds in which the mouth is blocked centrally by the tongue and air is allowed to pass out over the sides.

Lingua-Alveolar—The consonants produced as a result of contact between tongue tip and alveolar ridge (gum ridge).

Liquid—A class of sounds that are characterized by a vowel-like quality.

Morpheme—The smallest unit of speech that carries meaning.

Nasal Consonant—The speech sounds produced with nasal reinforcement.

Palatal Sound—Any speech sound articulated with the tongue arched in the region of the hard palate.

Phoneme—The distinctive sound elements of a word.

Plosive Sound—The sound produced with a complete closing of the breath channel.

Semi-Vowel—A voiced glide.

Sibilant—A speech sound where there is high pitched, turbulent noise.

*Recall Answer Sheet—Words*

Church—ch = affricative
Paw—a = back vowel
Mother—m = bilabial consonant
Feather—er = central vowel
black—bl = cluster
today—t & d = cognate sounds
Life—l = continuant consonant
ice—i = diphthong
Family—f = fricative
Meet—ee = front vowel
Yellow—y = glide sound
Hat—h = glottal sound
Land—l, n, & d are all homorganic
Nobody—b = labial
Flower—f = labiodental
laugh—l = lateral
nap—n = lingua-alveolar
Run—r = liquid
Cat's—'s = morpheme
Man—m = nasal consonant
Young—y = palatal sound
Language—each letter is a phoneme
Pam—p = plosive sound
Weather—w = semi-vowel
Song—s = sibilant

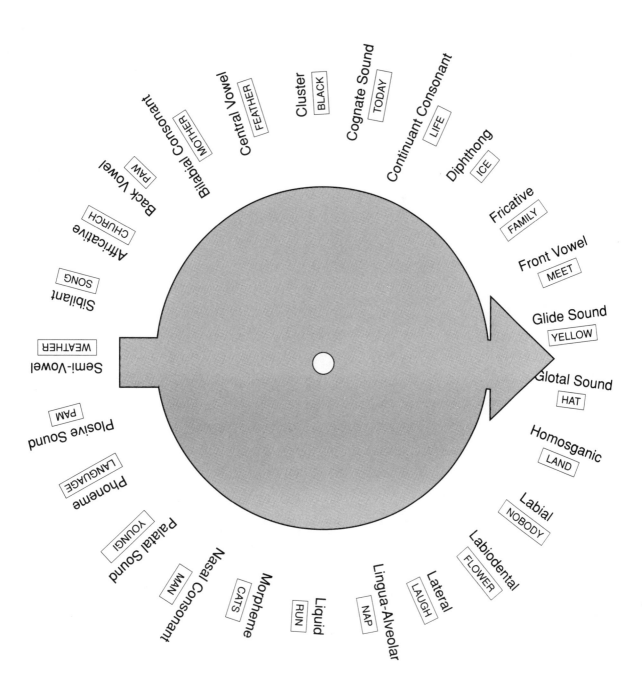

Central Vowel FEATHER

Cluster BLACK

Cognate Sound TODAY

Continuant Consonant LIFE

Diphthong ICE

Fricative FAMILY

Front Vowel MEET

Glide Sound YELLOW

Glotal Sound HAT

Homosganic LAND

Labial NOBODY

Labiodental FLOWER

Lateral LAUGH

Lingua-Alveolar NAP

Liquid RUN

Morpheme CATS

Nasal Consonant MAN

Palatal Sound YOUNG!

Phoneme LANGUAGE

Plosive Sound PAM

Semi-Vowel WEATHER

Sibilant SONG

Affricative CHURCH

Back Vowel PAW

Bilabial Consonant MOTHER

117

# CHAPTER FIVE

# *Reading Comprehension*

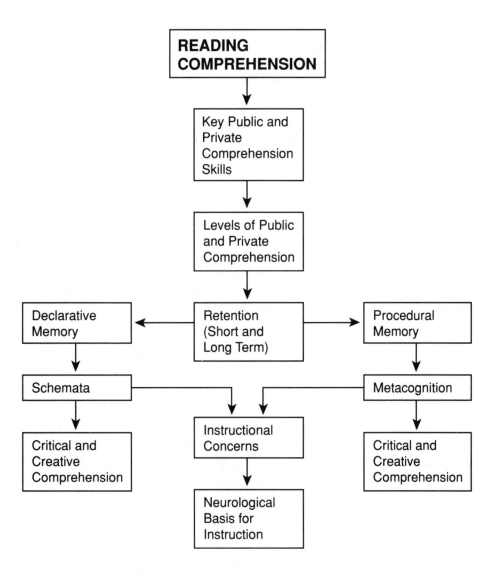

"I understand what the teacher explains but I just can't make it work for me in the book."

This 14-year-old student is talking about comprehending the information in her mathematics textbook. Her problem also extends to history, English, and science textbooks. What this student needs to learn is that comprehension, or getting meaning from a textbook, requires learning strategies that make her independent of the teacher. She must view reading comprehension as an active, not passive, process. In order to give meaning to reading, students must become involved and make their own meaning. After giving a brief background of reading comprehension and how teachers and textbooks influence this process, this chapter will provide teachers with activities that make reading comprehension an interesting, active experience.

The various comprehension needs in each content area are frequently not considered a part of the instructional process. For example, in social studies, students must comprehend material from many disciplines: maps for geography, tax returns and contracts for civics, diaries and primary sourcebooks for history, and graphs for sociology. Comprehension in science demands understanding flowcharts in chemistry, diagrams in physics, and paradigms in fields like electricity and astronomy. Of course, everyone can read sentence diagrams, math word problems, music score sheets, and make sense of them. These are reading comprehension tasks that are needed in the different subject fields. But first, teachers must identify the comprehension skills they are teaching when they provide classroom instruction.

## Key Public Comprehension Skills

*Reading comprehension* is defined as getting meaning from the printed word. As Farr (1989) describes it, that meaning can be both public and private. The *public meaning* occurs when the reader obtains the same information that the author intended to convey. The *private meaning* is the personal understanding that the written material has for the reader. For example, a piece of literature could be publicly described by its plot, setting, characterization, writing style, and theme. The same work could have a personal meaning for a reader that is quite separate from its public meaning. Reading comprehension instruction must consider both public and private meanings.

In the public or general meaning, reading comprehension consists of the skills identified in basal readers and other books and tests that measure comprehension. With some variation in terms, reading comprehension skills are identified as the following:

1. Recognizing the main idea of paragraphs
2. Noting important details
3. Using context; word meanings
4. Identifying sequence of events or categories
5. Predicting outcomes
6. Understanding cause-effect relationships
7. Understanding comparisons
8. Drawing conclusions
9. Distinguishing between fact and fiction
10. Using context; figurative language

Most of these skills are identified as being taught in elementary reading textbooks or basals, secondary remedial reading textbooks, and reading comprehension skill series. These behaviors can be considered products of the comprehension process. When a student can produce a conclusion, predict an outcome, and identify a detail or main idea, the teacher assumes that reading comprehension has taken place.

In the past, these skills were assumed to have been learned in the bottom-up model, where readers work their way up a scale of sequential units. First, they learned letters, then words, then sentences, and, finally, passage meaning. The emphasis was on both the textbook and teachers asking questions requiring lower level comprehension skills labeled as *literal, interpretive,* and/or *translation* actions. The upper level (or more difficult comprehension), called *critical thinking,* included application, synthesis, analysis, and evaluation skills.

The levels of comprehension as variously labeled by Bloom (1956), Barrett (1972), Sanders (1966), Herber (1978), and others provided the basis of a step-by-step teaching process in reading comprehension instruction. The only confusion seemed to be what to call the different levels of comprehension skills. Comprehension within this model is considered to be a very rapid process through which information is understood in a series of stages independent of students' background knowledge, information provided by the textbook, or individual processing strategies. In the interactive model of reading comprehension, the private comprehension skills drive understanding and are acquired first in the comprehension process.

## Key Private Comprehension Skills

Although levels of comprehension have not been abandoned as components of reading comprehension instruction, a second model for teaching, called the top-down model, has emerged. This interactive model focuses first on private meaning where such factors as the role of individual background and experience as well as self-awareness of comprehension acts are considered more important to the understanding processes. Students are now being taught to use their own background and experience, and to set goals when reading. They are even being shown how to be aware of their thinking processes, which is called *metacognition.* Each of these processes is highly individualistic and private. Reading comprehension is viewed here as an active construction of meaning that is monitored and checked according to experiences held in long-term memory, personal goals, and text-created difficulties.

Some reading researchers think that trying to determine meaning controls top-down information flow at all levels. The reader overcomes comprehension difficulties by using background knowledge and prediction skills. Readers then formulate a hypothesis and read to confirm whether or not their prediction was valid. Despite gaps in explaining just what the reading process is and a lack of overall precision and clarity, this model clearly reflects reading as a predictive process.

The emphasis on teaching reading comprehension now includes both the top-down and bottom-up instructional sequences where meanings, *public (bottom-up)* and *private (top-down)*, are considered appropriate places to begin instruction.

Finally, there are other models of reading comprehension where readers are assumed to be using both models for obtaining text concepts. Readers use the context to influence the reading process, which indicates that the textbook format plays an important role in ease of understanding. Decisions about when to pause, reread, and skim or skip material are strongly influenced by the visual attributes of a textbook, or what is called the *topography*. Topography can either enhance or diminish comprehension of a text. It is one range of a comprehension keying system. Background knowledge of semantic, syntactic, graphic, and phonology skills is a second keying system that influences concept attainment on two levels: vocabulary and sentence interpretation. In each case, readers check to see if vocabulary or organized information (called *schema*) is in their personal background or memory. Then they add it to a running clause interpretation. According to Just and Carpenter (1987), the system is called a *recognize-react cycle*. The *react* includes use of heuristics, which allows students to detect an error more efficiently. Integration, then, may occur at the end of a sentence, clause, or thought unit. Although interactive models are good at explaining reading behavior, it has not yet been determined how well they predict comprehension (Rayner & Pollatsek, 1989) (see Figure 5–1).

The *private-meaning aspect* of reading comprehension occurs when the readers' background purposes for reading are applied to the passage. As demonstrated by the comprehension process model, private meaning takes place when individually developed learning processes and knowledge structures are applied to a written passage. Learners bring ideas, beliefs, and self-perceptions with them to the learning situation. They access new information and form the perspective of their existing knowledge. As a result, successful instruction facilitates construction of understanding rather than presenting information to be absorbed. Effective instruction finds a "way in" to the ideas of students in order to change them (Linn & Clancy, 1990). For example, when a preservice teacher is asked to react to reading an article on teaching technical vocabulary in art class, the public meaning is for her to learn strategies for teaching vocabulary in her content area. However, the private comprehension is as follows:

> I believe that vocabulary introduction in the art class is important because the students will need to learn abstract concepts in art. By using technical vocabulary in the classroom, the concepts are reinforced verbally and visually with the art lesson. The point that made the biggest impact on me was not the major point of the article. The author taught each grade level (550 students in all) for forty minutes per class. I think that weekly classes and the time limit of forty minutes is appalling. I wonder how a teacher can manage to offer continuity and knowledge in this brief period of time. She somehow

**Figure 5–1**  *Comprehension Process Model*

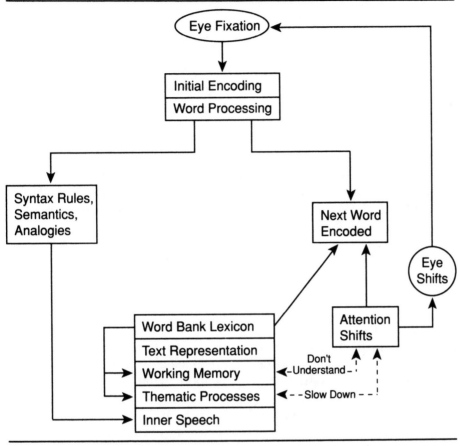

*Source:* Adapted from Rayner and Pollatsek (1989).

managed to teach the students reading skills and art. It would be hard to complete an art project in such a short period of time!

As noted, the comprehension of the article occurred in both the public (general) and private meaning areas. However, the importance of the article was given by personal, not public, meaning. The student quoted above obviously knew the main idea of the article. She was also able to understand the cause-effect relationship as evidenced by the statement referring to abstract art concepts reinforced by technical vocabulary instruction. However, when she predicted outcome from applying the number of students, content delivery time, and curriculum demands, she personalized the meaning and did not like the prediction. The personal, not public, meaning of this article assured its impact on the student.

*Summary*

In both public and private realms, meaning obtained from reading comprehension can be taught as an active process. Obtaining meaning is considered a result of a top-down, bottom-up, and/or interactive process. Performance skills have been identified that indicate to teachers which students are comprehending the text. Whether they retain the information or not is another matter related to memory. The more meaning is manipulated, the longer it stays with the reader. For example, students may be reading about coral and where it is found. Activities related to the reading may include the description of the what, where, and when of coral creation. Higher-level thinking strategies would be employed by an activity where students try to determine if coral could be found near their home. Whether these are called *hands-on* or *extension activities*, the point is that the meaning the student has for coral is more likely to be retained the more it is used and transferred. The importance of all forms of comprehension is they must be taught and not just expected to occur when students read. (Stevens, Slavin, & Farnish, 1991; Reutzel & Hollingsworth, 1991).

## Levels of Public and Private Comprehension

Vacca and Vacca (1989) and Herber (1978) condensed Bloom's taxonomy into three different levels: literal, interpretive, and critical thinking. *Literal thinking* is considered easier to learn, as questions on the literal level locate public facts about what, where, and when, and essentially provide a summary of what was directly stated. *Interpretive reading comprehension* is obtaining meaning found between the lines (Gray, 1960). Because the answers to interpretive questions are not directly stated in the text, they are considered more personal reading and depend on examining the language structure, determining the patterns of relationships and applying personal experience to the works. For example, in literature, interpretive reading means identifying character motivation and setting when not directly stated. In other subject fields, interpretive reading can be considered determining the sequence, cause and effect, or comparison-contrast relationships between facts, events, or problems.

Higher-level comprehension, called *creative, critical*, or *reading beyond the lines*, is considered more difficult for students. It occurs when reading material is manipulated according to the procedural operations that are required. For example, if a student is asked to read a laboratory experiment and then conduct it, the student is required to read and produce a thinking product on the *application level*. If a student is asked to determine whether a passage is well written, the student must read and produce a result on the *analysis level*. If a student is asked to develop a city government for the future or predict outcomes or conclusions that are not given in the text, the student is comprehending and then producing on the *synthesis level*. And finally, if a student is asked his or her opinion of the reading, the assignment includes identifying the personal values or criteria for having that opinion. The student is then comprehending on the *evaluative level*.

The importance of mastering the levels of comprehension is that purposes for reading and levels of comprehension are related. Teachers should not ask questions on the literal level in class and then test on higher levels of comprehension. This is unfair for students, as they have not practiced thinking and comprehending in the manner that prepares them for the teacher-made test. An example of a teacher-made test for a developmental reading class is found in the Teaching Activities section of Chapter Three. The first part of the text asks questions requiring literal and interpretive thinking, which were congruent products practiced in class. The essay asks for analysis, evaluation, and synthesis. Most of the class did not pass the essay portion of the test, which asks for thinking skills that were not practiced in class. Comprehension levels, then, are both public and private in origin of the products. Teachers must recognize and teach that reading comprehension results from the interaction between public and private sources of meaning.

# Retention of Reading

Beyond the public and private comprehension skills and levels of comprehension performed, there is the issue of how all these skills and operations influence retention. When students have read passages and say they comprehend them, teachers and even parents expect them to be able to recall the material later. Although Farr and Carey (1986) do not consider retention a part of reading comprehension, Manzo and Manzo (1990) and Richardson and Morgan (1990) devote portions of their books on reading in the content area to memory training.

This book takes the perspective that comprehension and storage or retention are two steps of understanding. A student is not able to relate reading to previous experience or previous knowledge if the memory facility is not in place. Thus, reading comprehension, in its most comprehensive form, cannot take place without some retention. Reading without retention does not seem to be a profitable use of instructional time. Likewise, comprehending without the ability to communicate understanding later introduces the possibility that the reader did not comprehend the material in the first place.

Memory takes place in two forms: declarative and procedural memory (see Figure 5–2). *Declarative memory* is the retention of information or facts for later use. The strengthening of neural pathways that permit long-term storage takes approximately 25 minutes (Kolb & Wishaw, 1990). If facts and information are not manipulated for that period of time, they will be placed in short-term memory and not retained. *Procedural memory* is the knowledge of how to do something. For example, when dialing a telephone number, both the

**Figure 5–2**   *Memory Model*

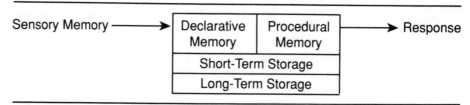

*Source:* Adapted from Mayer (1989).

number being dialed and the process of how to dial are stored. The process of how to dial would be called procedural memory. Reading comprehension, then, is a matter a understanding the material presented and knowing the procedure of how to read. Some educators refer to teaching procedural memory as study skills or having basic reading skills. At any rate, in any storage activity, dual input takes place in both declarative and procedural memory.

It is the teacher's responsibility to teach both declarative and procedural understanding when teaching reading comprehension in different subject fields. The importance of this aspect of comprehension is that each content area has its designated tasks for students and the specific process by which students are to interact with those tasks. The differences in disciplines in both procedural and declarative memory tasks were identified in Chapter One.

And finally, some relatively recent terminology has been coined by reading educators to use when describing reading comprehension.

*Metacognition* is the awareness and monitoring of procedural memory.

*Schemata* is the organized personal background knowledge one has related to declarative memory. The way one relates a fact, concept, or idea to previous meaning contributes to personal meaning and comprehension.

*Critical/creative reading* is the cognitive thinking skills of application, analysis, synthesis, and evaluation. These are sometimes given such labels as creative problem solving and logical thinking skills.

## Summary

Public and private meanings in reading comprehension can be manipulated for different comprehension products. The level of selection is largely based on the teacher's classroom assignment. Although there are limited data to support it, Pogrov (1990) has found that remedial students make exceptional gains in coursework when thinking skills are taught. This study recognized that all instructional events have both a procedural and a factual component. Relatively recent reading terms have been coined to explain personal and public meaning, and declarative and procedural memory, all of which take place during reading comprehension.

# Instructional Concerns

The importance of teaching reading comprehension beyond memorization of facts found in textbooks cannot be overemphasized. Democratic societies are based on the assumption that citizens can analyze, synthesize, apply, interpret, and evaluate information. Schools are the delivery systems where the knowledge and values of the society are learned. The public assumes that skills gained in school will be used or transferred into society. If students are taught to memorize facts and neither apply, evaluate, or even remember what they are taught, then the process or procedure is all that remains with them. Too often, school is the place where teachers force-feed facts to passive students in a manner that hampers and discourages individual thinking. This procedure demonstrates that the country does not value critical thinking necessary in a democracy. Furthermore, such an instructional process will not produce active readers nor a positive attitude toward any subject matter. If students do not understand the processes or content, they become as frustrated as the girl in the beginning of this chapter. Teaching reading comprehension is the active teaching of thinking processes and should be the emphasis of instruction in all subject classes. If content teachers are interested in teaching critical thinking, they should also be interested in learning how the teaching of reading comprehension can aid students in developing critical thinking skills.

Teachers who want their students to think critically about what they read usually test on different levels of comprehension. The examination of teacher-made tests and standardized tests described in Chapter Three shows how teachers and publishing companies test on different comprehension levels. The instructional concern is not only the testing of different levels of comprehension, but the problem is also that teaching reading comprehension on all levels does not seem to be consistently taking place in elementary, secondary, or college reading classes.

In the late 1970s, Durkin (1979) received a grant from the National Institute of Education to study "What Classroom Observations Reveal about Reading Comprehension Instruction." The study was conducted in 39 middle-grade classrooms (grades 3–6) with observations scheduled for three consecutive days. Durkin trained graduate students in the components of reading comprehension and what one would see when it was being taught. She then called school districts and asked the principals to identify their best elementary teachers and to find out when they would be teaching reading comprehension. The graduate students were then sent to observe instruction and record their findings. The uniqueness of this study was its size, the simplicity, and the fact the similarly trained observers were recording actual instruction of the best elementary teachers.

Results of Durkin's study showed that teachers were actually providing reading comprehension instruction 12 percent of the time they had identified themselves as teaching reading comprehension instruction. In elaborating on the findings, Durkin noted the importance placed on written exercises. In actual classroom practice, written exercises or workbook sheets were being viewed as comprehension instruction. Covering materials, making assignments, and checking written assignments seem to be far more important than teaching understanding or what was read. In fact, Durkin reported that, in many instances, teachers emerged as "mentioners," "assignment givers," and "assignment checkers." Over 12 percent of the time was being used in assignment checking. In summary, Durkin listed five concerns that have classroom implications for improvement of the teaching of reading comprehension skills:

1. Teachers were not observed teaching fundamental reading comprehension skills.
2. Teachers were observed to rely on written practice as a substitute for teaching comprehension skills.
3. In all classroom observations, the instructional sequence was determined by what came next in the textbook.
4. The proliferation of ditto sheets and other "busy work" seemed to usurp instructional time.
5. Teachers view themselves as instructors even when they are observed as merely "mentioning" a basic comprehension skill, or when they are giving a written assignment or checking an assignment.

When reporting her findings at the National Reading Conference in 1980, Dr. Durkin said she hoped her results were only a description of instruction in Illinois where the study took place. Unfortunately, the same results appeared in studies both before and after Durkin's investigation. Guszak (1967) assumed that levels of questions that the teacher asked in class indicated the levels of comprehension that were being taught. He found most of the questions teachers asked were literal (66 percent in second grade, 48 percent in fourth grade, and 47 percent in sixth grade). The second largest group of teacher-asked questions were evaluative. Although his study indicated an effort on the part of the elementary teachers to question students in both public and private meanings, the levels of comprehension, known respectively as applicative, creative, critical (or analytic), synthesis, and interpretive, were asked less than 20 percent of the time in teachers' questions.

In 1989, Wendler, Samuels, and Moore again asked how the best classroom teachers were instructing reading comprehension. Unlike Durkin, they identified the best teachers as those having a master's degree in reading and those having district awards for excellence. In the first observation, teachers were not told that they were being observed in reading comprehension instruction. In the second observation, teachers were told. Prereading activities and direct comprehension instruction were measured. No significant difference was found between master teachers and regular teachers in the percentage of time spent in prereading activities or direct instruction. When told that comprehension instruction was the focus of the observations, teachers did not increase the percentage of time for prereading activities or direct instruction. Instead, they significantly increased the percentage of time spent asking assessment questions, listening to students' answers, and giving corrective feedback.

There could be an explanation on the college level for the elementary teachers' instructional patterns. After examining textbooks that claim to train teachers to teach reading comprehension, Durkin (1986) found that reading methodology textbooks were inadequate and brief in providing specific reading instruction strategies.

If reading comprehension is not directly presented in reading methodology textbooks for teachers in elementary schools, the college professor must provide specific instructional strategies. If prospective elementary teachers are not fortunate enough to find professors who supplement textbooks with practical strategies, then, as new teachers, they do not know how to teach reading comprehension. They know the *what* but not the *how* of instruction. Thus, the basal textbooks used in 90 percent of elementary classrooms become the basis of comprehension instruction. A projection from such college training is that reading comprehension should not be more likely to be taught in secondary content classes where it is not considered the teachers' specific charge.

Direct reading comprehension instruction needs to be demonstrated for content teachers whose training has been in other subject fields. The teaching activities section provides examples that show teachers how to help students find the main idea, identify organizational patterns, support details, infer word meanings, identify sequence of events, and predict outcomes in content textbooks.

Personal or private comprehension skills can also be taught. The most frequently used format is the Directed Reading Activity, which helps students set the purpose and establish personal meaning in different subjects. Examples of DRAs conducted in science, mathematics, history, and music classes are also provided in the Teaching Activities section.

Memory, or the retention of what has been read, falls into two categories: declarative and procedural memory. Declarative memory instruction aids students in remembering facts. Strategies of overlearning, imaging, mnemonic devices, and clustering or chunking into what is known as schema are explained. Procedural memory is the retention of how to do something. Strategies of repetition, steps of scientific problem solving, REAP, PREP, self-questions, metacognition awareness, code, SEARCH, REST, and SQ3R are described. A procedure for note taking, which will aid in listening comprehension, is also provided.

The content teacher in every subject field can take one, some, or all of these strategies and apply them to the textbook, lectures, laboratories, or class discussions. By teaching students how to separate public and private meaning and the strategies for developing comprehension skills in both areas, student performance in class should improve. Furthermore, if strategies for procedural and declarative memory are taught, students will be able to remember more material.

# Neurological Basis for Instruction

Teachers have always had partial or indirect knowledge of how the development of the brain affects learning. Within recent years, however, that knowledge has increased significantly. The teaching profession is now on the edge of a major transformation that will relate instruction to the development, organization, and operation of the human brain. Teaching comprehension without an understanding of basic neurological functions of how the brain operates is like playing baseball without knowing where the bases are located. The new information not only will change instruction but will provide support for instructional practices now in place and those to come (Stevens, Slavin, & Farnish, 1991; Crano & Johnson, 1991).

## Development of the brain

The human brain begins to develop about three weeks after conception. Thousands of new cells develop each minute. By birth, the brain weighs about one pound and develops from the most basic functions of consciousness, monitoring circulation and breathing, to more complex functions. During the first year, the brain adds its second pound. Much of this growth occurs in the cerebellum, located under the bump on the back of the head. It is the brain's automatic pilot—coordinating the actions of muscle groups in order to crawl, walk, eat, and conduct other integrated muscle activities. As the cerebellum develops, a child crawls, walks, and then runs. The third and final pound of the brain develops between the ages of 2 and 16 years. This gradual growth stage moves the infant from gross motor development and speechless state to the comprehending and communicative state of a fully functioning individual (see Figure 5–3).

The brain is known to be ipsilateral with two hemispheres. In the late 1960s and 70s, Sperry, Galin, and Ornstein were three of the many researchers who investigated the right and left hemispheres and their functions and interactions. For many years, the third weight gain of the brain was ignored because 16 ounces of growth spread over the 14 years that followed acquisition of speech, seemed an insignificant factor in the developmental process. The attitude of indifference toward this growth period changed for educators when Epstein (1970),

**Figure 5–3**  *Brain Functioning*

The brain is a very sophisticated organ that weighs about three pounds. The cerebral cortex is divided on the grossest level into two hemispheres, left and right, which are connected by a large structure consisting of nerve fibers, the corpus collosum. The corpus collosum provides communication between the hemispheres and allows the transmission of memory and learning. The hemispheres appear to be organized bilaterally symmetrical (mirror images of each other). However, they are also organized asymmetrically (there are structural and functional differences).

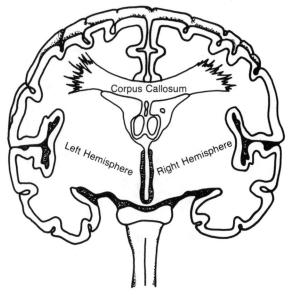

The Corpus Callosum

Professor of Biophysics at Brandeis University, examined his research and began to believe that the third weight gain was no inconsequential matter. He found the brain does not grow continuously at an ounce a year as supposed. Instead, it grows in four-year cycles during which periods of rapid growth are followed by the slower integration of that growth into the development of cognitive processes. This pattern roughly parallels the growth stages identified by Jean Piaget and researchers at the Gesell Institute of Child Development.

Thatcher, Walker, and Guidice (1987) studied the different rates of development both between and within the hemispheres and age-related growth spurts. They found a continuous overall pattern of growth in both hemispheres from birth to age 3. There was a left hemisphere growth spurt between the ages of 3 and 6 years followed by a period of continuous growth, and a pattern of continuous development in the right hemisphere with a small growth spurt in the right frontal cortex between the ages of 8 and 10 years. Smaller bilateral growth spurts occurred in the frontal cortex between the ages of 11 and 14 years and between age 15 and adulthood (see Figure 5–4). Their

**Figure 5–4**  *Cerebral Cortex*

The cerebral cortex can be divided into four major lobes: temporal, frontal, occipital, and parietal.

*Temporal Lobe*—primary auditory reception; may play a role in learning and emotional behavior

*Frontal Lobe*—important in planning and controlling behavior

*Occipital Lobe*—primary visual center

*Parietal Lobe*—primary kinesthetic (sense of movement in the body) center

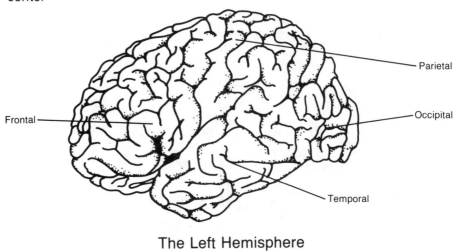

The Left Hemisphere

study paralleled the earlier work of Epstein (1970), which identified growth spurts in two-year periods, with girls' growth occurring before that of most boys. Epstein suggests that nongrowth periods might be viewed as important times for cognitive integration and for instruction that is compatible with the development that has just taken place.

Roberts's (1988) study on the effects of development on the ability to comprehend on literal and inferential levels demonstrates the important relationship between physical development and instructional content. Roberts found that experience and age had a significant effect on factual comprehension scores. She interpreted her findings as indicating that personal experience has a more powerful effect on both factual and inferential comprehension than prereading instruction. According to reading experts, a major factor contributing to comprehension is prior learning, or background knowledge. However, there is a smaller difference between all learners' comprehension ability when self-paced instruction is provided (Whitener, 1989). Individual growth rates are known to influence development of cognitive structures, which can be translated into self-paced instruction as a means for helping all students comprehend more effectively.

Another example of the relationship between neurological development and instruction is the obvious knowledge that younger students need to have concrete experience with a subject in order to do well with comprehension. In contrast, older students are able to activate and integrate relevant knowledge without concrete experience. Piaget's stages of cognitive development would identify younger groups in the concrete stage and older groups in the formal operational state. Thus, knowledge of the development of the brain combines with reading research to explain observations about learning (Crano & Johnson, 1991).

# Direct Instructional Strategies for Teaching Reading Comprehension

## Strategies for literal comprehension of main idea

*Determining the Main Idea.* Sometimes the main idea is directly stated in textbooks. Read the paragraphs taken from the following textbooks and identify the main idea.

### Example 1

Early, Canfield, Karlin, & Schottman (1979). *Moving Forward.* New York: Harcourt, Brace Jovanovich, p. 63. (English, sixth grade)

What do people think of when they hear the word Viking? They think at once of tall people sailing the North Atlantic in their dragon-like ships a long, long time ago. They remember that the Vikings visited the lands of Newfoundland, Nova Scotia, and New England almost five hundred years before Columbus discovered America.

How do we know about the Vikings? The information comes from several sources. First there are the writings and pictures made at that time by people other than the Vikings themselves. Then, there are the Vikings' own writing and their works of art. Those works help us learn about the Vikings.

### Example 2

*Basic: Concepts and Structured Problem Solving* (1984). St. Paul, MN: PCL Textbooks, p. 460. (computer science, eleventh grade)

Decomposing a problem into smaller pieces (modules) allows you to focus more easily on a particular piece of the problem without worrying about the overall problem. The tasks become easier to solve and are more manageable since each performs a very specific function. Typically, you can code each module independently of the other and even test and debug each module separately. Once all modules are working properly, you can link them together by writing and coordinating code (generally called the root segment or the main code.) The coordinating code activates the various modules in a predetermined sequence. Consider [the following figure] which illustrates these principles. Note that the resulting program consists of 5 modules: the coordinating module and the four modules A, B, C, and D. It is, of course, conceivable that a particular module itself might be broken down into other modules.

Sometimes, textbook headings tell students what the main idea will be for the chapter. Other texts write the main ideas in the introduction section or to the side of the chapter text. These chapter aids should be shown to students in addition to organizational patterns of textbooks, which place the main idea in other locations in the paragraphs such as the middle or the end. Even if the main idea is not always found at the beginning of the paragraph, the concept that it can be found somewhere in the paragraph should be introduced.

Another way of approaching the identification of main ideas is for students to write thesis statements. They simply take the topic of the paragraph and write that as their subject in the sentence and then add the verb to the sentence. Take the stems for the three examples listed above and have students write the main idea or thesis.

Vikings. . . .

Computers. . . .

Identification of the main idea can be written, worked out in small groups, or given to students in samples taken from standardized tests. In most reading tests, the comprehension paragraphs will ask students to recognize the main idea in a multiple-choice format. These paragraphs can be borrowed from old tests or practice test books for exams such as the California Achievement Test, Stanford Achievement Test, or American College Test. Regardless of where they are placed or what strategy is used for identification, all students should be told that main ideas are in every paragraph in their text.

The only exception to the main idea in every paragraph is literature books where stories and essays have main ideas that have to be interpreted (usually called *themes* in English terminology). The best strategy for inferring themes in stories and essays is to have the students answer the following questions:

1. What is the problem in the story?
2. How is the problem solved?
3. What are you supposed to learn from the resolution of the problem?

When they finish answering these three questions individually or in a group, they will have identified the theme or main idea with the last question. The details of the story such as setting, point of view, and characterization should be in the details supporting that theme. Content subjects that do not contain pieces of literature do not have to interpret the details and be close to the main idea. The skills of identifying the main ideas and details are supportive of each other and hence are related. Other teaching strategies to show this relationship between main ideas and details are outlining, making time lines, and writing summaries.

## Strategies for identifying types of supporting details

The importance of teaching students how to identify the main idea and supporting details by location and relationship cannot be overemphasized. Every comprehension passage on standardized achievement tests of any form contains paragraphs followed by questions that ask the students to pick the right main idea, or theme, or title and to answer questions about the supporting details. Generally these questions are literal and the answers can be found in the passage. But in order for students to do well on standardized tests, they must be able to find the main idea and identify supporting details on their own. The following examples can be copied and given to students to help them see the types of comprehension relationships between sentences in a paragraph.

### Example 1: Main Idea and Example Details

Peragallo (1981, July). Incorporating reading skills into art lessons. *Art Education*, p. 31.

Following directions in art classes can include such activities as clean-up procedures, mixing paint, warping a loom, assembling a coil pot, etc. Unlike the detailed directions found in many arts and crafts books, the directions can be general procedural steps that allow for divergent outcomes. [The following figure] is a good example of how specific, ordered procedures still allow for a diversified product. Posting or listing instructions on a bulletin or chalk board can end students' constant questions about what to do next. Whenever possible, the instructions should include visual illustrations. Posted instructions give students a sense of independence, the teacher more freedom to offer assistance where needed, and "non-readers" the opportunity to practice the skill of following a series of series of procedural steps.

### Example 2: Main Idea and Descriptive Details

Alvino, J. (1990, February). Building better thinkers, a blueprint for instruction. *Learning, 90:* 40.

Asking a group of teachers if thinking skills are important is like asking a group of scientists if the earth is round. But ask teachers to define the ability to think or to describe state-of-the art thinking-skills instruction, and the questions and conflicts abound. Should the emphasis be on critical or creative thinking? On the cognitive or metacognitive functions? On separate or an integrated approach? How do you evaluate skill in thinking?

### Example 3: Main Idea and Expansion Details

Reis, S. (1990, February). Teaching techniques. *Learning, 90:* 46.

Students who are taught fewer thinking skills, but in greater depth, learn them better. That's what our field testing with children in Connecticut schools has shown. We found that students who'd really mastered a thinking skill or skills had worked with teachers who'd introduced a few skills, taught them step by step, demonstrated how to use them within the content areas and with special projects, and made sure students practiced each one several times during the year.

We also found that students who succeeded best learned a skill in the early grades and relearned it, through more complex applications, in subsequent years. For example, 7th graders who'd been introduced to the steps of problem solving in 3rd grade and who'd reviewed them in 5th grade could effectively use those steps.

### Example 4: Main Idea and Contrast and Comparison Details

Hudgins, B. B. (1977). *Learning and Thinking.* Itasca, IL: Peacock, pp. 88–89.

Samuels (1970) conducted a review of research on the role of pictures in the reading process, including their effects on comprehension. The weight of the evidence does not show that pictures enhance a child's comprehension of what he reads—neither do the pictures except in a minor way, interfere with the child's comprehension. We need to take into account, though, the kind of content, and therefore the types of pictures under discussion. Samuels's focus is principally upon the process of learning to read. The material in readers, for example, does not tend to be specific or detailed. Thus, drawings or pictures such as those in Dwyer's study are not considered. Nonetheless, Samuels points out that the absence of positive facilitation of pictures is not a sufficient reason to omit them from children's books. They frequently have aesthetic values, and they may also improve the child's attitude toward reading.

### *Strategies for inferring word meanings*

Determining what a word means by the surrounding sentence is really a logical thinking exercise that employs distinct thinking strategies. Context clues fall into the following types. Once the types are learned, then the inductive thinking strategies can be applied to determine word meaning.

1.  *Association* clues identified by appositives or adjective strings: The queen was tall, regal, and *opulent* in her crown.
2.  *Contrast* or *Compare* clues found by opposites or similar words in close proximity: *Lank* rather than squat, the soldier stood in the formation.

3.  *Summary* clues that conclude an idea or description: He was mean, odiferous, and a snarly, *malevolent* type of a fellow.

The skill of identifying a word of figurative speech in context could also be considered a vocabulary skill. Context clues are often given in vocabulary sections of reading or achievement tests.

### Strategies for identifying the sequence of events by cause and effect, comparison, or chronology

Sequencing seems to be a major comprehension skill. When examined closely, it requires that the reader be able to identify the events or categories that are related and the organization of the passage itself. For example, students have to know when an episode ended and a second began before determining that sequence is predicated upon knowledge of clusters. Textbooks often identify clusters by headings. The sequencing of clusters can then be taught by time lines, loops, or any pictures that seem suitable. The easiest way to demonstrate both the segmenting of content and the relationship between events and episodes is through the use of cartoons. Cut them up and then have students put them in sequence as a first step in teaching this comprehension skill that requires analytical thinking strategies.

### Strategies for predicting outcomes or drawing conclusions

The most obvious strategy for predicting outcomes is to have students predict outcomes or conclusions before reading a passage. These skills are practiced in such teaching strategies as anticipation guides, student-generated anticipation reaction guides, and REQUEST. A simple form is to have students write their own conclusion after reading portions of the story or assignment. Examples of strategies mentioned above are found in the back of this chapter.

### Strategies for identifying private meanings

Students will remember what they read if it is important to them. Unfortunately, textbook reading does not arrive with the personal meanings established. For example, chemistry, history, or mathematics could have a personal meaning for many students. They can see the course as preparing them to major in the subject, explaining why their city has historical significance, or enabling them to figure mathematically how to expand their bedroom. These meanings could be introduced by the teacher. In this case, the teacher would be activating the students' schema, or background, prior to reading the textbook. This is known as making the material relevant to students' needs, relating it to their background, or providing a purpose for reading. Personal meaning can be provided by the teacher or the student setting the purpose for reading.

One strategy for setting purpose and establishing personal meaning is using the Directed Reading Activity (DRA). This strategy includes a personal meaning or motivation section, a purpose-setting section, and key vocabulary identifiers. In the DRA, the teacher establishes the purpose for reading. In a more recent modification of the DRA, called the DRTA, the students practice predicting skills and setting their own purposes. Most basal reading program's teacher's manuals use a form of the DRA or DRTA to introduce reading lessons. Thus, most elementary teachers are familiar with the strategy, but it may be new to secondary content teachers. Examples of the DRA and DRTA for different content classes follow this explanation.

Developing private meanings is the secret to student retention and comprehension. If it has meaning within their background of what is important or relevant, then the material will be either accommodated or assimilated into understanding. If it has no personal meaning, the reading will be forgotten. In obtaining either public or private meanings, the reader must be active and involved. Reading comprehension is not a passive process.

### Directed Reading Activity (DRA) format

**Background Motivator.**   Identify a need of your students for this material. Do your students want to become more competent, learn something unusual, learn a new skill? This section of the DRA establishes a personal meaning or activates schema. Background motivators can be unstructured, like webbing, or structured, such as a series of questions built around the theme.

**Vocabulary.**   What key concept vocabulary words are needed to understand the passage? Teach five or less of these words at the beginning of the lesson and see if the students retain them at the end of the lesson. For example, a health lesson about halitosis would need to include definitions of halitosis as a key concept word.

**Purpose.**   The students' and teachers' reason for reading the assignment needs to be stated before the reading: "You are reading this material in order to take a test on Thursday." "You are reading this assignment to determine why the South needed industrial strength." "You are reading this chapter in order to answer the questions at the end of the chapter (give a speech over the material, prepare a medieval fair . . . etc.)."

**Silent Reading.**   The students read the passage in class or as homework.

**Follow-up Activities.**   What is done directly after the reading? A check should be made on the vocabulary taught at the beginning. Other follow-up activities could include answering the questions at the back of the chapter, doing an experiment, giving a speech, dividing into groups to prepare the fair, and so on.

**Extension Activities.** Once an assignment is completed, it should be linked to following assignments and activities. For example, a lesson on caterpillars could be extended by a movie, a building of a tree to house cocoons, reading about caterpillars, or writing a paper relating the caterpillar to others in that species.

Specific Directed Reading Activities and lessons can be found at the end of this chapter.

# Declarative and Procedural Memory

*How to teach declarative memory*

The following strategies help students remember what they have read.

**1.** *Overlearning.* When facts or procedures are overlearned until they are automatic, material is retained in long-term memory.

**2.** *Imaging.* Meaning is constructed by visualization. Bartlett (1932), whose influential book *Remembering* covered almost 20 years of research and thought, stated:

> Remembering is not the re-excitation of innumerable fixed, lifeless and fragmentary traces. It is an imaginative reconstruction, or construction, built out of the relation of our attitude towards a whole active mass of organized past reactions or experience, and to a little outstanding detail which commonly appears in image or in language form. It is thus hardly ever really exact, even in the most rudimentary forms of rote recapitulation, and it is not at all important that it should be so. (p. 213)

**3.** *Mnemonics.* This is the ability to recall facts through location and pegwords. Based on the results of Bower (1973), these two methods of mnemonics yield comparable results. The location methodology's origins lie in the work of Simonides, a fifth-century poet. Simonides was invited to sing at a banquet given by an Olympic winner to celebrate his victory. During the banquet, Simonides was called from the hall, and shortly thereafter the floors collapsed, killing all the guests. The bodies were crushed beyond recognition, but Simonides was able to help relatives identify their dead kinsmen by recalling who was seated at each place. The method of location as devised by Simonides is still a fundamental mnemonic devise. The learner calls to mind places he knows very well, such as his bedroom, and then figuratively stores items he wishes to remember in furniture in the bedroom. For example, a list of famous writers of the Neoclassic period might be remembered by visually locating them in the dresser, on the bed, in the closet, and so on. Professional mnemonists divide rooms into a series of squares then recall by associating the number of the square with the location and the object stored there.

The second mnemonic devise is the pegword, which links series of words by sequentially identifying them with any items or subitems that may be requested. For example, the pegword *Persia* enables students who are taking essay exams in history to recall all of the significant areas to be discussed: politics, economics, religion, society, intellectual contributions, and aesthetic characteristics. Mnemonic devices can help students retain information that is low in meaningfulness. A mnemonic substitutes a more familiar or more easily learned expression, or a rhyme, for the learning task, which is then associated with it.

**4.** *Clustering or Chunking.* Historically, the mind can remember 7 plus or minus 2 items. This means that those with good memories in certain areas can remember 9 items and those with poor memories can remember 5 items. It then makes sense to cluster or chunk information together under concepts. The association or mediation is better if the students rather than the teacher establish the chunking pattern.

## How to teach procedural memory

The following reading strategies help students remember procedures and processes:

**1.** *Repetition.* This could be another form of overlearning.

**2.** *Procedural steps.* Identify procedural steps such as those in scientific problem solving:

   a.   Gather background information.
   b.   Generate a hypothesis.
   c.   Test the hypothesis.
   d.   Redefine the hypothesis.

**3.** *REAP.* This strategy was devised by Earnet and Manzo (Manzo & Manzo 1990):

Read—Reading to discover the author's ideas
Encoding—Writing it into your own language
Annotating—Writing your interpretation of the author's ideas
Pondering—Deciding whether the article as text information is significant.

**4.** *Internalized questions.* Develop standard internalized questions that students will ask themselves as they read:

   a.   Does it make sense?
   b.   Is this relevant to the purpose I have for reading?
   c.   Does the conclusion follow from the body of the material?
   d.   What can I conclude about what I have read?

**5.** *Metacognitive awareness.* Examples of metacognitive awareness are SEARCH (Indrisano, 1982) and metacognition awareness code (Smith & Dauer, 1984). Smith and Dauer's concept was to have students monitor their comprehension by using a code to record their cognitive and affective responses to materials they read. Students are to record their responses on narrow strips of paper placed in the textbook. This method was tested with students who were given different codes for different subjects. The science code was C = Clear, D = Difficult, I = Important, and S = Surprising. The social studies code was A = Agree, B = Bored, C = Confused, D = Disagree, and M = Main Idea. These codes have been modified by the author into affective and cognitive codes, which would simplify the number of codes learned and divide them into public or cognitive and private responses.

### Metacognitive Awareness (modified)

| Cognitive code | Affective Code |
|---|---|
| C = clear | A = agree |
| H = hard to understand | Co = confused |
| D = disputable | I = important |
| M = main idea | S = surprising |

*SEARCH* also provides a strategy for metacognitive or procedural awareness:

S = Set goals
E = Explore source and information
A = Analyze and organize information
R = Refine and rehearse
C = Communicate with others
H = Help yourself improve

**6.** *PREP.* This strategy, devised by Langer in 1981, provides a procedure for analysis of information.

a. Consider initial associations with the concept during brainstorming or initial introduction of the topic.
b. Reflect on responses to concept, which builds awareness on prior knowledge and associations.
c. Reformulate knowledge when new ideas are learned.

**7.** *REQUEST.* Manzo and Manzo (1990) conceptualized a procedure for students to construct informed questions. The procedure is as follows:

a. The teacher and students have copies of the selection to be read before them. The teacher states the basic goal: "Our intent in this lesson is to improve your skill in setting a purpose for reading."
b. The teacher guides the students through as much of the selection as seems necessary to formulate a logical purpose to continue reading silently. Students ask questions of the teacher, trying to imitate the process and type of question that the teacher usually asks.
c. For each sentence, the students ask questions of the teacher

and the teacher asks questions starting to integrate information from the preceding sentences.

   d. The request procedure should continue until students can:
1) Decode and derive proper meanings for all the words in the initial paragraph(s).
2) Demonstrate a thorough understanding of the sentences read.
3) Formulate a reasonable purpose for the silent reading of the rest of the passage.

   e. Following silent reading, the teacher's first question should be "Did we identify the best purpose for reading this selection?" The next question should be the actual purpose question that was to guide silent reading.

**8.** *REST.* This system of note taking, devised by Mogan, is:

Record
Edit
Synthesize
Think

**9.** *SQ3R.* This strategy is:

Survey text material for number of pages, format style, and so on.
Question (or identify) the purposes for reading.
Read to answer the questions.
Recite the answer to the questions.
Reread to find answers to the questions that were not recalled in recitation.

# Summary

Reading comprehension is the development of relationships that provide meaning. Its development is the result of the direct and indirect teaching of how to find the components that organize these relationships. The components are identified in both public and private realms. In essence, reading comprehension is a matter of obtaining public and private meanings that are retained through the use of declarative and procedural memory. Reading comprehension is also not a single-dimension process. Declarative and procedural comprehension can be manipulated on what has been historically called levels of cognitive thinking. The ability to use and transfer information gained from reading for different purposes is one of the most important procedures for teaching reading comprehension in all classes. Also, instruction in reading comprehension is not directly conducted in all elementary schools. This finding is based on observational research conducted over a 20-year period.

Furthermore, teacher training programs that use reading methodology textbooks will have a dearth of adequately described specific teaching strategies. Thus, teachers are forced to be "mentioners" and "assessment" evaluators. They have not been given the tools to teach reading comprehension directly. A developing relationship between neurological and reading research has resulted in a criterion by which new and traditional instructional patterns can be understood and evaluated. There is no indication that literal and interpretive reading comprehension cannot be taught in content classrooms by using the simple strategies given in this chapter and the Teaching Activities section.

# Application Exercises and Teaching Activities

## Application Exercises

**1.** Examine the following questions and identify on what level of comprehension they are written.

*Level*

___ a. How can a flat sheet of paper be manipulated to show dimensions?

___ b. Why is negative space an important element in a work of art?

___ c. What does the term *picture plane* mean?

___ d. Discuss the aspects that flatten the picture plane in a work of art.

___ e. Discuss the differences between one-point linear perspective and two-point linear perspective.

___ f. What is a necessary element in seeing dimensional space correctly?

___ g. Name three Cubist artists mentioned in the chapter.

___ h. What do you think is the most important element in a Cubist painting?

___ i. Draw three separate pictures of a still life showing three different points of view. Then combine the three different points of view into one drawing, taking only parts of each of the separate drawings. This exercise will give a student an understanding of the Cubist concept.

**2.** After completing activity 1 above, identify the levels of questions that were not represented. Write sample questions for the missing levels of comprehension. For example, if there is no literal-level question, write one.

**3.** Design projects for your content area that would require thinking strategies above the literal level.

**4.** Observe reading comprehension instruction in a classroom in your geographic area. Record the percentage of time spent in direct instruction.

**5.** What questions would you like to ask the reading teacher interviewed in the following report?

I interviewed Mrs. Trisha Dillon, who teaches reading in a private school. She has taken six hours of reading instruction. She is discussing a seventh-grade class of 29 students, most of whom are better than average ability. Mrs. Dillon has the entire class in one reading group.

She states that the major problem she is encountering is in the poor comprehension exhibited by the students. She states that the students tend to read on a word-for-word basis, rather than read in phrases. She also has noted that some students give evidence of good verbal ability, but are poor in reading and writing. These students are being checked for hearing and sight. Comments on the results of these children's exams were not immediately available.

Mrs. Dillon stated that another problem she is having is the lack of basic study skills. Although reading in this school is taught in a phonics-oriented fashion, the students are weak in phonics. Vocabulary and dictionary skills are of a poorer quality than she expects. Mrs. Dillon would also like to see more study stalls, tape-recorded materials, and an additional reading area made available to her.

# Teaching Activities:
# Examples of Directed Reading Activities

*Music*

*Background and Motivator:* Play recording of Beethoven's Fifth Symphony.

*Questions:* What kind of mood do you think the composer was in when he wrote this piece? What type of events would make a person feel this way?

*Purpose:* Determine how the events in a composer's life can affect his or her music.

*Vocabulary:* Direct instruction of the key vocabulary needed to understand the chapter.

*Silent Reading:*

*Follow-up Activities:* Vocabulary puzzle to see if students have remembered the meaning of the key vocabulary

Discuss other composers studied previously and how events in their lives might have influenced their music. Discuss contemporary composers such as Irving Berlin and Aaron Copeland. What contemporary events might have influenced their lives and music?

*Extension Activities:*

Listen again to the symphony and draw a picture representing the mood of the music. Listen to recordings of other composers, read their biographies, and compare their music to the experiences of their lives.

*History*

*Background and Motivator:* Discuss what students think causes war.

*Purpose:* The reading assignment is to finish the section on the immediate causes for the Civil War.

*Vocabulary:* Handout given with key vocabulary words and literal definitions. Students will use these words in an exercise to place them in the proper context within sentences.

*Silent Reading:*

*Follow-up Activity:* Students as a class will prepare a chart that shows a time line of the events leading up to the Civil War. During this time, key vocabulary concepts will be used and an attempt will be made to establish personal meaning with any of the students (e.g., family involved, family that were slaves, family killed in other wars, etc.).

*Extension Activity:* Class will be divided into two groups. Each group will take a side, with one being the North and the other being the South. Each side will be asked to defend its position in the war.

*Science*

*Background and Motivator:* Identify need by testing for coronary heart disease risk. Everyone should be interested in maintaining their heart.

*Vocabulary:* Systole, diastole, blood pressure, hypertension, athersclerosis, sphygmomanometer, stethoscope. Instruction in word roots, such as *dia, hyper,* will be given. Students will then be asked to define the above words.

*Purpose:* The students will learn about blood pressure and coronary heart disease and will be able to evaluate their own health status.

*Silent Reading:* Material from the heart foundation

*Follow-up Activity:* The class will take their individual pulse rates and blood pressures. Health care professional will take cholesterol screening.

*Extension Activity:* The students will complete a family tree indicating blood type and occurrence of coronary heart disease.

*Math*

*Background and Motivator:* Knowledge in first chapter will help students give directions to their home, balance checkbook, do taxes, and shop intelligently.

*Vocabulary:* Opposite, origin, absolute value, technical, and general meaning of words will be shown in semantic map.

*Purpose:* To review principles of number lines previously learned and to prepare you to give directions, balance checkbook, do taxes, and shop.

*Silent Reading:* Math textbook chapter on number lines

*Follow-up Activity:* List as many opposites and absolute values as you can in one minute (example of opposites—boy/girl)

*Extension Activity:* Write how you would give directions to your house from school and how this relates to number lines.

*English/Speech*

*Background and Motivator:* How many of you would like to get your own way most of the time? Being able to do so is called *persuasion.* In this chapter you are going to learn how to be more persuasive through writing a speech.

*Vocabulary:* Introduction, body, conclusion, list all similar words to help with semantics and understanding of the chapter.

*Purpose:* To improve personal skills of persuasion through reading, writing, and speaking.

*Silent Reading:* Chapter in speech book on persuasive speeches

*Follow-up Activity:* Write a persuasive speech to be given to your family that will enable you to change someone's mind.

*Extension Activity:* Deliver persuasive speech to class, to family, to video.

# Strategies for Activating Prior Knowledge

**Definition**     Helping students build bridges between what they already know about a topic and the new information they are reading about the same topic.

**Strategies**     BRAINSTORMING/TALK THROUGH—This strategy aids in surfacing what students know—provides the teacher with an idea of the kind of pre-teaching that must take place.

Teacher lists major vocabulary words or concepts on the chalkboard, then simply asks students to tell all they know about the concepts OR to define the vocabulary words. This strategy may be done orally with groups or in written form with individual students.

PREP—This strategy allows the teacher to introduce a topic by focusing on what students know and aids students in making relationships between what they know and are learning. It's done in a group setting—discussion style.

The teacher introduces a topic and records student responses to the following statement/questions:

"Tell me all you know about _____."
"How did you know _____?"
"What more do you still want/need to learn?"

**Advantages**     Provides instruction to counter strength of students' tendency to maintain misconceptions and challenges student to utilize prior knowledge.

Provides teacher with diagnostic information concerning how much pre-teaching of vocabulary, concepts will be necessary.

Aids in identification of varying knowledge of students.

Identifies student resources.

Provides all students an opportunity to participate.

*Source:* Langer, J. (1981). From theory to practice: A prereading plan. *Journal of Reading, 24,* 152–156. Reprinted with permission of Judith Langer and the International Reading Association.

# Using Story Grammar to Develop a Schema for Reading Narrative

First ask pupils to supply answers to the questions listed. Record their answers and then have them rewrite the answers as an original story.

1. *Setting:*
   a. Where will our story take place—at the beach, in an airplane, in a classroom? What is the place like?
   b. Who is the heroine or hero? What is she or he like? Describe.
2. *Episode:*
   a. What will happen?
   b. How will the heroine or hero (protagonist) feel about what happens?
   c. What does the protagonist want now? What does the protagonist plan to do? What does the protagonist do?
3. *Consequences:*
   a. What happens when the protagonist carries out the plan?
   b. Does the protagonist succeed or not?
4. *Reaction:*
   a. What did the protagonist learn from all this?
   b. What do we learn from this?

*Source:* McConaughy, S. H. (1980, February). Using story structure in the classroom. *Language Arts, 57:* 157–165.

## 35 Comprehension Activities for Any Subject

Try one of these activities to teach reading comprehension in any content class.

1.  Draw a picture to illustrate the selection you read.

2.  Make a list of words that describe the selection you read. You may use words from this list: funny, exciting, sad, pleasant, depressing, strange, unbelievable, not true, believable, humorous, true, odd, thrilling, happy, unpleasant.

3.  Write a letter to a friend and tell him or her about the selection you read. Tell your friend why you think he or she should or should not read the selection.

4.  Write a poem about the selection you read.

5.  Write a letter to the editor of *Reader's Digest* and tell her or him why you did or did not like the selection you read.

6.  Write five questions about the selection you read.

7.  Make a list of 10 key words from the selection you read. Use the words to make a puzzle (crossword, seek and find, word train, word scramble). Let a friend work the puzzle.

8.  Copy five sentences from the selection you read. On a second sheet of paper, write the sentences with one word missing from each sentence. Write the missing words at the bottom of the second page. Let a friend try to put the missing words in the right sentences.

9.  Pretend you are a television news reporter. Tell about the selection you read as if it were a top news story.

10. Write five sentences about major concepts or events in the selection you read on five separate index cards. Shuffle the cards. Let a friend try to put the cards in order. When he or she is finished, correct any errors your friend made.

11. State the main idea of the selection you read in one sentence.

12. Write a skit or play based on the concepts in the selection you read.

13. Write an epilogue to the selection you read. (An epilogue tells what happens after the passage or story ends.)

14. Pretend you are the author of the selection you read. Change the ending.

15. Write the title and author of the selection you read on your paper. Answer these questions.
    a.  Did you like the selection?
    b.  How did the selection make you feel?

c. Do you think the selection was accurate/true?
d. Was the selection interesting?
e. Will you tell a friend to read this selection?

**16.** Choose three paragraphs from the selection you read. Practice reading the paragraphs. Take turns with a partner by reading your paragraphs to your partner and then listening to your partner read her or his paragraphs.

**17.** Read your favorite part of your selection out loud to a friend. Listen to your friend read his or her favorite selection out loud. Discuss which selection you think is the best.

**18.** Pretend you are a newswriter. Write an article about the selection you read. Make up a good headline (title) for your article.

**19.** Was the selection you read taking place in the past, the present, or the future? Draw a picture of something in the passage to show how you knew when it took place.

**20.** Suppose you had written to a person in the selection you read and asked what he or she would like for his or her birthday. Make a list of 10 presents the person might have asked for. Explain why he or she would want those presents.

**21.** Choose a place mentioned in the selection you read. Write a story, a legend, or a factual report about that place.

**22.** List five characters from the selection you read across the top of your paper. Write five characteristics of each person under each name. Then write the opposite of each of the descriptive words you wrote.

**23.** Write three questions that can be answered by reading the selection you read. Answer the questions.

**24.** Make a poster advertising something in the selection you read. Make it bright, bold, and simple.

**25.** Who was the main character in the selection you read? Write that character a letter. Suggest what might have happened if she or he had acted another way.

**26.** Write 10 words of a certain type that you found in the selection you read (big words, feeling words, color words, etc.). Alphabetize the words.

**27.** Write sentences from the selection you read that tell:

a. how something works
b. how something sounds
c. how something feels
d. how something looks

**28.** Write a comparison of one character in the story you read to a real person you know. How are they alike? How are they different?

**29.** Tell how you felt about some character in the selection you read. Tell why you think you felt that way.

**30.** What day of the month is your birthday? Count the words in the selection you read until you come to the number for your birthdate. Write that word on your paper. Write every tenth word after that until you have a list of 15 to 20 words. Group the words into categories of words that are alike and words that are different.

**31.** Write a story using the main idea of the selection you read. You may change the time, the characters, or anything else as long as the main idea is the same.

**32.** Write a play based on the selection you read. Make a list of the characters and who in our class you would have act the parts.

**33.** Make a puppet show about a part of the selection you read. Color or draw a few pictures to be shown on the commercial.

**34.** Write a television commercial for the selection you read. Color or draw a few pictures to be shown on the commercial.

**35.** Choose a friend to be a news reporter. You pretend to be an object, insect, character, or element in the selection you read. Give the reporter 10 or 15 questions for him or her to ask you in an interview. Perform the interview for the class.

# Patterns of Nonfiction

| Name of Pattern | Parts |
|---|---|
| **I PROBLEM-SOLUTION**<br>Purpose: To move to action | **PROBLEM-EFFECTS-CAUSE-SOLUTION**<br>The PROBLEM in this pattern is a situation causing distress or tension; the EFFECTS are the results of this situation (waste, suffering, etc.); the CAUSE or CAUSES are the factors that produce the situation; the SOLUTION is the action the author suggests to remedy the situation. This pattern may have a SIGNIFICANCE, which is usually a specific call to action. |
| **II-A THESIS-PROOF**<br>Purpose: To prove something | **THESIS-BACKGROUND-PROOF-IMPLICATION**<br>The THESIS is the proposition the author wants to prove; the BACKGROUND is the information the author gives the reader so that he or she can understand the PROOF. PROOF and IMPLICATION are self-explanatory. |
| **II-B OPINION-REASON**<br>Purpose: To prove something | **OPINION-BACKGROUND-REASON-RECOMMENDATION**<br>The OPINION is one side of an open question (debatable topic); the BACKGROUND is a "briefing" to make the proofs more understandable; REASONS are arguments to support the author's OPINION; RECOMMENDATION is the ACTION suggested by the author. |
| **III INFORMATIONAL**<br>Purpose: To give information | **ASPECT-ASPECT-ASPECT-ASPECT-ASPECT**<br>Each section of the material is devoted to an ASPECT of the overall SUBJECT MATTER of the article or book; the ASPECTS vary according to the author's plan, which can be chronological, spatial, a process, etc. |
| **IV THE NEWS ARTICLE**<br>Purpose: To inform about an event | **WHO-WHAT-WHEN-WHERE-WHY**<br>The News Article describes an event. It is about something (WHAT) that happens at a certain time (WHEN) in a certain place (WHERE) to certain people (WHO) usually for certain reasons (WHY). These "5 Ws" are the ASPECTS of this pattern, which is a variation of the INFORMATIONAL pattern. |
| **V HOW-TO**<br>Purpose: To instruct | **IMPORTANCE-STEPS-SIGNIFICANCE**<br>In this pattern, the author usually attempts to show why the subject he or she is discussing has values for the reader. The STEPS part is the instruction itself; the SIGNIFICANCE usually urges the reader to follow the steps or adhere to the instruction. |

# Inventory of Comprehension Skill

1. Does he associate experiences and meaning with the graphic symbol?
2. Does he understand words in context and can he select the meaning that fits the context?
3. Does he have the ability to give meaning to units of increasing size:
   a. the phrase
   b. the clause
   c. the sentence
   d. the paragraph
   e. the whole selection
4. Does he have the ability to detect and understand the main ideas?
5. Does he recognize significant details?
6. Does he follow directions?
7. Does he perceive relationships:
   a. part-whole
   b. cause-effect
   c. general-specific
   d. place
   e. sequence
   f. size
   g. time
8. Does he make inferences and to draw conclusions, to supply implied details and evaluate what is read?
9. Does he identify and evaluate character traits, reactions and motives?
10. Does he anticipate outcomes?
11. Does he recognize and understand the writer's purpose?
12. Does he retain ideas?
13. Does he apply ideas and integrate them with one's past experience?

*Source:* Dechant, V. (1964). *Improving the teaching of reading.* Englewood Cliffs, NJ: Prentice-Hall. Reprinted with permission.

# CHAPTER SIX

# *Reading and Writing: Avenues to Critical Thinking*

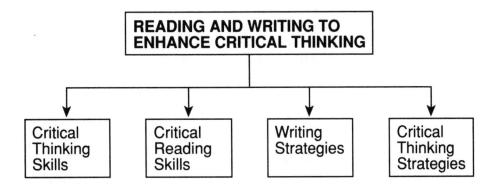

Reading and writing instruction should be focused on teaching critical thinking. Every content area teacher is either directly or indirectly teaching reading and writing as well as the critical thinking that is a part of the process. Critical reading and writing are independent of intelligence and can be taught for remedial, developmental, and gifted students, beginning on the primary level.

Reading is no longer defined as the sounding out of words and the ability to recall written information. These two skills might be included as some of the first to be mastered in the reading process but they certainly are not the purpose for reading. If the two skills of word attack and literal comprehension are emphasized, reading ceases to be a fulfilling experience. Students who are avid readers do not engage in reading because they enjoy hearing themselves sound out words or giving themselves quizzes over what they have read. People read because they want to learn about something they are interested in, they want to talk with their friends about what they have read, and they want to feel competent and intelligent. Yet, much of students' time in school is spent documenting that they know vocabulary words and facts, which associates reading with drill. Little attention is paid to instruction in critical reading, which increases the enjoyment of all students and improves future citizens' ability to form intelligent opinions about what they read.

If there is not enough time in class for all students to discuss their opinions and reactions to what they have read, then integrating reading and writing is a very expedient means for teaching critical thinking. Activity is critical to thinking and learning. To know something is to see, modify, change, transform, and act on it through writing. Thinking and knowing, then, are a part of structuring and restructuring knowledge. Student learning is not enhanced by less active modes of listening to teachers, watching teachers and other students, or attending and following action in the class. Both writing and reading are active processes whereby the students must structure and restructure content.

The mastery of just one critical thinking technique, detecting bias, was described by a redcap at Los Angeles International Airport. He felt it was the only useful thinking skill he learned in school and he learned it in his English class. Whenever he read the paper, watched the news, or listened to a conversation, he asked himself who was the "protagonist." Next, he asked who was the "antagonist" and then he asked what were the problems. After asking and answering these three questions, he often found himself disagreeing with the conclusions reached by those reporting. Using this strategy, he was able to judge the veracity of what was read and seen, make distinctions between relevant and irrelevant data, and examine the writer's attitude. He was able to form an independent opinion about what he had read. Some people have seen the effect of the media on the general public, while others have witnessed its effect in rising misinformation and gullibility. Just as the redcap demonstrated through critical thinking, well-educated citizens should not only be able to sound out words and to recall information but to digest, synthesize, evaluate, and formulate intelligent opinions about what they see and read.

Our schools are the place to learn these skills. More than 20 years ago, Lee (1969) believed that students did not lack reading comprehension skills; they lacked meaning skills. Meaning occurs when one is able to think about what has been read and apply, analyze, criticize, and hypothesize. These skills are observable and they lend themselves to systematic instruction. D'Angello (1972) found when readers were unaware of viewpoints that either differed from their own or the author's, their comprehension did not match with the public meaning. Critical reading and the understanding of bias may be prerequisites to accurate comprehension. No student should be expected to find his own meaning if he has been taught primarily to decode and recall information from a single source. Similarly, no student should be expected to write with clarity if she has only been taught to spell and copy information from an encyclopedia or other sourcebooks.

Criticial reading, writing, and hence critical thinking can begin with a single source of information. The skills taught would be the following:

1. Determine the relevance of information.
2. Distinguish between fact and opinion stated in the piece.
3. Make a reasoned judgment.
4. Identify unstated assumptions.
5. Detect bias.
6. Detect emotional language or appeal.

7. Identify propaganda techniques.
8. Label value orientations and ideologies.
9. Judge authenticity of the author.

Within the problem-solving framework:

10. Recognize adequacy of data.
11. Identify the reasonableness of alternatives and solutions.
12. Predict possible consequences.
13. Test conclusions or hypotheses.

When examining these skills collectively, the definition of critical thinking demonstrated through reading and writing emerges as the ability to manipulate, reflect, compare, and evaluate data. Traditionally, critical thinking has been categorized in the upper levels of cognitive and reading comprehension taxonomies. In this way, it has been labeled as application, synthesis, analysis, and evaluation of material. In the reading instruction sequence, critical reading and thinking skills follow the students' acquisition of literal and interpretative meaning. One source or textbook can be used for instruction. However, the definition of critical thinking implies at least two perspectives, which is where student writing becomes important as the second perspective. If there is only one source of information that is accepted and memorized, then the learning process is called *indoctrination.* As Singer and Donlan (1980) proposed, the goal of reading instruction is to develop single-text strategies that are then used on multiple texts with increasing student independence. Similarly, Russell (1950) described critical thinking as the reactions to other's ideas or to one's own previous ideas. Two perspectives and student independence are found in both experts' definitions of learning. Obviously, though, a truly informed and educated person is able to read, write, and think. These skills can be taught at the same time.

Critical thinking instruction in this chapter will be discussed as the outcome of reading and writing strategies. The questions answered will be the most frequently asked questions of content teachers.

1. How do I encourage students to think and read critically?
2. What are some writing strategies to use to avoid controversy when teaching critical thinking?
3. What are critical thinking strategies to use in the classroom?

# Critical Thinking

*How do I encourage students to think and read critically?*

The simplest way to encourage critical thinking is to make sure the questions, activities, or problems in the textbook provide practice in reading, writing, and thinking beyond the literal and interpretive levels. Using Bloom's levels of cognitive thinking, the instructor can encourage critical thinking by teaching both declarative and procedural reading comprehension. When thinking on any one of the levels, a different process or procedure is used to organize information. In most cases, students will be asked to think on different levels in different classes. For example, working mathematics problems is a major procedural comprehension activity in math classes. In order to do well, a student has to be able to apply facts learned earlier in the chapter to work the problems. In social studies, students are asked to answer questions that follow the reading assignments. Depending on the level of the questions, the readers must use literal, interpretive, application, analysis, synthesis, or evaluation skills.

Thus, the first step in teaching students how to think on critical levels is to examine the questions at the back of the textbook chapters. If they are consistently literal, the teacher will need to construct his or her own questions to add to those in the book. Suggested formats are presented in Figure 6–1 (elementary) and Figure 6–2 (secondary). The elementary questions can be used with learning disabled and ESL students.

**Figure 6–1**   *Making a Literal Test a Critical Thinking Test*

A 14-question chapter test may be found at the end of Chapter 4: Rocks in *Holt Science 3.* All 14 questions are literal questions, as the answers can be found on the following pages: 60(1), 60(2), 59(3), 60(4), 61(5), 61(6), 61(7), 65(8), 64(9), 64(10), 64–67(11), 65(12), 65(13), and 65(14). Understanding that literal questions only require that the student look back in the textbook to find the answers, students need to write and think on the application and analysis, synthesis, or evaluation levels. Sample questions on other critical thinking levels follow the original questions.

**1.**   (original question) Which of the following does not describe a property of a rock?
   a.   dull   c.   striped
   b.   loud   d.   blue
**1a.**   What would a dull rock be used for?
**1b.**   What criteria are used for determining if a rock is smooth?
**2.**   (original question) Rocks found at the beach are usually
   a.   round and smooth   c.   hard and rough
   b.   round and rough   d.   soft and rough
**2a.**   Why are round and smooth rocks found at the beach?
**2b.**   Will rocks found on the beach always be round and smooth?
**3.**   (original question) Rocks that are formed in layers are often found
   a.   in flat areas   c.   in hilly areas
   b.   at the beach   d.   on mountain cliffs
**3a.**   What are layered rocks used for?
**3b.**   Why are rocks that are formed in layers found in flat areas?

If the teacher assigns questions provided by the textbook, then those questions should ask students to comprehend on different cognitive levels.

*Source:* Compiled by Dennis Ball, science teacher. From Abruscato, J., Hassard, J., Fossaceca, J., & Peck, D. (1984). *Holt Science 3.* New York: Holt, Rinehart and Winston.

**Figure 6–2** *Making Textbook Questions on Different Critical Thinking Levels*

Compare the thinking skills found in the textbook questions with those written by the teacher. As in the science example (Figure 6–1), it is clear that more active participation and understanding is required of the readers when writing answers to teacher-developed questions.

*Music Textbook Test*

Write the letter of the correct answer in the blank.

*Music Textbook Test*

Write the letter of the correct answer in the blank.

1. Melodies move by ___ , ___ , and ___ .
   - a. step          c. leap
   - b. reverse     d. repeat
2. A major scale is a pattern of whole steps and ___ .
   - a. half backs       c. whole notes
   - b. half beats       d. half steps
3. A key signature shows what ___ are needed.
   - a. sharps or naturals     c. heels or flats
   - b. sharps or flats          d. flats or naturals
4. A minor scale sounds different from a major scale because it has a different ___ .
   - a. step pattern      c. key signature
   - b. melody             d. rhythm
5. A scale of only five notes with a step-and-a-half between the third and fourth notes is called a ___ .
   - a. pentatonic scale       c. a fish scale
   - b. a twelve-tone scale    d. a chromatic scale
6. In a sequence, a melodic pattern is repeated ___ .
   - a. at higher or lower levels       c. backwards
   - b. once                                   d. with other instruments
7. In music, an interval is the span between two ___ .
   - a. rests               c. notes
   - b. key signatures    d. bar lines
8. "This Land Is Your Land" was written by ___ .
   - a. Arlo Guthrie        c. Woody Guthrie
   - b. Tyrone Guthrie     d. Frederick Guthrie

The following teacher-made questions test students on different cognitive levels.

1. All songs are melodies. True_____ False_____ (literal)
2. Identify which are whole steps and which are half steps in the following example.   (Interpretation or Application)
3. Write the key signature for the key of E-flat major.   (Application)
4. What would be the key signature for a major scale beginning on D? (Application and Analysis—one would have to write a scale beginning on D and then analyze where the whole and half steps must be to make it a major scale.)

Continued

**Figure 6–2**   (cont.)

---

5. Does the following example use a major or minor key? (Analysis of a minor key)
6. Write your own sequence based on this pattern, beginning a whole step lower.   (Application and Synthesis)
7. Name the following intervals.   (Interpretation)
8. Would you consider "This Land Is Your Land" by Woody Guthrie a good folk song? Why?   (Evaluative)

---

Like those in Figure 6–1, questions in the music book are written on the literal level.

*Source:* Compiled by Ted Grille, music teacher. From Culp, Eisman, and Hoffman (1988). *World of Music.* Morristown, NJ: Silver Burdett and Ginn.

The direct relationships between Bloom's taxonomy and critical reading skills, as traditionally defined, are described next.

**Analysis.**   In analysis, a complete statement is broken or separated into its component parts for individual study. In addition, a student thinking on the analysis level must be aware of the precise thought process being used.

1.   *Detecting authenticity and/or choice of a source of information.* Who is the best person to make an accurate and unbiased statement about a subject?

2.   *Discriminating between fact and opinion.* Students must learn to distinguish between what can be proven objectively and what is an interpretation.

3.   *Recognizing propaganda techniques.* The language of propaganda is designed to sway and influence people. Propaganda can be good or bad. Students should be made aware of these techniques so that they are able to evaluate when their emotions are being manipulated.

4.   *Detecting fallacies of reasoning.* Some of the methods of using false reasoning are slanted arguments, false analogies, guilt by association, assumptions, ambiguity, and statistical fallacies.

5.   *Judging logic of actions.* To judge logic of actions is to assess the practicability, utility, and applicability of a procedure or method.

**Synthesis.**   Synthesis is the act of combining or unifying separate elements into a coherent whole.

1.   *Building hypotheses.* To build hypotheses is to construct tentative assumptions that appear to account for an observed effect, which may be used more fully to examine a specific situation or to provide possible conclusions or proofs.

**2.** *Conducting projects.* A student must describe the important elements of a task and explain the ways in which the task can be completed successfully.

**3.** *Developing conclusions.* A student should be able to use the information given to decide what feasibly could come next in the sequence.

**4.** *Determining alternate actions.* Explore and develop different approaches to the solution of problems.

**Evaluation.** The highest level of the cognitive domain is evaluation, which includes two steps. First, the student must set up standards against which he or she will judge the value of an idea, or complex of ideas, or an object. Second, the student must judge the correlation between the standards and whatever it is that is being evaluated.

**1.** *Evaluating value conflicts.* Assess the coherence of specific actions and ideals and determine the compatibility of personal desires and social sanctions.

**2.** *Testing generalizations.* Determine whether or not declarations, conclusions, or other articles are justified and acceptable on the bases of accuracy and relationships to relevant data.

**3.** *Assimilating or accommodating information.* Establish whether information fits within the student's existing value structure or whether the values need to be altered to accept information. Rejection of information based on established values is also a part of this process.

**4.** *Examining values of the teacher and the author.* Gray (1969) states that by the eleventh grade, attitudes and values are very set and determined. Certain attitudes, if the readers are unaware of them, can lead to a lack of comprehension of what is read. Therefore, students should be taught before the eleventh grade to examine their own attitudes as well as those of the authors they read.

A teacher is not expected to use every one of these skills in every lesson, but he or she should be aware of them so that these skills can be recognized in textbook activities and questions. The teacher can also construct discussion or essay questions.

Many teachers in our educational system today depend largely on questions and techniques that require only literal comprehension from their students in daily assignments. Much has been written and spoken about critical reading/writing/thinking skills, yet the frequency of their use in many classrooms is limited. There are several reasons for this.

**1.** For students to think at these higher levels, they must use a wide variety of materials and be able to relate their previous experience to these materials.

**2.** Frequently, students attach a halo to the printed word, thinking that anything that is in print must be true.

**3.** When controversial issues are being studied, it is difficult for students not to get emotional; instead, they should examine both points of view, looking for the rationale behind each perspective.

**4.** The classroom atmosphere must allow for divergence in opinions, with freedom of expression for each.

**5.** The longer teachers teach, the less they emphasize critical thinking in their classrooms.

**6.** The management of students' thinking is demanding and can not be routinized in a lesson plan format.

**7.** Providing organized lectures makes it easier for students to take notes and memorize the material. Content is isolated, categorized, and simplified for the convenience of teachers and students.

Despite these obstacles, comprehension questions on different levels can be used to promote oral and written discussion before, during, and after the reading of a selection. Such questions become much more than comprehension checks. In fact, Reutzel (1985) even recommends going backwards in the reading lesson to help teachers and students achieve more expanded thinking patterns. He suggests beginning with the extension activities and then going to the comprehension questions, reading the selection and then having vocabulary study to follow. Robert Yeager, former president of the National Science Teachers Association, recommends conducting experiments, providing the science experience, and then making reading and writing assignments.

However teachers organize their instruction, teachers' questions and tests are important determiners of the "attention-to-task" revealed by students as they read and write. If teachers ask questions that call for simple recall at the literal level, the students are more likely to practice and become proficient in reading and writing for simple recall, but not become proficient in reading or writing with critical depth. As questions are asked, pupils are guided to read and then write for certain purposes—the purposes represented by the types of questions used in the guided reading.

It would be a mistake to assume that intellectual ability, or the lack of it, should determine whether or not we deal with comprehension questions beyond the literal recall level. A research study by Caskey (1970) supported the conclusion that, providing the materials are at the students' reading level, higher-level comprehension is more dependent on how we teach than on the students' intellectual ability. In other words, the national decline of senior high school students' ability to answer higher-level comprehension questions is a reflection on their instruction, not their intelligence (Rothman, 1990; Roberts, 1988). Gray (1969) found that even children in first through sixth grades were capable of judging the relevancy of information and the authenticity of information. It seems only logical that if we are going to expect students to use critical reading and writing skills in the upper grades, a foundation must be prepared in the early grades. Similarly, if we are going to test on application, synthesis, and analysis levels on national tests such as the SAT and ACT, then students should have extensive experience with critical thinking in their junior high and secondary coursework.

Boyles (1988) developed the following critical reading strategy for first-graders, but content teachers with ESL and learning-disabled students might be able to use it for critical thinking instruction in secondary classrooms.

*REACTION*
*Reward*—Read books for fun.
*Extend*—Do something with art, music, or poetry.
*Assess*—What is the lesson, moral, theme, or main idea?
*Change*—Rewrite parts.
*Take apart*—This problem wouldn't have happened if . . .
*Investigate*—Choose an idea to find out more about . . .
*Organize*—Sequence events.
*Name*—List.

Another twist to the questioning process can be verified by recent studies that have shown that when students, as well as teachers, formulate questions about materials they have read, both parties' comprehension will improve. This activity has been formalized into reciprocal teaching by Manzo and Manzo (1990). The teacher first shows students how to answer questions. When the students can replicate the teacher's model questions, then the process becomes a reciprocal one where the teacher answers students questions and vice versa. The QAR presented by Rapheal (1981, 1984) basically looks at the four places where an oral or written answer can be found: right there in the text (literal), in the text but not spelled out for the student (interpretive), in what students have learned and what is in the text (application), or in their own heads (Right There, Think and Search, You and the Author, and On Your Own).

Another instructional strategy to teach critical thinking is to use "talk throughs" where the teacher explains how she or he comes up with the answer to different questions. The important aspect here is that emotion must not control the process that the teacher uses to answer questions. Lack of emotional control allows biases, which, when the teacher/readers are unaware of them, prevent comprehension of what they read and bias what they write. Therefore, comprehending and answering material on different levels must involve the suspension or awareness of emotion involved in the process. Critical thinking involves using judgment based and defended on sound criteria.

One of the most limiting influences on the ability of children to think is the teaching situation. In elementary school, there is an

*". . . After preheating the oven, pour batter into lightly greased pan and bake 20 minutes at 350 degrees."*

overemphasis on the mechanics of reading, with too much phonics or undue attention to the parts of words rather than the meaning or messages they convey. Undue emphasis is placed on letter-by-letter sounding approach to unfamiliar words, isolation of sounds, and synthesizing these isolated sounds into words and/or nonsense syllables. Too much attention is given to rules, drills on words out of context, and routine procedures that are more mechanical than meaningful, such as ritualistically writing vocabulary words in sentences, copying meanings out of the dictionary, and completing one page after another in the workbook without reference to how the information relates to reading and why it is important to know. And finally, there is too much emphasis on names of various punctuation marks rather than their application to making the text meaningful.

The overemphasis on mechanics of reading is supported by the undue pressure that is placed on elementary children to succeed. Children are expected to bring home perfect papers and perfect report cards. This is difficult when they are consistently reading at the frustration level in material that is too difficult. The mountains of papers that have been graded by teachers and completed by students on the mechanics of reading have led to the belief that the only requirement of a good reader is that he or she be able to decode well. These conditions work against elementary children learning critical thinking skills.

Another issue is that social, emotional, and physical problems are much too prevalent in schools. Physical problems such as inadequate nutrition, lack of sleep, and hyperactivity exist. Severe emotional problems are present, resulting from disruptive family relationships, child abuse, emotional neglect, and unusual fears. Social problems also occur, such as the inability to work alone or in groups, or students so insecure in sharing attention from others that they cannot attend to the task at hand. There has to be a degree of self-confidence for one to be able to criticize the written word, and students with problems may not have the personal security to do so. And finally, emotional obstacles such as fear of failure, poor self-concept, inadequate response to stressful situations, and difficulty in controlling feelings all contribute to difficulties in learning how to think critically. Lee (1969) found that children with self-confidence developed better critical reading skills. Subjects that were interesting to children also encouraged their critical reading and writing ability.

Jenkinson (1965) believes that the reason secondary students are not writing, thinking, and reading critically is because they are not trained to do so in earlier years. Watson (1974) thinks that critical reading should begin in kindergarten. His idea is based on Taba and Bruner's spiral curriculum, which states that anything can be taught if it is presented on the developmental level of the child. The teacher should ask questions such as *why?* and *how?* as opposed to *what?*, *when?*, and *where?* Children think more deeply when the expectation is there.

Wolf, Huck, King, and Ellinger (1968) conducted a large study to investigate the critical reading of elementary school children. All groups of children receiving critical reading instruction made significant gains over the control groups. This study reinforced the fact that children, even in the primary grades, can be taught critical reading.

Over 30 years ago, Williams (1959) surveyed the critical reading skills found in basal readers. From 80 basals, Williams identified 186 critical reading skills. She condensed these into 33 skills. The highest number of skills found in any publisher's series was 24; the lowest was 11. This study indicated the need for elementary teachers to teach from supplementary basals that provide additional higher-level thinking skills.

Apart from the prior influence of elementary textbooks and teaching, the direct teaching of critical thinking influences secondary students' abilities. Denberg and Jones (1967) conducted a study with seventh- and eighth-grade students to see if training in critical thinking would result in improved critical reading ability. At the conclusion of the study, the researchers noted improvement in critical reading ability in all cases. In a study by Arlo (1969), ninth-grade students who were taught by inductive and expository methods scored significantly higher (.05) in critical reading than the control group taught by the usual curriculum. Downing (1974) found a significant increase in critical reading ability from grades 13 to 14. This study shows that students continue to grow in critical thinking and reading skills throughout college if they are directly taught. Thus, it might not matter that the curriculum has changed little in 40 years in social studies (Dynneson & Gross, 1983) or in mathematics, if critical thinking skills are being taught. Research over the last 30 years has found that critical thinking skills can be taught and such instruction makes a difference in student performance.

The main strategy for finding what influences critical thinking has been to compare the differences between skilled and less skilled comprehenders. Oakhill (1986) found that skilled comprehenders engage in more constructive processing and that retention ability has no relation to comprehension ability. The one important difference between skilled and less skilled comprehenders is that the former are better able to integrate information in a text and are more successful in drawing appropriate inferences from sentences and texts. Such studies indicate that the differences between skilled and less skilled readers could be eradicated by direct instruction in critical reading and thinking.

## Summary

The questions students are expected to answer shape their thinking. If students spend most of their time answering factual and evaluative questions, they will read all material for the purpose of answering recall and opinion questions. This repetitive process deadens students' ability to read, write, or think critically; instead, they become memorizers.

Second, all students, not just the brighter ones, can read beyond the simple recall level and should be expected to do so if one instructional goal is to develop critical thinking skills. Unless teachers can make life for the slower students less complicated and difficult, then they too will need analysis, synthesis, and evaluation strategies as much as the more intelligent students. All students' comprehension skills will improve significantly when they, as well as the teacher, are involved in formulating questions. And finally, it is not enough to enhance the textbook questions and teacher-asked questions. Students must also be taught how to answer questions where the product is not found directly in the text.

Limitations on the development of critical thinking skills can be identified in elementary reading curriculum content and evaluation. Another limitation can be found in the social, emotional, and physical problems of the students. However, the most significant limitation is that secondary students are not directly taught how to think critically. According to Oakhill (1982, 1986), the better readers are those who can think critically about their reading. Direct instruction in critical reading might improve reading comprehension and thereby reduce the number of remedial readers.

# Writing Strategies

*What are some writing strategies to use that encourage critical thinking?*

The most frequent criticism of school by students is that classes are boring. One reason classes are boring is that most of the time there is only one source of information and one perspective presented. Textbooks and teachers are usually in agreement, as it is safer for both to avoid controversy or a second point of view. Having multiple textbooks is financially prohibitive for most school districts, and preparing lessons by reading two or more sources is not expedient for the busy teacher. The result is that teachers end up amplifying what is in the text, and texts have been censored to the point that they are bland and hence boring.

A teaching strategy that avoids controversy and makes the class interesting is to change the traditional question/answer/read/test instructional sequence. In life outside the classroom, conditions for applying prior knowledge are rarely sequenced, packaged, or clearly delineated. Application situations in life are subject to considerable variability and that variability requires flexibility of responses. Instructing students through a process that seeks only one answer does not translate well to situations outside of the class. Visual and perceptual forms of comprehension need to be emphasized. "Monolithic" representations of knowledge leave holders facing situations where rigid "plaster casts" do not fit (Spiro, 1987). In short, the same information must be represented in many different ways and numerous connections must be drawn for all types of learners.

Establishing possible procedural routes for future assembly and creating potential analogies and models is useful for increasing understanding, critical thinking skills and avoiding controversy. Critical thinking instruction, in this case, would emphasize methods for assembling information rather than the current emphasis on retrieving information. Multiple strategies for setting up connectedness between different content areas would then be important. The strategies would include learning from examples, case studies, tutorial guiding or learning in pairs, and analogies. As an example, science could use conceptual models to improve students' understanding of scientific explanations. Critical thinking would be enhanced by identifying the major objects and action in a system model as well as causal relations among them. These strategies would build on the lower-level comprehension activities that emphasize self-monitoring of comprehension through self-questioning, reconstructing memory, summarizing, and mastery of literal comprehension. In all cases, higher-level thinking skills would be encouraged, as the control of the linear mode of read/question/test would be abandoned.

Conflict resolution is another way of teaching critical thinking. Holmes and Ammon (1985) suggest using tradebooks rather than textbooks for instruction in content areas. Here, the conflict is introduced by a variety of books written on the same topic. With tradebooks, students can develop such skills as recognizing and evaluating the reliability and authenticity of printed materials. A textbook is usually written from one perspective, with few conflicting statements of fact. When a textbook is used as the only source of information, some students tend to accept the author's statements without question. Holmes and Ammon (1985) suggest setting tradebooks up with the help of the librarian and keeping accurate records on the books that have been read in order to resolve conflicts or content discrepancies. Tradebooks for social studies would be magazines, newspapers, journals, and critiques. Tradebooks for PE would be magazines on health, fitness, exercise, physiology, and sports. Each content teacher knows the tradebooks that would be appropriate for her or his class.

The constraints of not having multiple textbooks or even a well-stocked library may keep many teachers from focusing on critical reading and thinking skills. The second issue is the one that most teachers want to avoid—censorship or parental problems as a result of controversies. When operating a public school, only those materials selected by the school district can be assumed to be free of controversy. Therefore, the best method to teach critical thinking and avoid controversy is to include writing as a component of the reading lesson. When students are examining their own writing or that of their peers, critical thinking skills are automatically a part of the lesson. Writers must develop the ability to think by producing a number of questions, ideas, solutions, or alternatives. They can make different approaches to the same issue and they can think of novel or unique approaches when they expand on ideas.

All critical thinking skills are necessary when students write, and they can easily be related to reading extension activities. The following sample writing activities can be used in content classes.

**Social Studies or History Class.**   Students might be given information from a tombstone about a family. This would be the only information provided; from it they would have to re-create the lives of the family or one individual's life. The possibilities for critical thinking in a writing assignment like this one are endless.

Students should also be aware of the differences between social studies disciplines, and might write about how they feel about history as opposed to civics. Writing assignments could also include research reports on time periods, cultural groups, or famous persons. Newman (1988) believes that critical thinking can be assessed and can occur in "conventionally" organized classes among all students, on all levels of grades and achievement.

**PE Class.**   Students might write to clarify thoughts and feelings after PE activity or write a description or interpretation of team responses and reactions. Writing could also be a problem-solving activity, where students look at specific offensive and defensive adjustments that could be made. A journal could be kept simply to document scoring information of games.

**Mathematics Class.**   Students could write out procedural steps to solve a problem. They could also write math problems in words. And finally, they could demonstrate their understanding of symbolic problems by writing their own problems.

**Science Class.**   A journal could be used for prereading predictions. Students could record laboratory observations and summarize learning. They could submit written questions regarding content confusions. And finally, they could use such a journal as a study support when they review learnings from the previous day.

**English Class.** Writing in English class could involve the creation of a short story, poem, or essay. Reports could be written on the theater or literary history of a certain period or about families. And, since speech is often a component of the English curriculum, students could write and deliver speeches on events of interest.

All these critical thinking activities are used in content classrooms. The purpose of this section on critical writing skills is to identify strategies that may not have been recently used. Writing skills are assumed to have been taught in English class, but, again, they need to be reinforced in all content classes. The point of writing across the curriculum is not to restrict the process to a simple formula like TDC (Topic sentence, Details, Conclusion). Writing, like reading, should be integrated to produce behavior that reflects critical thinking.

# Critical Thinking Strategies

*What are critical thinking strategies to use in the classroom?*

Karlin (1984) states that students should always have a purpose for reading. However, if students are involved and working with thought-provoking or challenging problem-solving situations, they will develop their own purpose for reading. Students should read a wide sampling of materials from various sources, such as text and reference sources, newspapers, and magazines. They can analyze the content of editorials and relate it to the presentation of news that is supposedly factual. They can evaluate the treatment given a news item by cartoons, editorials, news coverage, and news analysis. Two newspapers giving a different interpretation can be compared. Durr (1970) suggests interpreting cartoon strips by cutting away the "talk" shown in the balloons but leaving the characters intact. The students then devise the dialogue from strips, which requires them to use their insights into situations and characters. Odom (1971) gives 12 ways to use the newspaper in school. Cornish (1967) suggests that the intermediate grades pretend that they have discovered a new continent and they are responsible for its settlements. Thought-provoking activities can develop, such as what crops to grow, where to build railroads, what monetary system to use, and what form of government to establish.

Students can also read and analyze the characteristics of published book reviews. After this experience, they can write their own critical reviews. Several biographies about the same person might be read and compared. Davis (1967) recommends comparing books by the same author or the same topic. The students can do research papers on unsolved problems in literature or history. Roleplaying is also a good activity, where each student is motivated to do research on his or her character. Remedial students can make judgments and practice critical thinking, too. The text can be taped and the learner supplied with critical questions. A good discussion can follow using the questions. Students can read different accounts according to their reading ability. Reluctant readers might read William Bentley's *The Alligator Book: Sixty Questions and Answers* (Walker, 1972) while advanced students read Wyatt Blassingame's *Wonders of Alligators and Crocodiles* (Dodd, Mead, 1973). Also, Jean Fitz's biographies about famous Americans, like *What's the Big Idea, Ben Franklin?* (Coward-McCann, 1976) are excellent sources of enjoyment. Discussion comparing two nonfiction books on the same topic or comparing literature and nonfiction formats could follow.

All subjects can benefit from the study of analogies. Many people have been exposed to analogy questions on standardized achievement tests, but very few have ever experienced instruction in working with analogies. Ronan (1969) makes a case for teaching analogies. She states that one good logical thinking skill is the use, recognition, and evaluation of comparisons, or analogies. Another critical thinking skill is the identification of what are and are not important data. Being able to recognize missing facts or information is an important tool for evaluating the validity of a piece of writing, determining how to work a math problem, or deciding how to approach a scientific research project. The Teaching Activities at the end of the chapter provide a list of some of the common relationships found in analogies. Work on these relationships could help stop the decline in academic performance that appears to be afflicting our most able students.

According to Gregory Anrig (1984), president of Educational Testing Service, hidden in the celebrated decline of SAT scores since the high in the early 1960s is the fact that the most precipitous decline has been for those who rank highest in their high school class. From 1978 to 1984, the combined verbal and math scores on the SAT dropped an average of 10 points overall; for those in the top tenth of their class, however, scores dropped 26 points. The SAT scores have continued to decline from 1984 to the 1990s. Students are obviously having problems with higher-order thinking skills. They may be able to read a passage of literature but they have trouble critically interpreting it. They may be able to complete a mathematical computation correctly but they are unable to apply it in solving a problem. They may be able to spell correctly and demonstrate a knowledge of grammar but they are unable to introduce and develop a point of view in writing. These are the products of failing to teach critical thinking to teachers and students.

The activities listed are only a few of the many suggestions for teaching critical reading. Research indicates that critical writing and reading can and should be taught for all levels of intelligence, beginning with the elementary grades. Teachers, however, must be trained and begin teaching critical reading now.

# Summary

Critical reading and writing skills are important to the quality of thinking and to the functioning of our citizens. These skills must receive attention in all classrooms—kindergarten through graduate courses. To ensure the teaching of these skills, more research on specific skills that are factors in critical reading should be conducted. The single text and teacher agreement with the text have hampered critical thinking and reading instruction. Reading and writing strategies for the content areas are provided to help students and teachers learn how to develop their critical thinking abilities.

# Application Exercises and Teaching Activities

## Application Exercises

1.  What critical thinking skills are needed to solve the following social and political problems?

    a.  Industrial waste dumping has seeped into the water supply of your town.
    b.  The air pollution from cars is causing children to have to stay inside during play periods.
    c.  Many special education children in your school are being prepared for positions that will not exist when they graduate from high school.
    d.  The poverty in your area has greatly increased due to the increased number of teenage pregnancies.
    e.  Select a topic of current interest in your content area and discuss how critical thinking skills could be introduced in the reading, writing, and discussion of the topic.

2.  Using your critical thinking skills, examine the problems and solutions presented in the following teacher interview. Suggest alternative solutions.

### Interview with a Reading Teacher

The interviewed teacher teaches reading to the seventh grade. She had two classes consisting of 37 boys and 15 girls. She persuaded the administration to allow her to form three classes, one of which was mixed boys and girls.

*Problem 1:*   Students were unable to read the text.

(Solution)   I do not believe the teacher identified the reading level of the books used. I would do this before school started.

*Problem 2:*   Students were unable to follow directions.

(Solution)   I would give them a test on what their previous learning experience had been. I would check with last year's teachers for: (1) home background, (2) physical problems, and (3) emotional problems.

*Problem 3:*   Students complained that the work was unfamiliar and that they had no previous training in the handling of the material.

(Solution)   I would conduct a beginning-of-course survey to show students how to handle their textbook, what to do with the table of contents, how to read maps, and to be aware of the study aids provided them.

*Problem 4:*   Students were unable to apply their ability to figure out meanings and had inadequate vocabulary for their age and grade level.

(Solution)   I would give them a skills test to determine what specific skills were needed to develop a better vocabulary.

*Problem 5:*   Students read directions to the teacher and then told her they did not know what they were supposed to do.

(Solution)   I would give them a comprehension test to determine their ability to comprehend written instructions.

*Problem 6:*   Students complained that the material was boring and they saw no reason for studying it.

(Solution)   I would select material on their interest level and use this material to teach them how to (1) find the overall picture of setting, plot, and action; (2) appreciate the author's style; and (3) understand the sequence of development.

*Problem 7:*   Students said they were unable to understand poetry and dramas.

(Solution)   I would teach them to listen carefully and thoughtfully and try to visualize and hear the music of the words in poetry. I would encourage them to construct plays from some of the stories in the basal reader and give them time to act them out.

# Teaching Activities:
# Common Relationships in Analogies

1. Whole is compared to the part
    constellation : stars
    archipelago : island
2. Specific item is compared to its general class
    rodent : rat
    reptile : snake
3. The abstract is compared to the specific
    person : girl
    vehicle : car
4. The cause is compared to the effect
    rain : fertility
    drought : aridity
5. A word is compared to its synonym
    myriad : many
    sparse : few
6. A word is compared to its antonym
    neophyte : connoisseur
    tyro : expert
7. An object is compared to its function
    helmsman : steer
    monarch : rule
8. An object is compared to its characteristic
    telephone : ring
    clock : chime
9. Worker and article created
    carpenter : house
    writer : book
    composer : symphony
10. Worker and tool used
    carpenter : saw
    writer : typewriter
    surgeon : scalpel
11. Tool and object worked on
    pencil : paper
    saw : wood
12. The act the tool does to the object it works on
    saw : wood (cuts)
    knife : bread (cuts)
    brake : car (stops)
13. Time sequence
    early : late
    dawn : twilight
    sunrise : sunset
14. Cause and effect
    germ : disease
    carelessness : accident
    explosion : debris

15. Degree of intensity
    tepid : hot
    joy : ecstasy
    admiration : love
16. Class—species
    furniture : chair
    insect : grasshopper
    mammal : whale
    dog : poodle
17. Type—characteristic
    cow : herbivorous
    tiger : carnivorous
18. Grammatical relationships
    I : mine (first person nominative case : first person possessive case)
    wolf : vulpine (noun : adjective)
    have : had (present tense : past tense)
    alumnus : alumni (masculine singular noun : masculine plural noun)
19. Person and thing sought by person
    alchemist : gold
    prospector : gold
20. Person and thing avoided by person
    child : fire
    pilot : reef
21. Part to the whole
    soldier : regiment
    star : constellation
22. Sex
    duck : drake
    bull : cow
23. Symbol—what it stands for
    flag : nation
    insignia : rank

# Creative Ideas for Critical Thinking at the Intermediate Level

1. If a tornado destroyed this school building, what suggestions for temporary classrooms could you suggest?

2. Think up five new inventions made by combining two (or more) objects and/or inventions. (Example: a washer-dryer combination, a chaise lounge.) Attempt to convince the class that the whole is better than the sum of its parts.

3. Name three new regular newspaper features that could be added to increase circulation by appealing to young people. Suggest titles for the features and explain the material to be featured.

4. What if you suddenly became 10 feet tall while the rest of the world remained as is? What changes would you have to make in your life? What would be the advantages? Disadvantages? (Variations: What if you suddenly became 2 inches tall? Only 1 inch wide?)

5. Suggest three get-rich-quick schemes.

6. Design an undersea city. What are some problems you would encounter if you tried to actually build your city?

7. List every possible use you can think of for an ordinary coat hanger.

8. List at least 3 ways the movie rating system in your town could be improved.

9. What if people had a third hand? Where on the body do you think it should be located so that it would be most useful? List some advantages of having a third arm. Can you foresee any problems?

10. Suppose for one afternoon all inanimate objects could talk. What inanimate object do you think it would be most interesting to talk to? Why? List five questions you would ask it.

11. Give five reasons you think our grading system is a good one, or give five reasons why you think it should be changed.

12. A new soda pop has been invented! It is blue, tastes like broccoli, has no fizz, and people always get the hiccups after drinking it. Suppose you have been hired to advertise this product in such a way as to get people to try it. What would you say?

13. Think of your favorite song. Suggest five other titles that you think might have been chosen.

14. List every possible use that might be made of an old rubber boot.

15. Suppose you have invented a new cereal. Write a commercial advertising your new product.

16. What new improvements could be made on the modern bathtub?

17. Devise three ways to adapt an old television cabinet to other uses.

18. Think of at least three things in your home or school that operate basically on the principle of the simple pulley.
19. Think up 10 uses never heard of before for glue.
20. How would you plan the building of a new home that would be burglarproof?
21. You have just received 50 acres of land. How would you cultivate the land to make the greatest profit?
22. List some ways that you could teach younger children to respect fire.
23. What are some ideas for getting more miles per gallon of gasoline?
24. Name some ways of dealing with the predicted shortage of food in the future.
25. List every possible use that might be made of a round oatmeal container.
26. Devise three ways to adapt an old (half flat) beanbag chair.
27. List all the words, phrases, and figures of speech (including slang) that you can think of for the word *clue.*
28. Name three ways in which a barbeque grill could be improved.
29. You have invented a new type of weather-detecting device (barometer, thermometer, hygrometer). List five ways in which you might test it before offering it to the public.

# CHAPTER SEVEN

# *Study Skills*

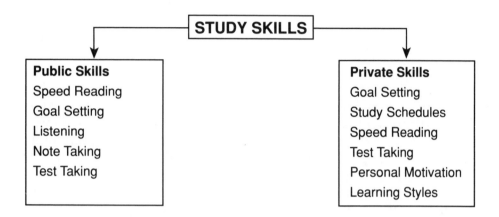

Studying can be an enjoyable, growth-promoting process if students have the time and the skills needed to make it so. When studying, an individual can meet the greatest minds and explore subjects that will lead him or her in new directions. Unfortunately, few students are taught study skills nor introduced to studying as a necessary part of classroom instruction. Since reading has been defined as an interactive process among the student, teacher, and text, it makes sense that teachers would want to have students extend their learning beyond the classroom. Students would not only interact with one text but with multiple texts.

This chapter will address both the personal and public (or general) study skills needed to survive well in school and to develop a lifelong interest in learning outside of the classroom called studying. Public (or general) study skills should be familiar to almost everyone, whereas personal study skills are individual learning needs not shared by everyone. Specific lesson plans for teaching study skills teaching strategies are in the Teaching Activities section at the end of the chapter.

Public study skills should be introduced in elementary school, and private study skills should be developed as the students become more secure with the general skills. The main assumption in this chapter is that study skills enable students to become independent learners.

Such independence was demonstrated in a freshman sociology class at Harvard University. The teacher was a famous sociologist who delivered an excellent lecture. In answer to the question as to why she took no notes, a freshman replied, "I know he is famous and all that, but I want someone who makes me think. I don't want to learn someone else's ideas as the end result of what I learn." The student to the right spent the better part of the lecture writing a short story in Spanish. The drowsy student to the left asked what the lecturer called a "penetrating question." All were, in their own ways, independent learners who were not dependent on the words of the instructor, no matter how world reknown he was.

If the student is independent of the teacher, he or she does not want to become dependent on a textbook. Study skills also relate to how one reads a text and integrates knowledge (Hamachek, 1990). Few textbooks begin or end with interesting passages. And since required reading is often boring or difficult, it takes students longer to study than it should. The choice is not pleasant—limiting personal time in order to read and hopefully be successful in class, or feeling insecure in class because assignments were not completed. A solution is to read faster, remember what is read, and survive better in school as study skills improve. Study skills publication series support their teaching in many classes by recommending their books for at-risk programs, social studies classes, athletic clubs, mandatory study halls, life skills classes, bands and drill teams, seventh through twelfth grades, and college preparation courses (Skipper, 1986). The point is that study skills may become a separate class in each of the instances cited above and they also should be an important component of content classes.

The purpose of study skills instruction is to teach students to become independent of the teacher and the textbook. In many cases, students are too dependent on teachers, and in return, blame teachers for their failures. To these students, an unfair test question would come from an outside reading assignment that the teacher did not remind them to read. The major way for independence to occur is for students to set their own goals and demand high-quality work from themselves rather than doing the minimum for assignments. To quote William Glasser:

> It is apparent, however, that students have a good idea of what parts of their schooling are of high quality. I have talked at length to groups of high school students about this subject. Most of them see quality in athletics, music and drama and few find quality in advanced placement courses or in shop classes. Almost none find anything of high quality in regular classes. All except a very few admit that, while they believe that they are capable of doing high-quality work in class, they have never actually done any and have no plans to do any in the future. . . . Students are not simply the workers in the school; they are also the products. Once they see that they, themselves, are gaining in quality, they will work to continue the process. (Glasser, 1990)

The first goal that students should be taught is to aim for excellence. The second goal is to establish their own criteria for excellence. And the third goal is to demand instruction beyond the literal level, which is where study skills are the most useful.

# Public Study Skills

## *Speed reading*

Just how fast should students read? Authorities state that 800 to 900 words per minute seems to be the maximum reading speed. Of course, students would not want to read that fast all of the time. The rate decision must be based on the purpose for reading. The average high school senior reads between 200 and 250 words per minute as an average rate. One of the first things teachers can do to increase students' reading efficiency is to realize that there are different reading rates for different kinds of materials. James Joyce once spent three days writing one sentence. Materials such as his, containing a great many ideas, would be read at a different rate than an advertisement or newspaper article.

Speedreading is the rate (usually measured in words per minute) at which a student can read printed material with adequate comprehension measured by accurately answering 75 percent or more of the comprehension questions, technical reading, or a combination. Speed reading is perhaps more properly called *rate of comprehension*.

Students should have at least three different reading speeds. The most rapid is *skimming*, which is used when students skip over unrelated or unusable material. Most people use skimming to locate or preview materials, to find the summary of a chapter, or to search for the answers to literal questions. Skimming requires alertness and intelligence. It also requires a certain self-confidence in that one must believe that the parts skipped are not important to comprehension. That attitude is justified the day the reader returns to some material skimmed and, after reading through it slowly, finds almost no added comprehension in the content.

Skimming a textbook chapter means examining the following:

Title

Introduction (if any)

Boldface headings and subheadings

Typographical aids

   italics

   heavy type

   underlined words

   colored ink

   definitions

   enumerations

   signal words

   key words

Graphics

  graphs

  charts

  pictures

  illustrations

Last paragraph

Summary

End-of-chapter material

The second rate of speed reading is called *rapid comprehending.* This is when the reader reads every word and tries to get the general idea of a chapter. Rapid comprehending is reading for the purpose of gaining meaning rather than skimming and reading for the location of specific information. Teachers can increase rate in this area by improving students' ability to understand units of thought. Provide interesting but relatively easy materials and simply encourage students to read as quickly as possible. Timed exercises are useful to increase rate. Rapid comprehension is also useful after concepts have been learned in some subject, such as science, or when studying for a test.

The third rate, *technical reading,* is the speed used for material that requires slow, careful reading and even rereading. Technical reading requires effort and a positive attitude toward the material. The reader must understand the material before it can be remembered. Technical reading occurs when students follow directions, use interpretive and critical thinking, conduct an experiment, remember details, discover related ideas, or draw conclusions. It is important to take notes during technical reading. Students should make an outline or write a brief summary of the important concepts. Technical reading is required in different subject areas. The student does not read science material the same way he or she reads a poem. (The reading skills needed for technical reading in each subject field are discussed in the Teaching Activities section of Chapter One.)

### Reading for a purpose: Goal setting

No matter what kind of material students read, they have to start by knowing their purpose for reading. This purpose can be set by the teacher saying, "You are reading this chapter to learn five characteristics of Teddy Roosevelt as President." Or the purpose can be set by the student saying, "I am going to see if Teddy Roosevelt and I have similar aptitudes." Once the purpose is set, then students can decide what type of reading would be best and when to vary the speed.

Improving reading speed skills means increasing the number of words taken in during each eye fixation, previewing material to establish purpose, and overcoming obstacles such as regression, subvocalization, and building background and vocabulary. Each of these speed-reading skills frees the reader to become more flexible in reading rate. For example, *previewing* simply means finding out what the book is about. In any book studied, the readers must find out if the book will give them what they want and what parts of it are needed. They must learn to look at the dust jacket, the foreword, the chapter title, and the paragraph heads. From chapter titles and paragraph heads, they find the part they want within the topic sentences or by going to the index.

While previewing, the readers must keep in mind their purposes and the type of books they are reading. Sample purposes might be the following:

1. Novel or short story
   a. Read for enjoyment.
   b. Read to interpret.
      i. What are the most significant events?
      ii. How do the characters react to each other? Do they change or develop?
      iii. Does the story carry a message or some deeper level of meaning?
2. Information books
   a. Read for relevance—does what the students are reading relate to what they're studying?
   b. Skim to get the general idea. Read more slowly to get details.
   c. Set a deadline, which will ensure studying with more concentration.
   d. Students should decide if they are going to take notes or underline.
   e. Read over main points.
3. Reference material
   a. Decide what kind is needed—encyclopedia, dictionary, yearbook, magazine, etc.
   b. Use the index or alphabetical guide quickly and intelligently.
   c. Don't waste time on information that isn't needed—skim first to find out where to start.
4. Research paper
   a. Identify the books needed.
   b. Search for ideas in different texts.
   c. Read to support ideas that students have.

## Obstacles to speed reading

One obstacle to speed reading, *subvocalization*, is saying the words in the mind. The reason the average reading rate is around 250 for high school seniors is that 250 words per minute is the average rate of spoken language. Evidence of this difficulty can be seen when readers move their lips while reading silently. This may simply be a bad habit or the reader may need feedback to comprehend the material. Other readers do not move their lips but they say every word in their mind. Subvocalization usually happens when a reader finds it difficult to understand the material. Beginning or poor readers need to subvocalize but better readers find it is an obstacle to increasing reading speed.

When attention is directed to this problem, subvocalizing readers find they either move their tongues slightly, say the words to themselves, or hear the words in their head. Subvocalization is a hard habit to break. The reader can check for subvocalization by placing fingertips on vocal chords to feel any possible movement. Rather than subvocalizing, the object is to concentrate on going directly from the printed word to the meaning. Some feeling of inner speech may be so closely related to understanding that it never disappears altogether, but most students do not need to subvocalize to the extent that they do.

Improving students' speed means forcing them to read faster. Even if comprehension suffers at the beginning, their pace will improve rapidly. Set a time limit for the students to cover a given amount of material. Give them something specific to look for in the chapter. Emphasize that they always read for the idea or what the author is trying to tell them. Tell them to read words in groups, never singly; that is, they should read phrases and sentences and not single groups of words. Although all the skills needed for teaching speed reading have not been presented, the central skills have been discussed. All students can benefit from speed reading instruction, even remedial readers. Furthermore, remedial readers are more likely to be motivated by both the lack of social stigma in speed reading instruction and the benefits as they study in other subjects.

As if reducing study time were not enough, the advantages of staying informed, speeding up the process of finding information for research, and controlling learning with confidence provide further motivation for learning how to speed read.

### Listening skills

The biggest obstacle to being a good listener is self-involvement. It is a rare person who can listen to a lecture for more than five minutes without having his or her mind wander. Value differences or personal preferences also keep students from receiving information even if it is understood. One of the best ways to teach listening is to begin by having the students keep a time chart for the whole day of how long they are able to listen without thinking of something else. Call it "click in and click out" assessment. This procedure will help make the students aware of how much time they spend in class daydreaming. Once they are aware that they are not the best of listeners, the following skills can be taught as guides for being a good listener.

**1.** *Relax your body to help you listen with attention.* Avoid any physical action that will take your mind off what is being said.

**2.**  *Listen intently at the beginning of a speaker's talk to make sure that you understand his or her introductory ideas.* The ideas should arouse your interest and give you a hint of what is to follow.

**3.**  *Watch the speaker's nonverbal vocabulary.* Do not let your gaze wander around to objects or persons in the room.

**4.**  *In conversation, do not pretend with facial expressions to be listening while you are actually thinking of something else.*

**5.**  *If you have the habit of losing interest in a speaker's words and letting your mind wander, admit that to yourself.* Practice bringing your attention back to the speaker.

**6.**  *As you listen, distinguish between main and minor ideas.* Practice summarizing mentally the main ideas you have heard.

**7.**  *Take notes of the main ideas to help you concentrate on what is being said.*

**8.**  *Ask questions when you do not understand.* There is little point in trying to listen if it is not clear to you what the speaker is talking about.

**9.**  *If you get bored in class, don't doodle; instead, look over previous notes.*

Listening carefully is one of the most important study skills. All students can learn this skill and all can benefit from improving the skills they already have.

## Note-taking skills

Notes provide a record of what students hear. Taking notes helps in concentration, both in reading and in listening. They also help retention by providing additional material manipulation (the actual writing of the notes). When students hear and write, they are encountering the same material twice. Note-taking skills from lectures and textbooks differ. Both formats will be discussed in this section.

No one seems to take lecture notes in the same way. Students develop their own abbreviation systems, their own awareness of what is and is not important, and their own organizational system. Some take notes occasionally and spasmodically, others write in a jumbled and disorderly manner, and still others spend hours recopying notes with the idea that writing orderly notes from messy ones helps them learn. Whatever style the student uses, the notes must be orderly and arranged in such a manner that the student can pick out the main points.

Some students prefer to outline, but this method is difficult in some lectures and discussions. Some students connect their notes in paragraph form, which is readable but can take too much time. Others record snippets, which are collections of key words and phrases. This method is fine if it is clear to the reader. And finally, some students use file cards, which gives students the opportunity to make organizational arrangements later. (File cards are excellent if students are getting material ready for an essay.)

Before class, the following points should be considered:

**1.** Is there enough space in my notebook to keep notes and handouts organized?

**2.** Take notes on only one side of the page. Later, spread the pages out to see the pattern.

**3.** Draw a vertical line about two and one-half inches from the left edge of each sheet. Record classroom notes in the space to the right of the line. Write questions, test ideas, and personal comments to the left side.

**4.** Before each lecture, take a few minutes to look over the notes on the last lecture so you can connect them with what your are to hear.

**5.** Predict the lecturer's purpose and write your own prupose for taking notes before the lecture begins.

During the lecture, students should write when the lecture or discussion seems important. Listen for phrases like "The four causes were" or "To sum up," which indicate significant ideas. If the information is not important, it should not be written down. Skip lines to show the separation of ideas. Indicate the subheads and supporting details with numbers of letters under the main ideas. Draw pictures to show relationships of ideas to each other. For example, if one could fill in the graphic organizers at the front of each chapter in this book, he or she would have notes of significant points or main headings in the chapter.

After the lecture, consolidate notes as soon as possible. This helps place information in long-term memory. Make scribbles legible and fill in blanks left during the lecture. Then underline, draw, or box in the words containing the main ideas. In the recall column at the left side of the page, jot in key words and key phrases that will stand as clues for the ideas and facts on the right. In making these jottings, the student rereads all the lecturer's notes and thinks about the ideas, which can be rethought in the student's own words. He or she should be encouraged to reflect on the notes as they are summarized in a phrase or key word. This organizes and structures notes in the student's mind.

For review, cover the right side of the sheet, exposing only the jottings in the recall column. These jottings help students recall the body of notes. Recitation also helps review. Then uncover the notes in the right column and verify what has been said. And finally, review for 10 minutes or so each day, regardless of whether or not students are reviewing for a test. This procedure, called *overlearning*, aids in placing information in long-term memory. Recall for a test is then much easier and study time for tests is greatly reduced. When the time comes for the test, reading the key words and reflecting on them helps retention. The student is providing his or her own personal meaning to the notes through this reflective process.

Taking notes from books or articles requires that the student first get the big picture. What is the author's purpose? Look at chapter headings and subheadings and decide if that is what is needed. Note key points, which are often found in summary paragraphs at the beginning and end of the chapter. And remind students to keep a sensible proportion of notes to original. For example, it is not necessary to have one page of notes for one page of text.

When taking notes from a book, it is useful, if possible, to underline key statements in the text. Bracket key phrases and put light check marks around significant points. After reading a few paragraphs, return to marking and underline the phrases and sentences that seem most important. If the student has underlined well, he or she will have a clear picture of the most important material for review.

Writing in the margins can also be helpful. Challenge the author directly in the margins of the text. Ask questions, disagree, change statements, rephrase concepts. Do anything to involve the reader actively with the author. By actively changing the author's ideas, the reader will be more alert and remember what he or she has read. If it is not possible to write in the textbook, a journal or reading log will accomplish the same purpose. After reading a section or a chapter, record thoughts so that there will be a personal and active response to the textbook. Again, draw pictures or formally synopsize whole chapters in brief paragraphs. In any event, the transfer of thoughts to paper will be of great help in reviewing and writing essays or term papers later on.

## Test-taking skills

The type of test the students will be taking determines the review and test-taking procedure. Here, procedural memory takes over and students use the processes they have used since childhood. These may not be the best strategies, however. Students in all classes can benefit from direct instruction in how to review for and take tests effectively.

If the tests are standardized, they usually have a preparation manual that accompanies them. Although test developers are trying to test beyond the literal and interpretive levels, they have not been able to do so comprehensively. The result is that standardized exams like the Stanford Achievement Test or California Test of Basic Skills test recognition and speed-reading skills. The correct answers are listed and the student must recognize them within the framework of the time given. For these tests, it is important to increase students' reading speed so that they have time to answer questions and to prepare them for the test format in which the recognition takes place.

Preparing for a teacher-made tests means both understanding the teacher and the format of the test. Multiple-choice and true/false tests measure recall but essay tests require a recitation form of studying. Comprehensive reviews involve thinking on higher cognitive levels. First, a clear-cut impression must exist. Students cannot remember concepts whose outlines are blurred. Remembering comes from repetition, so notes must be reviewed. The notes from class should be combined with notes from the text, which should reveal a relationship. The next step is to link ideas and chain them together. The student should be able to take an overall view of what has to be memorized. The Association of American Publishers (1981) describes reviewing for tests in this manner:

> Reviewing is a cumulative discipline and ought to become a habit of study. You review a phrase or sentence by underlining it. You review a page after reading it by simply recalling the major points. You reassess the meaning of a chapter by noting some of the main ideas on a piece of paper. You re-evaluate the material when in class by joining the discussion. You record varied points of view and interpretations in your notebook as you listen to the professor and other students. You make your final review before the test by re-examining your own textbook underlining, your notes in the margins, lecture materials and notebooks.

The easiest way of reviewing is to assemble your summary notes of each chapter, converting the statements into questions and checking the individual chapters to see if you are answering the questions fully and accurately. Your questions in the margins and your underlining will help you to recall details. If you have kept a reading journal, your own reflections will be a further aid in remembering particular ideas. Your class notes will reinforce your reading. Pose rigorous questions to yourself, but as you approach the examination, remember one important point—do not clutter your mind with details. If you have read the text carefully and can identify major ideas, you will easily remember supporting information and data.

Beyond these processes, students should study their weak points first and be selective. Students cannot remember everything. They should pick out the most important points and then think of the *why:* Why is something important? Why is a given relationship established? They should be critical of the material read as writers are not always right. Students should be taught to clarify to their own satisfaction points those that are not clear. They also need to work on a deadline. Teach them to set a time limit to their studying.

Thus, test taking is the measurement of studying and review skills. Provided the students are properly equipped, comfortable, and calm, the testing skills listed below should be easy to follow.

1. Read directions carefully and understand what they say.
2. Read the whole test.
3. Budget time. Leave 10 minutes for review.

4. Make an attempt to answer every question.
5. As you read, if you get ideas or if facts come to mind, jot them down for reference. This may help answer questions.
6. Do only what the questions ask.
   a. Particularly in essay questions, make sure you have interpreted the question correctly.
   b. Stick to the point. Get the important details down. If generalizations are made, they should be supported with evidence.
7. Think before you write.
8. Check answers for meaning, the connectors betwen paragraphs and sentences, grammar, spelling, and clear handwriting.
9. Guess whenever it is best.
10. Read the exam carefully. Specific words such as *always* and *never* are clues that the statement is generally false.
11. Answer the easy questions first. On objective tests, do not waste your time worrying about a difficult question. Skip it and if you have time, go back to it.

These test-taking skills can be learned by all students. Teachers should also put into place a test-taking skills development program that includes elements of learning about tests. About 60 days before test administration, the teacher should introduce the students to worksheets and provide practice in answering in the test format. Students cannot be expected to do well on a test that has a format unfamiliar to them.

Test vocabulary should also be introduced as frequently as possible. It is the teacher's responsibility to make sure the vocabulary is on the test. Mimette Bradshaw, a first-grade teacher, described the anguish of other first-grade teachers as they prepared their students for the newly adopted state exam. In April, teachers were given a list of 350 words that were supposed to be on the test. They sent the children home with 25 words a week that students had to learn. Most of the classroom time was spent drilling the vocabulary words. When the test was administered in May, only 2 of the 350 words were on the test. Although it was not possible to get an old copy of this particular exam because it was a newly constructed state test, other state-required tests do provide material on measured vocabulary skills that teachers could use in their curriculum and avoid teaching-to-the-test disasters.

And finally, students should be given practice in self-pacing, following directions, and marking answer sheets. How many students have not paced themselves and thus not finished the test? How many students have marked the answer sheet in the wrong manner and lost valuable testing time? How many students have misread the directions and discovered their error only after the test was over? Practice on the elements of test format, vocabulary, self-pacing, following directions, and answer sheet marking should be in place in every content classroom to help students demonstrate more effectively the knowledge they have acquired.

## Summary

To make progress in any subject or field, students must learn the basic content or principles to a level of mastery. They must master the basics, or they will have nothing upon which to build more sophisticated understanding. Mastery converts the ideas and principles into "magnets." These magnets draw the supporting facts and details around themselves naturally like iron filings. Unless the material is mastered, students are going through the mere motions of getting an education. They will be putting in time without having anything to show for it.

By using study skills, any student should be able to master any assignment equal to the level of even the most excellent student. It may take some twice as long as others to master the same lesson, but, after all, mastery is mastery. If students keep practicing, they can cut down on the time it takes to master assignments. In other words, if students are willing to put in sufficient time and effort, and if they are willing to follow an efficient set of study skills, they should be able to master their assignments as well as the best of students. Study skills are designed to help students do the very best with what they have.

# Private Study Skills

## Individual goal setting

Individual goal setting is probably the most important aspect of all studying. When children are in elementary school, their goals are more likely to be to please their parents and teachers and not to look ignorant in front of their friends. As they grow older, students' purposes may still include those developed in elementary school. Others may add or find new goals that relate to wanting to graduate, needing the knowledge for their career, or avoiding having privileges taken away from them (or other family-imposed sanctions). All of these purposes are examples of externally controlled motivation. The objective of developing private study skills is to provide students with internally controlled motivation. They can complete an assignment because it is required (*external motivation*) or because they want to master the concept (*internal motivation*). As very young children, students cannot initially be expected to establish their own purposes. They must be given the purposes. But as they become older, students can develop both external and internal goals. However, like many other study skills, private goal setting must be directly taught.

One of the many study strategies teachers can select for helping students learn how to establish personal goals is Indrisano's (1982) *SEARCH*. The procedure is as follows:

*Set* goals.
*Explore* sources.
*Analyze* and organize information.
*Refine* and rehearse.
*Communicate* with others.
*Help* yourself to improve.

Teaching and providing practice in a strategy such as this helps students become independent studiers. Once they have started to use this strategy in class, they will start to use it outside of class and become excited about their own control of learning and their involvement with what they are reading and writing.

Another strategy for helping students set goals and become independent readers is called *SQ3R*. This is a familiar procedure to many teachers and is becoming a popular component in junior high reading programs. Content teachers would want to make sure their students know how to use this strategy also.

*Survey:*   Preview or skim a book or chapter. Ask yourself the following questions:

1.   What do I already know about the topic?
2.   What more would I like to know?
3.   What new material have I learned about the topic?
4.   What other questions would I like to have answered about the topic?

*Question:*   After surveying a chapter, formulate questions from the chapter, boldface headings, and subheadings. Good questions give students a purpose for reading and help in finding answers quickly. To formulate questions, use this guide:

If you want to know a reason, then ask *why.*
If you want to know a way or a method, then ask *how.*
If you want to know a purpose or definition, then ask *what.*
If you want to know a fact, then ask *what.*

These questions require students to think and to consolidate information and ideas. Students then read to answer questions, revise their questions as needed, and formulate new questions. They should be told not to forget to form questions about illustrations and graphs and to combine headings and subheadings. Also, the questions may come from the back of the book or chapter if these are assigned. Review questions might also serve as good purpose setters.

*Read:*   Read to answer questions one section at a time. Once the answer is found, then start to read for another question.

*Recite:*   Once the chapter has been read, close the book and recite the answers to the questions.

*Reread:*  Reread to find the answers to the questions that the student couldn't answer in the recitation.

These purpose-setting procedures for reading and studying can be introduced in the classroom. The more they are used in the classroom, the more likely they will be used by the student outside of the classroom.

## Study schedules

The second personal study skill is scheduling the studying. The usual advice about studying indicates that one should find a quiet place to study with all equipment needed close at hand. Reading lights should be over the left shoulder (if the student is right handed). Reading material should be held at least 14 inches away and held at a 45° angle. However, those who have lived in a dormitory, lived with teenagers, or lived in crowded housing know that most study rules should be flexible. For example, a college freshman once came to the author disturbed because each time he got out his textbook and went to the kitchen table to study, he fell asleep. The textbook and kitchen table were his cues for falling asleep. Developing a study schedule for him and other students is a personal activity that takes into consideration physical requirements, learning style and capabilities, and living conditions.

The only factor that is constant in all students' schedules is that each person has 24 hours in a day. They should be able to make a schedule of when and how much they need to study for each subject. For college classes, three hours of outside study for every hour of class is a good rule of thumb. For high school students, extracurricular activities, sports events, work, and social life often take priority over study time. Study halls are not standard in some school schedules. High school students must set their own study schedules and make them a priority. One way of doing this is to assign study partners who sign each other's study sheet. The study sheet is handed in like a homework assignment and receives a grade. Goals, accomplishments, and questions can be listed on the sheet. This teaching strategy involves external and internal motivations and peer pressure, which can be viewed as either form of motivation.

Students should also be encouraged to record distractions to find out what causes them to stop concentrating on studying. The distractions list will tell them what to control in order to increase study time. And finally, having high school students write or discuss the advantages and disadvantages of procrastination increases awareness of scheduling study behavior.

The study schedule or homework supervisor for junior high and elementary students used to be the mother. However, today many mothers are working outside the home and older siblings or after-school programs have replaced her supervision. In that case, after-school programs should routinely include a study time with an adult who helps students study. Junior high students who go to other homes or become "latch-key" children should be encouraged at school to study as soon as they get home from school. Training in school emphasizing the importance of study schedules and providing schedules to be filled out as homework should make studying outside the classroom improve. Even elementary students should be encouraged to set their own goals of quality, which may mean going beyond just what the teacher assigns. Teachers might consider that some families view reading and doing homework as unnecessary and as a form of escape from work. If the school can promote such independence and "escape," then the students will find studying an opportunity for enjoyable solitude.

## Speed reading

The causes of reading slowly are different from individual to individual: some subvocalize, some never try to read anything, some analyze every word, some have a limited vocabulary, some have poor study habits, and some have limited background experience. It is experience with material or background that enables a student to read faster. An interesting point is that the faster the students read, the more they concentrate. Teachers have opportunities through prereading activities to expand students' background. However, the primary responsibility for being aware of gaps in background belongs with the student.

Limited backgrounds make students bored or confused. An effort to expand one's background should involve the following:

**1.** Start a vocabulary development program for yourself. Use a thesaurus, word history book, and lexicon.

**2.** Read magazine articles, newspaper articles, encyclopedias, and books on the subjects you need to know. Not all knowledge on a subject is contained in one book. Find an abundance of easy reading material that is of high interest.

**3.** Keep a record of daily progress.

**4.** Interview friends, relatives, and neighbors who know about subjects in which your background is lacking.

**5.** Watch educational TV programs, computer programs, and videotapes on selected subjects.

Reading speed may increase with the expansion of background knowledge. However, concentration or paying attention to what is being read may sabotage students. A poorly defined purpose for reading will reduce concentration. And if the text has too many unknown words or difficult concepts for particular students, they may start to think of other things.

Another factor that is hard to control is the interest of the textbook. Few students would read a textbook for enjoyment if given the choice. All would agree that it is difficult to concentrate when the material is uninteresting. Concentration in this case must be developed by the student taking an active position and challenging or mentally rewriting the text. The final textbook obstacle to concentration is the language structure or writing style, which may be different from the ones to which students are accustomed. Corrections of these problems are not possible in many cases. The teacher cannot rewrite the textbook language or make it more interesting. Concepts may be clarified but it is difficult to teach everything that all students must learn in order to read faster. The best approach is to address individual student concentration needs. These steps will help improve concentration when reading and studying.

1. If the mind wanders, find out why.
   a. If it's a deed to be done, do it.
   b. If it can't be done, make a note of it and then forget it.
   c. If it's a plan, finish it or make a note to do it later.
   d. Come to a decision about what is bothering you, and then plan to carry out your decision.
2. Set a definite goal.
   a. If the task is too big, break it into a number of small tasks and do one at a time, crossing them off a list. A feeling of satisfaction will follow.
   b. Decide the order in which you will do the tasks and then do them. Ten minutes of planning are worthwhile.
3. Compete with yourself. Set a time for the task you wish to do. Then finish it in less time. Increase the work you have to do each day in this time and try to finish it ahead of time.
4. Pace yourself. Set your alarm clock or have someone call you at the end of a certain amount of time and see how many pages you can read in that time. The next night, see if you can read more pages in the same length of time.
5. Time yourself. Read a certain number of pages; look at the time it took you to read. Tomorrow try to read the same number of pages in less time.
6. Keep asking yourself, "What is the author saying to me?"
7. If you have trouble concentrating, use a magic charm, like a scarf or a paperweight to help you concentrate, or stand up and stretch, or go for a quick walk and clear your mind. Then come back and continue reading.
8. If you cannot concentrate on your reading, slowly count to 10 and read again.

Lack of background and problems with concentration reduce students' reading speed and comprehension. An additional personal characteristic that increases reading speed is self-confidence. If a student is not familiar with the material or if the material does not seem worthy of attention (concentration), students may react by either speeding over the material or reading it slowly so that they will master every word. It takes a self-confident individual to dismiss material as irrelevant. It also takes a risk taker. Students who do not feel confident will read slowly to make sure they understand everything.

## Test-taking skills

Students should first prepare for teacher-made tests by asking the following questions:

1. How many questions will be on the test?
2. What format will the questions follow?
3. How much will the test contribute to the final grade?
4. How much time will be allotted for taking the test?
5. Is the test going to cover all the material from the beginning of the course or will it cover only material from the last exam?
6. Is there a penalty for guessing?
7. What materials do I need or am I allowed while taking the test?
8. If the test is an essay test, find out what criteria the teacher is using to grade the test. For example, a math analysis test may give partial credit for the right process even if the answer is wrong.

As they take tests, they should follow these tips:

1. Arrive early.
2. Choose a seat carefully.
3. Stay with your daily routine—skip breakfast if that is your normal routine.
4. Be prepared and tell yourself that you are prepared.
5. Talk to yourself in a positive manner.

Table 7–1 lists words found in essay questions that should help students read the exams more effectively.

The object of teacher-made tests is to demonstrate to the teacher what the student has learned. Assuming that a teacher knows what the testtaker means is a frequent problem. General statements have little meaning unless they are supported by specific examples. Test taking demands that students use all of their personal knowledge of the teacher in order to predict the type of tests he or she will design. It also demands that the student be able to control his or her anxiety and use of time. Self-discipline is one of the most important personal characteristics of good test takers.

## Personal motivational strategies

Marilyn von Savant, listed in *Guiness Book of Records* as one of the most intelligent human beings, started exercising her mind when she

**Table 7-1**  *Key Words in Essays*

| Type—asked to: | Definition—then: | Key Words |
|---|---|---|
| Compare | Show how two things are alike. | similarly; likewise; in like manner; equally important |
| Contrast | Show how two things are different. | but; yet; however; on the other hand; nevertheless; on the contrary |
| Discuss Describe | Give as much information as possible. | that is; as has been noted |
| List Name Enumerate Outline | Identify major points. | first, second, . . . ; finally; next; too; in addition; last; furthermore; and; and then |
| Explain Defend Document | Give reasons. | because; as a result; therefore; then; hence; thus; for that reason; for these reasons |
| Relate Associate | Show how two things are connected. | (Use words from Compare-Contrast) |
| Summarize Compile Paraphrase | Briefly tell the main points (omit details). | in short; in summary; in conclusion; in other words; on the whole; to sum up |
| Sequence Arrange Trace Rank | List information in order or progress of a subject or event. | (enumerations) |
| Demonstrate Illustrate Show | Provide examples for . . . . | |
| Apply | Show use for . . . . | |
| Construct Develop Devise | Create . . . . | |
| Evaluate Criticize Analyze | Give your viewpoint—give reasons or defend. | |

was very young. Her belief that intelligence and thus thinking can be learned resulted in her book on the subject. Studying should be considered the training of the mind, but students do not know how to train their minds to think about imformation unless they are given methods of doing so. Expanding their competence in thinking is an excellent personal motivation. Expanding thinking skills is one of the private study skills that should be taught.

Early in the twentieth century, John Dewey identified five phases of reflective thinking process.

1.  Suggestions—the mind leaps to possible solutions
2.  Intellectualization of difficulty that has been felt into a problem to be solved
3.  Hypothesis to initiate and guide observation in the collection of factual material
4.  Mental elaboration of idea or supposition
5.  Testing hypothesis by overt or imaginative action

More recently, college students have been found to be one of the following types of studiers:

**1.** *Good Strategy Users:* Students who have good self-awareness and good product outcomes and who use a variety of study strategies including paraphrasing, mental integration, and self-questioning

**2.** *Information Organizers:* Students who are text markers and note takers and whose primary mental learning tactics are mental integration, rote learning, and relating information to background knowledge

**3.** *Flexible Readers:* Students who place heavy emphasis on reading tactics using relatively few text-noting and mental-learning tactics

**4.** *Text Noters:* Students who almost exclusively rely on text-noting tactics and who seldom use mental-learning tactics or reading tactics

**5.** *Mental Integrators:* Students who interact with the text actively and who try to link sections of the text together into a whole by using self-questioning and self-checking processes

**6.** *Memorizers:* (the largest cluster) Students who focus their study of factual material on the text's major propositions (Wade, Trathen, & Schraw, 1990)

An interesting finding of the Wade, Trathen, and Schraw (1990) study, which identified diverse clusters of students and their study behavior, was that there seemed to be no significant difference between the six types of studiers in the amount of information recalled immediately from the reading of the text. An important question for teachers and students to ask would be: Which group had the best delayed recall and retention? Being able to remember later what has been learned is the personal goal of many who study.

Gestalt psychologists believe that remembering is a result of a searching/thinking process. The searching and thinking results in restructuring the field of knowledge. This restructuring often comes with insight, which Hilgard and Bower (1975) claimed had the following characteristics:

1. Occurs in a problem that has the capacity for solution.
2. Involves the use of relevant past experience of the thinker.
3. Includes the arrangement of the situation for clear observation.
4. Gives results after much fumbling and searching.

Dewey, Hilgard, and the gestalt psychologists all describe the thinking process as beginning with emotional disequilibrium. Dewey's (1933) term of *felt difficulty* identifies where studying should also begin. Emotional responses of confusion, curiosity, anger, and determination start the thinking process. From there, the thinking conditions described above begin to take place. They do not occur in sequence for all students but are part of a complex, personal process. Developing personal thinking while studying can be very enjoyable and motivating.

To simplify the motivational process, there are those who believe that motivation is externally conditioned (Skinner), those who believe that motivation is internally conditioned (Maslow), and those who believe that motivation is the result of an interaction between the individual and the environment (gestalt psychologists). Researchers such as Maslow, White, McClelland, and Atkinson believe that there is an internal motivation toward growth, competence, and achievement. Private or personal motivation concerns itself with this area of motivation.

The classroom methodology, then, means the teacher tries to identify or create sutdent deficiencies and then reestablish equilibrium through learning. A simple example would be if the teacher asks the students to describe three important characteristics of the praying mantis. When students are unable to do so, they are encouraged to read about the insect in the text, which is the means of reestablishing equilibrium. Such teachers encourage students to set personal goals and maintain realistic levels of aspiration. Strategies for encouraging this form of motivation include individual contracts, self-paced programs, and progress reports.

Studying can be motivating in itself if students view it as a time when they explore and develop their own minds rather than a time devoted to completing senseless work that they have been coerced into doing by parents and teachers. It should be a time of reflective development where students analyze the reading task, reflect on what they know and what they need to know, and deveise strategies for learning. The factors that influence students' personal motivation are the nature of the material, the level of reading and study skills they possess, and the characteristics of the learner.

*Learning styles*

What are people talking about when they refer to *learning styles*? In the past, educators were recognizing that individuals prefer different delivery methods: *auditory* (they like to hear the information), *kinesthetic* (they find physical movement and touching makes information clearer), and *visual* (they can learn easier if they see information). Teachers were urged to present lessons that appealed to all of the senses in order to capture all of the learning styles of their students. Grace Frenald's kinesthetic remedial reading process followed this line of thinking. For example, her students read the word and simultaneously said and wrote the word. This procedure had students using visual, kinesthetic, and auditory channels for learning. Today, learning styles consider the work of neurologists, psychologists, and educators. Mutual interest in learning abilities has been a factor in each discipline, but more recently, work in the three different fields has begun to be specifically helpful for teachers.

In the late 1960s and 1970s, brain researchers discovered that the two hemispheres had different functions in behavior and most specifically in language reception and production. The right hemisphere was found to understand and relate intonation and to determine context, humor, and metaphor. The left hemisphere is the center of the understanding and use of phonology, syntax, and semantics of spoken and written language. Thus, the left hemisphere is sequential and extracts information from the environment in a time-ordered sequence. The right hemisphere is simultaneous or spatial and processes the gestalt or whole experience.

The processing difference between the two hemispheres was best described by Roger Sperry's (1968) experiments with split-brain patients whose two halves of the brain were separated and did not communicate (hemidicorticuts). To normal readers, it would be like looking at a group graduation picture and searching for a specific person. The right simultaneous processor would look at the entire picture and then begin to find configurations. The left sequential processor would go row by row and person by person, looking for the specific individual. Tests, clinical exercises, and books were written about left-brain and right-brain children, teachers, and even corporate managers. What is apparent is that both processes are integrated in most persons. There may be a preference for approaching learning from the overall gestalt, or meaning emphasis rather than from a sequential skill sequence.

Individual preferences for learning in this manner have resulted in students being labeled *right* or *left brain, simultaneous* or *sequential, field dependent* or *field independent,* and *global* or *analytic learners* (Sperry, 1968; Corballis & Morgan, 1976; Carbo, 1990; Dunn, 1990).

Learning style can also be considered a cognitive or thinking style. Roswell and Natchez (1989) differentiate learning styles as individual preferential use of particular problem-solving strategies. For adults and older children, the use of a learning or cognitive style, then, reflects an initial approach to solving a problem, which is complemented by the simultaneous contribution of the alternative approach. According to Roswell and Natchez (1989), the learning preferences of young children are not as clearly developed as they are with adults and older children. Thus, children, with the help of hours of television viewing, enter school more global than analytical.

The workings of the brain that produce thinking and learning preferences are far from random. In fact, many behavioral scientists and neuroscientists now believe that much of the brain's activity is preprogrammed and that some unknown portion of it is genetically determined. Although environmental surroundings, upbringing, and interpersonal relationships are still believed to influence emotions and learning to an extent, some researchers are placing growing emphasis and responsibility for behavior on the neurochemical and structural components of the brain.

Larry Stein of Wyeth Laboratories in Radnor, Pennsylvania, states, "All decisions of the learning in the end basically have to do with the 'decision' of whether a neuron will fire or not." The firing of a neuron is a result of the orchestrated flow of intertwining chemical rivers that branch through various areas of the brain. Learning is not a matter of just one neuron firing. The chemical aspect of learning now lies with the research of neurotransmitters and the mapping of their functions. Specific diseases such as Parkinsons Cholera is known to involve the deficiency fo the neurotransmitter dopamine. The chemical processes that contribute to memory and learning in the brains of children can be expected to be affected by heredity, pre- and postnatal care, nutrition, and the use of mind-altering substances on the part of the mother or child.

Thus, learning style becomes a much more individualistic preference and more specifically defined than presenting material visually, auditorily, and kinesthetically. Learning style relates to information reception and processing influenced by the chemical and structural functioning of each student's brain. It can be identified through study strategy clusters preferred by a student or through self-description. At this time, it is not a process that a teacher can easily determine for classes of 30 or more students who rotate on an hourly basis. Because of these institutional constraints, the student, not the teacher, must take responsibility for identifying his or her learning style characteristics as they influence studying and learning.

## Summary

To become independent learners, students must have strong desire and encouragement to establish and follow their own goals, set their own motivations, and develop their own learning style assessment. When studying is not done voluntarily for personal gain and development, studying becomes coercion rather than pleasure. There is a great difference between reading and studying, and the emphasis should be on studying. Reading skills can be defined as an ability that is essential to successful performance in reading: vocabulary knowledge, comprehension skills, and organization of learning into memory. Study skills, however, involve understanding, mastering the lesson, note taking, skimming and scanning, and technical and rapid comprehension reading. If students are having trouble in school with academic work, the chances are exceedingly high that this trouble stems from not knowing how to study. Consequently, if steps are taken merely "to read better," then the real problem of not knowing how to study is being overlooked. Reading is one step in effective studying.

To improve study habits, students need first to analyze the qualities of their own minds and personal situations. Are they letting personal problems and plans interfere with their studying? Have they set goals? In their efforts to memorize material, do they not understand it? After students analyze their personal needs, the process of developing study skills begins. Instructional strategies for teaching study skills in content areas are provided in the Teaching Activities section.

# Application Exercises and Teaching Activities

## Application Exercises

**1.** Describe the personal and general study skills needed in these two schools:

I interviewed Mrs. Adams of Elder Middle School in Fort Worth. She had just recently moved to this region from the small border town of Eagle Pass, Texas.

How does reading education differ in Fort Worth in goals and aims as opposed to Eagle Pass?

I think the basic objectives are the same; however, I think we concentrated more on teaching fundamentals of reading, such as word pronunciation and vocabulary expansion, than they do here. In Fort Worth we tried to concentrate on comprehension and speed in reading. There is a far greater emphasis on phonics in Eagle Pass than there is in Fort Worth due to the bilingual differences that Eagle Pass encounters. Also in Fort Worth they tend to give many more standardized tests, such as the Nelson Denny Reading Test.

What is your biggest problem in teaching reading in Fort Worth as opposed to Eagle Pass?

First of all, it's so much different up here. For example, the children have many more activities than the children do back home. For instance, after school, children here have a million and one places to go and many things to do to divert their attention. They have all kinds of sports and recreational facilities to go to and most all of the kids up here watch so much more TV than the kids back home. In Eagle Pass there seems to be a greater pride in the accomplishments of small children in school. Up here it is assumed by parents that a child will learn normally, advance into high school, and then into college. This is not to say that there is a noncaring behavior of the Fort Worth parents for the education of their children. The caring is very much there and the desire to "keep up" with their children's school achievement is also very much there. In Eagle Pass, reading seemed to be a little more fun for the kids, although it was a little bit more work. They could sit down and read a story or read a book and become exposed to a world of imagery—but this is exactly what the kids up here obtain through TV.

What are some of the specific reading problems you encounter here?

Reading problems here are really quite individual; however, they are also quite universal. We have children who are quite slow in their reading ability, have poor comprehension, and exhibit word reversals, and we have children who have as much trouble properly pronouncing words as spelling words. Many of the kids find reading boring and their attention span is very limited. Therefore, the teacher finds herself often trying to create motivation tactics in reading. For each of these reading difficulties, we can help the child if he or she is willing to cooperate with us. I find that, for the most part, an overall poor reading ability can be helped simply by practice. With a lot of my kids, I recommend to their parents that they sit them at home for 45 minutes with the TV off and have them read any material that is of interest to that child. I think this is the most effective remedy or aid for the child.

# Teaching Activities:
# Listening Guide for Social Studies

*Sixth-Grade Text:*
*Soifer, Israel, and Leferts, Walter (1982).*
*Nations of the World. New York: Macmillan.*

*Study Skills Lesson: Outline for Lecture*

## Great Britain

I. Assessment of prior knowledge of students on subject.
   A. Student's impressions of England.
   B. Location relationship to Central Europe. (Map)
   C. Use map to locate British Isles. (Wales and Scotland)
   D. Climate, harbors (picture), homes (picture)
II. Early history of Great Britain.
   A. Roman and Norman Conquests.
   B. Roman Baths and Hadrian's Great Wall (pictures).
III. Developments of English Government.
   A. Discussion of similarities between U.S. and British government.
      1. Two party system
      2. Trial by jury
      3. Elected representatives
   B. From council to parliament form.
   C. Prime Minister (name).
   D. English Jury System.
   E. The Great Charter (Magna Carta)
      1. Why cornerstone of English liberty?
      2. What is U.S. cornerstone of liberty?
IV. Great Britain as World Power.
   A. English colonies (where) (map).
   B. English Industrial Revolution (what did it begin?).
V. Students to summarize this lecture with a *question annotation form of summarization.*

*Study Skills:* Assessment—Map use—Picture use—
Teacher modeling with questions—Summarizing

*Listening Guide for Lecture of Great Britain*

I. Significance of Britain's location to:
   A. Central Europe
II. Climate and its effects:
   Crops—industry—harbors
III. Two conquerors of British Isles.
   What was left behind them?
IV. Magna Carta?
   The rights of . . .
V. Form of Government:
   English government and U.S. government.

**201**

Vocabulary: Jury
Parliment
Baron
Prime Minister
VI. Colonies.
Where and how many?
VII. English Industrial Revolution.
Spinning jenny
Factory system
James Watt

*Directions for Studying Effectively the Lecture on Great Britain*

We will discuss this procedure before the lecture, in order for students to raise questions and think through the process before they are to use it.

1. How to organize information from lecture and prepare for test.
   a. Use the *note-taking system for learning (NSL)*. Use a sheet of paper with a margin line 3″ from left margin. Take lecture notes in right margin. Use labels in left margin to organize lecture notes. (Fill in labels soon after lecture notes in order to reinforce short-term memory.)
   b. Make your reading notes on another sheet of paper and you can then insert these notes to your lecture notes in the left margins along with your labels that you inserted after the lecture.
   c. You now have complete notes from lectures and for future tests.
2. Following are some guidelines to help increase your reading speed.
   a. Preview your textbook material on pages 334–347. Determine your *purpose for reading,* which, in this instance, should be for information. This will help you formulate questions about the material as you read.
   b. Improve your rate of reading by looking at more than one word at a time.
   c. You can focus your eyes on the empty space immediately above your line of reading. This will help you to phrase read, which in turn should improve your rate of reading. Experiment with covering the bottom half of a line. You will find that you can still read the line! The upper part of the written line is composed of the distinguishing characteristics!
   d. Speed up your reading rate when reading material you already know and decrease it when you come to more difficult areas.
3. When summarizing a lecture and listing your various topics, they should be a continuous train of thought in your own words.

# Practicing Guide for Music Class
## Skills Taught: Work-Study and Organizational

*Direction Sheet*

1. *Posture:*  Play your instrument in front of a mirror to determine whether you are holding it as shown in class.
2. Just look at (or visualize) your instrument to determine what are the specific skill requirements of playing an instrument. (Think separately of the left hand and right hand.)
3. *Intonation:*  Have someone play a C major scale on the piano. Try to duplicate *exactly* each note of the scale on your string instrument.
4. *Bowing:*  Experiment with varying degrees of speed, location, and pressure to play both loud (ff) and soft (pp) with your bow.
5. Device for memorizing the note names corresponding to the lines and spaces on the staff: Spaces = FACE; Lines = *Every Good Boy Does Fine*
6. Device for memorizing the sharps and flats in a key signature: Sharps = *Faces Can Get Dirty After Eating Bologna;* Flats = *Betty Eating Apples During Gym Class Failed*
7. Use the following checklist derived from exercise #2 to divide your practice time.

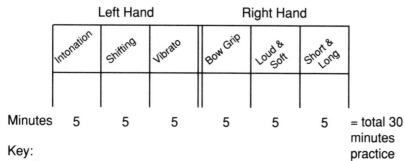

| | Left Hand | | | Right Hand | | |
|---|---|---|---|---|---|---|
| | Intonation | Shifting | Vibrato | Bow Grip | Loud & Soft | Short & Long |
| | | | | | | |

Minutes    5      5      5      5      5      5    = total 30 minutes practice

Key:
1 = Can do well
2 = Needs improvement
3 = Very weak

## Semantic Mapping for Art

Art is an easy subject to study because all the concepts can be related visually as well as verbally, thus committing these concepts to your memory by the process of application.

1.  It is important to have organized notes when studying for a test. Since art is a visual subject, your notes will contain many sketches, outline maps, and some charts. Outlining the units in your notes will help condense and organize your notebook. Look at the table of contents in the text, *Exploring Visual Design*. Map the first unit, "Elements of Design."

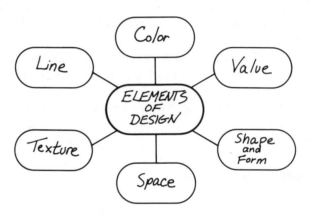

You could also outline the chapters in the same manner. For example:

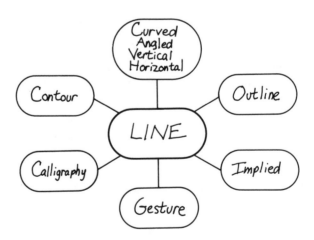

2.  When taking notes from your reading or from lectures, slides, or videos, simply divide the page in half. You will use one side to list your concepts and facts, and the other side to make sketches to help convey the message. For example:

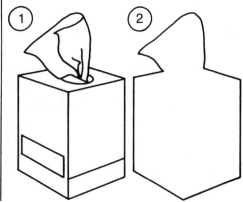

**1** Contour--single line drawing that defines outer and inner edges of an object

**2** Outline--line that describes outside edge of an object

**3.** The text contains many photographs to refer to when you do not understand the concepts in the lectures or the text. There is also a glossary in the back of the text to help you define the concepts.

**4.** You must be able to show a relationship between the written concepts and the visual concepts. An example would be the color wheel. The theory of color is complex, but the color wheel organizes the information concisely. It is helpful in learning to read the wheel that you learn to draw the wheel. First, you start with a triangle. Then you add the primary colors at each angle, like this:

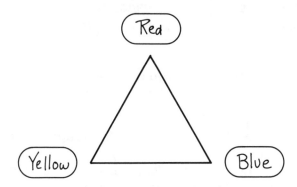

Then you add the secondary colors, like this (Remember that the secondary colors are made by adding the primary colors together):

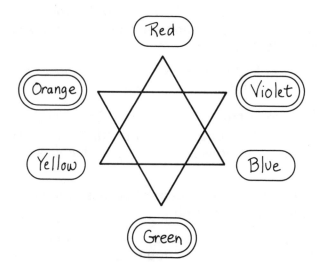

# You Can Study Better and Faster with "PQRST"

*Step Up Your Studying the Air Force Way*

PQRST is the Air Force name for a "package of effective study skills." This systematic study method, often known as SQ3R, is based on studies by Frances P. Robinson at Ohio State University.

PQRST proved itself in the crisis of World War II when young men were rushed through training courses. Fast, efficient methods, called "higher-level study skills," were scientifically designed to help them.

There are several approaches to study-type reading, and the student-reader should "size up the reading task," then vary his or her approach accordingly. *PQRST is just one of these approaches.*

*PQRST has proved useful to many students when the reading task is thorough reading and retention of information* in chapters of a science or social studies textbook. It is often useful with an expository chapter in English or any other subject.

## 1. Preview

Spend a few minutes in an advance survey of the chapter. Previewing is like getting an aerial view of the terrain.

*Read the introduction.*
Here, the author briefs you on what to look for in the chapter. *The author tells you what he or she is going to tell you.*

*Hit the headlines.*
Examine the boldface section and paragraph headings, some of the topic sentences, and any sentences containing terms printed in **boldface** or *italic* type. If you find no boldface headings, examine the topic sentences at the first or last of paragraphs.

*Read the concluding paragraphs and/or the summary.*
Here, the author carefully *wraps up the principal points* he or she has made. By reading the summary first, you learn major points to look for in your reading.

*Note:* If you find no introduction, headings, or summary, scan the material itself for general content.

*The "Preview" Step Should Pay You Well:*

This step should *subtract from your study time.* By investing five or ten minutes in previewing, many students save at least twice that time.

*You should concentrate better* because you will know what to look for as you are reading.

Because you know the author's organization in advance, *main points should stand out* as you read.

*Details should fall into place* and be more easily remembered.

## 2. Question

*Go in with a question—come out with an answer!* Be a human question mark!

As you approach each section, *turn the boldface heading into a question.*

In the heavy black headings the author is shouting to you, "I am giving you these headings as clues to major points. Change them into questions, and you'll be routed to main ideas."

AND/OR

*Turn topic sentences into questions.*

If boldface headings are missing, look for topic sentences and turn them into questions, or use the questions at the end of the chapter.

*Note:* If both boldface headings and topic sentences are missing, formulate questions yourself from scanning the material.

*The "Question" Step Should Pay You Well:*

Instead of being purposeless, your reading will now become an *active search for answers.*

You should *comprehend difficult reading material* more easily.

If a "miracle cure" *for trouble with concentration exists,* it is approaching reading with questions.

Questions should help *awaken interest* if the assignment seems boring.

You should be *guided to main points.*

*Test questions should seem* more and more *familiar* as you perfect the question technique.

*Note:* Steps Q, R, and S are completed in order—one right after the other—as you work carefully through the chapter one headed section at a time.

## 3. Read

Now read the section thoroughly and find the answer to your question. After you do this intensive reading, make mental or written notes of important points. Quick, labor-saving notes are your long-term insurance against forgetting. Only you can decide the method of marking main points or taking notes that is best for you.

1. Use the quick *draw-a-line system.*

Draw a single line down the margin next to a main point and a double line next to an important detail. You may wish to go back and record these points in note form after you have finished reading a section.

OR

2. *Underline* selectively.
   You might underline main ideas with one line, key words in major details with two lines, and, in some cases, key words in minor details with three lines.

   _____ = main idea          _____ = important detail

OR

3. Make *marginal notes*—just brief jottings of key words or "cue phrases."
   Main headings should be close to the margin. Subpoints should be set in a little. Later, these marginal notes can be used in studying to recall the facts.

OR

4. Use the *divided page.*
   Make a dividing line down the center of a sheet of paper. Write important questions on the left side and the answers on the right. Use the self-recitation method of study. Test your memory by covering the right-hand side and trying to find the answer. Check and recheck until you know the material thoroughly. Questions and answers may be greatly abbreviated. You will find the "divided page" an especially convenient device for later review.

OR

5. Place *numerals* in the margin.
   As you read a paragraph (or longer unit), *place numerals* in the margin *beside points to be remembered.* If you like, you might use a and b to indicate subpoints.

OR

6. *Outline the chapter* if you prefer.
   Rephrasing the author's words as you outline helps make what you read your own.

*The "Read" Step Should Pay You Well:*

As you read to answer questions, you should now *cut through* what is less important *straight to main points.* You should be better able to select what is important and to disregard what is unimportant.

All the devices above should promote *concentration* and *retention.*

### 4. State

Use self-recitation to change "half-learned" to fully learned material.

*Look away from the book and try to answer your question.*
   See if you can recite to yourself the main idea and the impor-

tant details. Put the ideas into actual words. If you can't do this, reread the parts that give the answer.

*Keep the print out of sight* at least *50% of the time* you're studying.

A full half hour of every study hour should be spent in self-recitation.

*Note:* Do you have trouble concentrating? Try a "cover card." You can reread a section with your thoughts worlds away, but the cover card forces you to concentrate intently as your mind struggles to recall what you have read. A "cover card" is convenient for concealing material in your book as you *state* important points to yourself. Cover everything but the boldface heading, the heading of an important list, a term you want to define, a topic sentence, etc., while you recite to yourself on the material you have concealed. Cover the labels of a diagram while you see if you can name each part. Cover answers in your notes as you check on your retention. Reciting aloud or in a whisper will reinforce your learning.

*The "State" Step Should Pay You Well:*

The self-recitation step forces *concentration.*

Through self-recitation, you should *retain longer.*

Air Force instructors tell us that spending half your time in self-recitation should help you make *better scores on tests* taken immediately after study or several weeks later.

## 5. Test

Do self-testing later for purposes of review. This will retard the natural process of forgetting.

*Use as many different senses as you can.*
First, check your memory for the larger pattern by reciting the principal points the author makes in the assignment. Then use your "cover card" to conceal everything but boldface headings, topic sentences, or the headings of important lists while you recite to yourself on the subpoints you have concealed.

*Your "cover card" will be useful again.*
*See* the ideas as you reread parts you do not remember. *Hear* yourself as you recite them aloud or in a whisper. Use your *muscular* or *kinesthetic sense* as you write very brief jottings or cue phrases. Your senses are your avenues of learning.

*Do pencil work as you review.*
Your pencil will have a "no-doze" effect! Jot just a key word or two as you recite important points to yourself. Make quick lists of items. Pencil work will help concentration.

*Space out your reviews!*

Forgetting takes place most rapidly shortly after you finish studying a lesson. *Arrange your first review* from 12 to 24 hours after you first study the material. If you reinforce the original learning immediately, you will remember *much* longer. Other reviews should be spaced out after that—perhaps a week later, two weeks later, a month later, and just before the final examination.

*The "Test" Step Should Pay You Well:*

Through spacing out reviews, you should have *far better retention* after weeks and months have passed.

# Study Skills in Math

**I.** The study skills to be taught to the students are note taking during lectures and while reading, how to listen, and how to take a test.

**II.** The following is a direction sheet to be handed out to the class:

*So You Want To Make An "A"!*

Here are some tips on how to make a good grade in this course. If you will follow these guidelines and incorporate your own procedures that work for you, the course will be easier to pass with a good grade.

1. Taking notes during lectures is important. Do not attempt to write down everything that I say during class, but do take notes on:
   A. New terms
      - Write the word and the definition.
      - Write the equation associated with the new term.
   B. Any procedure that is not clear to you from the beginning, or the part of a procedure that is confusing.
      - Ask me to explain further. I will take the time to help.
      - If you are still confused, write down the equation and put into words what happens at each phase of the procedure.

   Do not write in complete sentences or abbreviate words. Be sure that you will be able to read your own abbreviations when you consult your notes at a later time.

   As you will be assigned homework daily, read your notes from that day's lecture prior to starting your homework. (Don't panic—here will be no busy-work or excessively time-consuming work.) This will refresh your memory and put you in a mathematical frame of mind.
2. While you are reading the textbook, it is very helpful to write down certain ideas.
   A. New terms—Write down the word and definition.
   B. Equations—Although the examples in the book explain procedures, write the examples down, step by step. You learn math by working math problems, and this will familiarize you with new methods.
3. The ability to listen is a lost art. Here are some methods to use to learn how to listen, not just hear.
   A. Watch the person talking without taking your eyes from his or her head (even if his or her back is toward you). This is not always possible when you take notes, but practice it as often as possible.

B. Concentrate on the topic and what is being explained at the time. Do not reflect on an earlier part of the lecture at this time, and do not try to anticipate what the speaker will say next.

4. Giving tests is a necessary evil; therefore, here are some guidelines for taking a test.

A. Work the problems that you are sure you know first.

B. Place a mark (a small check or dot) next to the ones that you aren't positive of when you first read them.

C. Other problems that you work may remind you of the procedures necessary to work the problems you checked; therefore, read them all again, working those you now remember how to work. (Erase the mark.)

D. Work the problems you are unsure of by whatever method you deem appropriate. You may incorporate the proper procedures somewhere along the way.

Above all, do not panic if you find that you do not know all of the answers to all of the questions. There are not many people who do know all the answers—just people who think they do.

5. There is no guarantee that you will make a grade of A, but if you attend class daily, do the homework assignments when they are assigned, and follow these guidelines, the possibilities of your making a poor grade are very remote.

# CHAPTER EIGHT

# *Remedial, Dyslexic, ESL, and Talented and Gifted Readers*

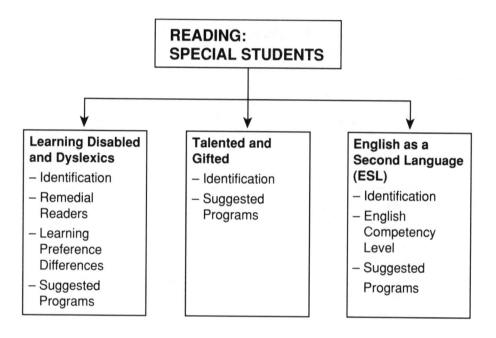

A tenth-grade history teacher assumes she will have a class of 15-year-olds who can read the textbook. This would be a fairly realistic assumption if the learning disabled, dyslexic, and ESL students were not mainstreamed from special programs into her class. She will be expected to excuse the special education students to be tested orally during exam periods and to follow a different modification of her teaching for each special education student. The bilingual teacher will want language modifications made for the ESL students. And, as many talented and gifted students are not identified or given special programs, they too will be in her class. The secondary classroom truly replicates the local citizenry. If this teacher has a typical sophomore class, she can expect a 10-year range of reading skills, with most ESL and LD children reading on the elementary level.

This chapter will discuss special students and their reading needs. It will also give examples of teaching methods and case studies that will provide practical classroom applications regarding these challenging populations.

# Remedial Readers and Dyslexics: Identification through Learning Disorders Label

*Learning disability, attention deficit disorder, minimal brain dysfunction,* and *dyslexia* are all terms that represent the multiplicity of learning disorders. Unfortunately, these terms are not clearly or exclusively defined. Individuals with quite different and distinct learning-related disorders are grouped together within one of these classification subtypes. As Martha Denkla, a child neurologist who studies dyslexia and learning disabilities, stated, it is much better to link characteristics than to lump them under one classification. But right now, almost any label placed on a student with a learning problem is not helpful to the classroom teacher. The reason is that labels provide little meaning or direction for the teacher. How do you teach a child with minimal brain dysfunction and attention deficit disorder differently from a child with learning disability? Rather than labeling a student as "dyslexic," "learning disabled," or "remedial," the teacher would be better served by identifying the specific characteristics of the student's learning problem.

The labeling process, however, is important in terms of getting support for or remediation for a student's learning problems. Not only is there a need for immediate coping strategies for daily academic tasks but there is little chance that the student will "outgrow" his or her learning problem (Dykman, Peters, & Ackerman, 1973; Gottesman, Belmont, & Kaminer, 1975; Klien, 1972; Rourke, Young, and others, 1986; Sarazin & Spreen, 1986; Bruck, 1990). So, regardless of its accuracy or helpfulness to teachers, labeling does enable teachers to get students placed in federally funded programs for the handicapped. The Education for All Handicapped Children Act (PL 94-142), signed in 1975 by President Gerald Ford, ensures the handicapped of an education. Of the 4.5 million students identified as handicapped in the 1987–88 school year, 47 percent, or 1.9 million, were labeled "learning disabled." The quickest identifier of learning disability is reading deficiency or remedial reading.

Unfortunately, the definition of *learning disabled* (LD) cannot be agreed upon by educators, psychologists, or medical practitioners. The American Psychiatric Association's Diagnostic and Statistical Manual-III-Revised refers to learning disabilities as "Specific Developmental Disorders" characterized by "inadequate development of specific academic, language, speech and motor skills that are not due to demonstrable physical or neurological disorders, or Pervasive Developmental Disorder, Mental Retardation, or deficient educational opportunities" (DSM-III-R, 1987).

Within the subclass of specific developmental disorders are those in areas of arithmetic, writing, reading, speech, expressive and receptive language, and coordination disorders. Attention deficit and hyperactivity disorders are also tied to reading problems and grouped under the subclass of disruptive behavior disorders and defined as

**Poem Written by 16-Year-Old Prisoner**

You Bless all men but if
I only had anything to give
To someone How it
Will help them to think of
themself
As you make them
not as man make them
But as you make them.

Yes But
Dear God I have done all I know how
to do. To make it sometime
it get so hard. But God
I know if you want me to make it
I will make it
But I've been down so long and
Now I want to be someone and I see
Myself saying Poor Me, How can
I make it.

But Lord I think I see my
Way
But Dear God you Don't have to think
You know me and Everything
I do and Everything I want in my
Life
Thank The God remember
Poor, Poor me.

"developmentally inappropriate degrees of inattention, impulsiveness, and hyperactivity." Although distinct terms for specific learning disabilities are available, subgroups are often referred to interchangeably.

So, while psychologists, psychiatrists, and counselors have the DSM-III definitions, the government provides a different definition of learning disability for federally funded programs. The 1987 definition by the National Institute of Health is as follows:

Learning disabilities is a generic term that refers to a heterogeneous group of disorders manifested by significant difficulties in the acquisition and use of reading, writing, reasoning, or mathematical abilities, or social skills. These disorders are intrinsic to the individual and presumed to be due to central nervous system dysfunction. Even though a learning disability may occur concomitantly with other handicapping conditions (e.g., sensory impairment, mental retardation, social and emotional disturbance), with socioenvironmental influences (e.g., cultural differences, insufficient/inappropriate instruction, psychogenic factor), and especially with attention deficit disorder, all of which may cause learning problems, a learning dis-

ability is not the direct result of those conditions or influences.
(Silver, 1988)

The difference between the two definitions lies in the assumed neurological or genetic etiology, which then determines the remediation the teacher is to provide. The similarity between both definitions is that neither provides a clue as to the degree of impairment necessary in order to identify "learning disability." The central problem for the content teacher, then, is to find a means to label remedial readers as learning disabled in order to provide them with additional learning assistance. In some school systems, this means administering an intelligence test and finding that the student has average intelligence but cannot read on the appropriate level. Other school systems administer multiple batteries of tests, the processing of which involves educational diagnosticians, special education teachers, school counselors and classroom teachers in multiple meetings, and months of administrative time but no assistance time for the child during the same period.

Regardless of the method used, identification will be based on one of three attributes: etiology (often inferred), performance on psychological cognitive measures, and performance on direct measures of reading and learning (called *achievement variables*). Test administrators can be psychologists, educational diagnosticians, or medical practitioners, each with a different theoretical and experiential background. But the most astounding aspect of this identification process is the fact that the test administrator is not required to communicate any information to the student's classroom teacher(s). In fact, most of clinical psychologists who tested clients for learning disabilities interviewed the parents extensively but never talked to the students' teacher. This means that junior high and high school teachers must make a special effort to obtain data from the learning disabilities identification process.

# Dyslexia

The most difficult student for content teachers to teach is the learning-disabled remedial reader. Special education labels are confusing, sometimes used interchangeably, and frequently not helpful in preparing content instruction. All special education students have an educational plan devised for them. Content teachers are supposed to follow this plan. A solution to the problems of confusing labels for remedial readers is to describe specific behavior rather than rely on the more vague descriptors traditionally applied to learning-disabled children with severe reading disorders found in special education programs.

The reading problems of dyslexics and learning disabled are initially caused by capabilities of the child, not the inadequacies of their instruction. As the AIDS and Crack children start to enter schools, they will display attention disorders as well as reading, writing, speaking, and listening problems, which can be more collectively identified than most current-day dyslexics. If the teacher knows a student's parents were on crack, the drug-related behavior can be identified. At this time, there are constellations of behavioral patterns that are not shared by all those who are labeled dyslexic.

## Characteristics of dyslexia

Many people label themselves dyslexic with little notion of what the term implies. They have a great deal of satisfaction, however, from knowing that their trouble with reading has a medical-sounding term. The problem is that the medical and educational communities rarely get together to make sure they are describing the same constellation of behaviors. Later in this chapter case studies of three dyslexics will be provided to give content teachers practice in identifying and designing possible remediation. Special interest in dyslexia, as opposed to other forms of reading disability, seems to come from the promise it holds as a distinct subtype of reading disability.

Almost a century ago, Dr. James Hinshelwood, an eye surgeon from Scotland, used the term *word blindness* to describe children who were intelligent and could learn if all lessons were done orally. They could not read words. By 1925, Dr. Samuel Orton had studied "word blind," or dyslexic, children and found additional characteristics such as left-handedness, ambidexterity, and a tendency toward reversals when trying to read and write. He believed that behind these phenomena was a basic state of confusion represented by a faulty patterning of brain function. As a result, many cases and characteristics of learning disabled were labeled *dyslexic.*

In 1968, the World Federation of Neurology adopted a definition of dyslexia: Specific developmental dyslexia is a disorder manifested by difficulty in learning to read despite conventional instruction, adequate intelligence, and sociocultural opportunity. The cause is assumed to be fundamental neurological disabilities that are frequently of constitutional origin. This is the medical definition of dyslexia. Educational definitions of dyslexia usually describe difficulties in the performance of language tasks in the classroom. No teacher needs these definitions to know something is wrong when an intelligent student cannot read, write, or spell as they well as he or she should or as well as others in the class.

Dyslexia will often include one, many, or all of the following characteristics:

*Alexia:*   The inability of intelligent people to recognize printed words. This is the behavior Dr. Hinselwood observed and termed "word blindness."

*Strephosymbolia:*   The inability to recognize and recall the orientation of letters and the order of letters in words.

*Dysnosia* or *agnosia:*   The difficulty in remembering specific concept-symbol relationships, as well as the partial inability to remember which concepts are represented by specific words.

*Dysgraphia* or *agraphia:*   Disorders in handwriting; specifically, difficulty in putting thoughts into written form and a partial inability to remember how to make certain letters of the alphabet; often a faulty sense of direction, left to right, top to bottom.

*Apraxia:*   Abnormal clumsiness suggesting tendencies to be messy or sloppy in written work.

*Aphasia:*   "Expressive" asphasia, is the inability to speak, although meaning is understood; "receptive" aphasia is the inability to comprehend or obtain meaning from spoken words.

*Dyscalculia* or *acalculia:*   The inability to comprehend relationships between math concepts and math symbols.

*Visual dyslexia:*   The tendency to see printed symbols upside down, backwards, or in scrambled sequence; the inability to comprehend items presented in a series.

*Phonological* or *auditory dyslexia:*   The inability to perceive separate discrete sounds of spoken language; the difficulty in translating speech into printed or written symbols; the difficulty in hearing discrete phonemic distinctions in speech, such as "big" and "beg."

Educators describe the following classroom behaviors associated with dyslexia:

Problems in learning the names of the letters of the alphabet
Difficulty in learning to write the alphabet in correct sequence
Difficulty in learning and remembering the printed word
Reversals of orientation of letters or the sequences of letters
Difficulty in learning to read
Difficulty in reading comprehension
Cramped or illegible handwriting
Repeated spelling errors
Degree of involvement may be mild, moderate, or severe

In addition, educators claim the following characteristics may be associated with "specific dyslexia":

Delay in spoken language

Difficulty in finding the right word when speaking

Late in establishing preferred hand for writing

Late in learning right and left and other directionality components

Problems in learning the concept of time and temporal sequencing

Family history of similar problems (Texas State Board of Education, 1986)

To simplify these characteristics and behaviors obtained from the medical and educational communities into an understandable format, normal reading behavior can be compared with dyslexic behavior. In normal readers, sense and sound are computed in parallel. In dyslexic readers, one or the other process may be totally or partially absent. The terms above describe those absences and the way they appear in behavior. The deficits can be in auditory comprehension, where certain grammatical constructions are not described properly, and/or in visual comprehension, which is a deficit in recognizing individual words in sequencing or attaching meaning to written symbols. For remediation purposes, these deficits found in dyslexics can be further divided into attentional, neglect, deep, phonological, and surface forms. The mother describing her dyslexic son in the Application Exercise that follows this chapter was told her son had stylistic dyslexia. *Stylistic dyslexia* is a label of little use to Matt's mother and teachers. Obviously, children identified as dyslexic cannot be clearly defined in an agreed upon manner (Presland, 1991).

### Case 1—Philip: Strephosymbolia, Dysgraphia, and Phonological Dyslexia

Philip, a college junior and the quarterback on the football team, was enrolled in a Reading in the Content Area course. He attributed his survival in school to memorization, help from his parents, and inordinate persistence. The following semester, he spoke to the reading class about his difficulties in school. Some teachers would not allow him to tape record classes or let him type papers (which helped him write). After his talk, a girl from his high school said that he was popular and considered intelligent. She said no one in their school had any idea of the difficulties he faced.

When he brought papers home from first grade, his mother would hold them up to the mirror in order to read them. He was always asking the teacher to repeat directions because what she said was jumbled. Every night after school, his mother would sit with him for at least two hours while he memorized what other first-graders could do in 15 minutes. But what hurt him the most was that he was always the last chosen for teams on the playground.

Elizabeth and Mark's learning disability was called dyslexia but the labeling itself was not helpful in remediating their problems. Terms such as *minimal brain dysfunction, specific learning disability, specific reading disability, specific dyslexia, developmental dyslexia, educationally handicapped* and *psycho-neurological learning disability* are used almost interchangeably in research and clinical practice. The terms refer to an elusive and heterogeneous group of characteristics in students who are having "unexpected" academic and/or behavior difficulties. By the time these same children reach secondary schools, their disabilities are still present and often compounded by psychological problems resulting from their inability to perform in the academic environment.

## Case 2—Elizabeth: Dysnosia or Agnosia, Agraphia, and Dyscalculia

When Elizabeth was 10 years old, her parents moved overseas. Her father spent night after night helping her with her homework and becoming more and more frustrated with her performance. He was trying and she was trying, but there seemed to be an inability to comprehend relationships in math or to remember what they had studied the night before. When Elizabeth's father would go to school and ask about her work, the teachers would say that she was doing excellent work but worked slowly and seemed to be tired. The discrepancy between what seemed to be good work at school and the inability to conceptualize even the simplest academic tasks at home made the father suspicious. When they returned to the United States, Elizabeth was tested and found to be dyslexic. She now attends a school for dyslexic high school students where 75 percent of the students are male, which is frequently the case with dyslexics.

## Case 3—Mark: Apraxia, Dysgraphia, and Strephosymbolia

Mark was 11 years old and had another year before entering junior high. He had been in special education since the third grade and still read on the second-grade level. When asked about his reading instruction, he said that the teacher gave him worksheets that he completed as best he could. When Mark had a question, he would go to the teacher and she would answer the question for him. After finding he had average intelligence, the teacher asked him to describe the alphabet as he saw it. He copied the word *basic* with the *b* and *a* reversed in script and the *a* and *i* exchanged in positions. Mark was an example of a dyslexic who has not been identified in the school system. He became a test case in a lawsuit against the school district because he was tested and received special education for three years, yet had never been identified as dyslexic.

## Summary

*Learning disability* and *dyslexia* are terms that have not been defined in the same manner by the educational or medical community. The confusion in referents is hardly helpful to the classroom teacher who must try to help these students. As demonstrated by the case studies, similarly labeled readers (dyslexic) display different classroom and reading behaviors. The best approach for the classroom teacher is to consider whether the student has learning disabilities that are global or language specific, as in dyslexia. Dyslexia should be viewed as a language disability occurring on a continuum ranging from a rather mild characteristic of symbol confusion to complex syndromes of language disabilities that are incapacitating. Once the breadth of the student's disability is determined, then the teacher should identify behavioral characteristics. Obviously, there is no single remediation program that is effective with a range of disabilities.

# Remedial Readers with Global Learning Disabilities

The following standardized test results are associated with global learning disabilities accompanied by reading disabilities. Any student exhibiting these characteristics should be carefully observed and further tested.

1. Global mixed language disorder, where all tests of language fall below age expectations, verbal IQ on the Weschler is below 90, and Performance IQ is at least 95.
2. Articulatory-graphomotor disorder, where fine-motor coordination and pencil use are deficient (dysgraphia, apraxia, or agraphia) and language tests are all normal; articulation is deficient.
3. Anomic-repetition disorder, where articulation and comprehension tests are normal and there is a scatter among subtests on verbal IQ on the Weschler.
4. Dysphonemic-sequencing disorder, which has substitutions, errors of sequence, neglect, "failed" sentence and digit span (by virtue of omissions with some naming errors), and complex syntactical constructions misunderstood. Articulation and verbal IQ are at least average.
5. Verbal learning disorder (memorization deficiency), dysnosia or agnosia, and sequential-simultaneous disorder. (Denckla, 1985)

Testing for these deficiencies involves assessing a number of skills, including motor, sensory, psychomotor, visual-spatial, language, reasoning, and memory. Intelligence, personality, and academic achievement should also be assessed on standardized tests. The interpretation of the test results should include evaluation of overall performance, intertest patterns, and the relationship of receptive to expressive deficits. Obviously this is not an identification process that the classroom teacher has time to conduct or interpret. Reading specialists, educational diagnosticians, and other professionals should provide support when a global learning disability is suspected.

Learning disability characteristics are assumed by some to be caused by a neurological deficiency—a deficiency that reveals itself on reading tests with low scores. In most cases, this is all the information the content teacher has to work with when beginning remediation. Elizabeth and Philip's teachers were further handicapped in their diagnosis by the students' physical beauty, agreeable personalities, and supportive families who worked with them to enable them to cope in school. Learning-disabled and remedial readers may demonstrate the same positive characteristics. Since both students were popular with other students and completed assignments at home, their only noticeable classroom behavior was slowness in verbal responses. Their teachers did not consider these behaviors as serious and had not considered either student remedial.

Learning disability characteristics can, however, translate into a number of disturbing observable classroom behaviors, provided the students have not learned how to disguise their disabilities. Such students may not be able to remember what they hear or retain what they read from one day to the next. They may be able to read but not comprehend what they read. The result may be that they seem not to listen or understand. Frequently, poor motor coordination produces poor handwriting, art work, or drawing. These characteristics may not be readily observable because the students' short attention span and lack of patience prevent them from completing or handing in assignments, or remembering to bring their assignment home from school. Unlike Philip, who was able to memorize textbooks and persevere, some learning-disabled students become so frustrated that they quit trying in a situation where they can not succeed. When trying to explain a math concept to a learning-disabled 11-year-old, a teacher watched as the boy, in frustration, curled into a ball beside her desk. Other students said, "Where is David? Is he gone?" But he had just gotten so frustrated that he had taken time out to get control of himself. Although other students may not be so physical about how they feel, they may wish they could just quit like David did.

It is difficult to determine whether the learning deficiency causes the emotional frustration or the converse. Certain affective characteristics also seem to be observable. The student develops a poor self-concept when he or she cannot accomplish assignments that are relatively easy for other students. The author investigated the social needs of regular and remedial readers in elementary and secondary schools. The most significant social characteristic identifying learning-disabled remedial readers of all ages was the desire to be included. Learning-disabled and remedial readers feel isolated and want others to take a greater interest in them. They want help. The second finding was that they feel powerless over their relationships in terms of power and control. Teachers should consider that remedial readers might need to counteract their reading deficits by controlling social relationships. And finally, the older they get, the more affection remedial readers require. Interestingly enough, there were no significant differences in emotional needs between elementary and secondary remedial readers in the study, but there were significant differences in the interpersonal needs of remedial and regular readers regardless of age (Cochran, 1980).

Some students merely sleep through class, while others become irritable when faced with an assignment that is beyond their capability. Some of all of these conditions are disruptive in a classroom and yet they are symptoms that the teacher must consider in the identification and remediation of learning-disabled remedial readers. Testing for special-education programs can be suggested by the teacher. The examples of student scores on the WISC and informal reading tests in the Teaching Activities section of this chapter represent material teachers may receive, read, and possibly have to interpret if learning-disabled students are in their classes.

Most remedial readers will be identified in the content classes by regular teachers. Content teachers may also find themselves with a student who does not show a large enough discrepancy between performance and ability to be classified as LD but nonetheless has similar learning problems to the LD identified student. These students will demonstrate inadequate development of specific academic, language, speech, and motor skills that are not due to demonstrable physical or neurological disorders, mental retardation, or deficient educational opportunities (DSM-III, 1987).

The different LD programs, if available, are as varied as the students themselves. Many of the programs are just more intense versions of remedial reading programs, whereas others use techniques and ideas that are unique to LD classrooms. The most important thing to remember when choosing a particular program is the behavioral characteristics of the student.

## Remedial Readers without Learning Disabilities

Remedial readers are generally defined as those reading two years below their appropriate grade level. When IQ is considered, it becomes possible for talented and gifted children to be remedial readers if they are reading on grade level, as they have the ability to read far above assigned grade level. This section will describe the types of educational deficits that can result in remedial readers. These students need only to be given appropriate instruction and they will read adequately in a short period of time. The school, not the child, needs to be examined.

> John was a 15-year-old boy who read on the fourth-grade level. Despite his getting good grades in school, John's mother was concerned that he would not be able to go to college and become a lawyer because he couldn't read well. After testing, John seemed to lack skills taught in fourth grade. Subsequent to the testing and interviewing, the mother met John's fourth-grade teacher in the grocery store. She discovered that this was the teacher's first year to teach and she had 35 students in the class. The teacher remembered Johnny being gone on a week's vacation and then she couldn't get the time to work individually with him to remediate what he had missed. That is where John's problems began and they weren't corrected until he became concerned at age 15. This is an example of how parental, teacher, and enrollment factors contribute to poor reading skills.

The question could be asked as to why it took so long to fix John's reading problems. This time, the answer is in the instruction. Reading instruction took place in groups followed by worksheets. For example, on Monday the story is read aloud. On Tuesday, the students fill out what the basal reading textbook calls a comprehension worksheet. On Wednesday, the students read aloud the story again. Thursday they fill in another worksheet. Friday they write a book report about the story. If a child pays attention and listens well in class, it is possible to get good grades on the worksheets and prepare ahead for the section he or she must read.

In secondary classes, where students rarely read aloud, remedial reading students have figured out all kinds of methods to avoid reading aloud. Ken used to always start a fight. Katie used to get sick and asked to leave the room. Salvador would read softly and slowly. Teachers would get so irritated with the slow pace and not being able to hear him that he would only have to read a few words. But when you consider that Rod was whispering the words over Salvador's shoulder, Sal was reading remarkably well for a nonreader. And then there was William who used to say "big word" when he came to a word he didn't know. The students would laugh and the terrible moment would pass. Ken described the feeling he had before being asked to read aloud like sitting and watching a fire come up the aisle to burn you. You had a choice either to get badly burned or jump out the window, which was what happened when he caused a problem. But for him, it was the lesser of two evils. Ken, Katie, and William all graduated from high school reading on the fifth, ninth, and preprimer levels, respectively. Salvador dropped out in the tenth grade, which was a testimony to his persistence, for he could not read at all during his 10-year educational experience.

Although it is logical to drop out of school when you spend eight hours a day pretending to do something you cannot do (read), many remedial readers continue on to college. Rick was a senior in a regular English class but read on the fourth-grade level. And although the results disturbed his mother, Rick accepted an athletic scholarship to a junior college and planned to be a highway patrolman. He may be successful if he has the determination of Pearl, who was the only girl in a family of 16 brothers. Her mother wanted her to go to college and was working as a maid to put Pearl through school. Pearl kept changing majors, trying to keep her grade point up so that she would not be on probation. She came from an inner-city high school where most of the "A" and "B" graduates tested on junior high reading level. Pearl was admitted on her high school grade average of Bs but read on the fifth-grade level. Pearl had performed well enough in school to get B grades but her basic skills were not adequate for continuing her education. Pearl was trying desperately not to disappoint her mother and her brothers and had done her best. This grading seduction occurs all over the country, where students can pass courses without reading or writing ability. In these cases, remedial readers are a result of educational deficits, not student inadequacies.

The last example of a remedial reader with educational deficits is Michael. A 39-year-old school board president, he could not read state mandates and discuss them. He had passed eleventh grade but could read only preprimer books, which are two levels below first-grade readers. He had never written his wife a note or read his children's report cards or a newspaper. When he was 6 years old and reading to his mother, she had a nervous breakdown. Reading for him was associated with this catastrophy. But at age 39, he decided he needed to learn to read. Like Salvador, Ken, Pearl, Katie, and John, he had not received or been ready for direct reading instruction. Because of looks, personality, family status, and his own verbal cleverness, Michael had been passed through the eleventh grade. The community elected him to the school board. No one knew he was an illiterate adult.

Although each of these students behaved differently, went to school in different parts of the country, and were motivated to learn to read by different events, they all were and are capable of learning to read quickly. Millions of other students in our public schools fit the descriptions of the students we have discussed. Regardless of where they live, their pain and skills in deception are the same. There is no emotional disturbance or learning disability. They simply failed to get basic instruction in the thousands of hours they spent in school.

These students were, if anything, too charming. They didn't cause trouble in classes (with the exception of Ken, who terrorized his teachers or charmed them into passing him). Even when courageous teachers identify students who need extra help, the students sometimes lack the maturity to know how critical the lack of reading skills will be to their future. Appropriate state-administered reading tests with mandatory program placement could have identified all of these students before they dropped out of school or graduated to continue suffering in colleges and on the job.

Without state-mandated reading tests, the responsibility rests on the local level to identify as well as remediate children with educational deficits. Parents, adminstrators, and school board members will tell teachers to pass students who have not done the work. Parents will insist that schools not label their children "remedial" by placing them in special programs. The school system can be controlled by such parents and school administrators and damage students who need additional reading instruction. Content teachers must look to the leadership of the school to determine if they will have support in identifying and remediating those who do not qualify for special education classes.

## Learning Preference Differences

Just as some people learn more from watching football and others learn more from playing the game, learning preferences reflect the best means of having information organized. Learning preferences are identified by different educational terms such as *impulsive* or *reflective, right* or *left hemispheric dominant, visual* or *verbal, simultaneous* or *sequential, global* or *analytic*. Remedial readers with an impulsive, right, visual, simultaneous, and global preference are identified by performing at least two years below grade level and show a talent or competency in spacial assessment and an expected deficit in language assessment (Bakker, 1990; Johnsen, 1990).

These preferences for simultaneious (spacial) and sequential (language) methods of processing that are related to right and left brain hemispheres have been called *global* and *analytical* by some reading educators (Carbo, 1988; Carbo, Dunn, & Dunn, 1986; Naidoo, 1981). Carbo, Dunn, and Dunn (1986) have even quantified the numbers of learners with global and analytic preferences into 20–30 percent analytic and 40 percent global, with the remaining being tactile or kinesthetic learners. Information-processing strengths have been identified according to learning preferences and have been translated into classroom practices. Content teachers are urged to provide a variety of activities in the classroom in order to address learing preferences or styles. The result is good teaching.

In contrast to identifying one learning style, Luria's (1966) studies in neurology have supported an integration of spatial and verbal processing procedures, not an isolation in normal subjects. And although remedial readers with learning preference differences may not be similar in brain functioning, few have been tested on neurological test batteries to determine if Luria's contention is valid. In order to accomplish the complex act of reading, many systems in the brain work together. The brain has three dimensions, which can be visualized as three axes. Each axis works in coordination with the other axes. None of them operates independently of the other. For example, the bottom to top axis regulates the arousal mechanisms of attention and acts as a filter for the sensory data of letters and language (recognizes messages in print). Another example of neurological integration occurs with arousal and rest. When the brain is at rest, electrochemical changes occur, which can be identified as alpha waves. When cognitive activity is undertaken in a certain area, alpha blocking occurs, keeping the rest of the brain at relative rest. This is a complementary interaction of functions. There is a need to conduct additional electroencephalogram (EEG) and neurological testing on remedial readers to determine if the observed relationships between neurological and educational functioning can be further defined (Hynd and others, 1990; Landwehrmeyer and others, 1990; Snowling, 1991).

In addition, common sense dictates that environment influences how the brain processes information and subsequent educational functioning. Experience-dependent neurological connections are made in the course of one's life as a result of differential life experience. New connections are generated in response to complex information-processing demands of the environment. For example, environmental conditions that result from poverty contain experiences of powerlessness, deprivation, insecurity, and simplification. Because environmental demands are different for individuals, the cumulative effect of experience is that the brain differs from individual to individual in connections (Greenough, Black, & Wallace, 1987;

Humphreys, Kaufmann, & Galaburda, 1990). Obviously, if remedial readers inherit eye color and other physiological characteristics from their parents, they could also inherit ways of selectively making connections and responding to their environment. A tendency for alcoholism is inherited; so could a tendency toward visual learning or visual dyslexia be inherited (Smith, Pennington, and others, 1990; Lewis, 1990). So far, researchers will only indicate that some forms of reading disorders tend to run in families. Again, additional information has to be obtained on linking environmental factors and heredity to reading difficulties.

## Summary

Learning preferences can contribute to reading difficulties. Although there have not been many studies linking neurological functioning to remedial reading, those that have been conducted indicate abnormal language-processing procedures. Furthermore, the influences of the environment, and specifically environmental deprivation and heredity, have not been studied as they relate to reading behavior. Since there is little work done in this area, the observation could be valid that remedial readers result from incompatibility between classroom presentation and learning strengths.

# Suggested Programs

At this point, experimentation is the traditional methodology for remediating LD students. Hospitals such as Scottish-Rite in Dallas have provided training in programs (e.g., Alphabet Phonics) for dyslexics. Societies such as the Orton Dyslexia Society conduct conferences yearly where topics are discussed, such as "Turning the Tables for Dyslexic Students" and "Dyslexia Teacher Trainees." Teachers are trained in tutorial methods such as "Reading Recovery" adopted from Marie Clay in Australia and "Learning Styles" developed by American educators Carbo and Dunn. There are also special schools for dyslexics and private boarding schools for learning-disabled students. Such schools claim to obtain excellent results (based on individual studies that test according to each school's teaching procedure). Some claim to teach to strengths, whereas others claim to remediate deficiencies. To the content teacher, these special schools offer a bewildering array of choices, all of which usually require expensive training taken outside of the public school system on the content teacher's own time.

The mistake in remediation is to look for one program that will address all difficulties. The author was once asked by a concerned professor if she could find a remedial reading program for black athletes. Basically, no such program exists for black athletes or remedial readers. Individualization, considering the student's environment, heredity, learning styles, and academic strengths, is what is necessary. The activities and instructional descriptions contained in the Teaching Activities section of this chapter should provide a beginning point for content teachers.

Remediation, in the past, has been based on the medical rather than educational definitions of dyslexia. The medical practitioners focus on remediation of neurological deficits believed to be functional in nature. Neurologist Samuel Orton believed that the two hemispheres of the brain were imbalanced in the way information got from one part of the brain to the other. The Orton-Gillingham technique, which is based on Orton's belief, is a synthesis, sound-binding remediation procedure. First, sounds of letters are taught and then the sounds are built into words. Emphasis is placed on associating deficiencies and linking kinesthetic, auditory, and visual information in order to "rebalance" the hemispheres.

Hinshelwood, another medical doctor, placed his emphasis on the structural aspects of the disorder—specific brain sites and hypothetical connections. Remediation, following his theory, focuses on defining the area of deficit, such as visual decoding (which takes place mostly in the occipital lobe). First, the observable classroom behavior is recorded, then auditory cues in the form of phonetic reading, records, tape recorder, and other methods of sound-complement, visual input, are provided.

A third neurological remediation has been based on the premise that there has been a lack of focus in processing information. When the right hemisphere is functioning, the left hemisphere closes down. This occurs when there has been clear lateralization. In some people, however, lateralization has not clearly developed and the two hemispheres interfere with one another and prevent complete input. The remediation process here is based on Kimura and McGlone's (1983) early dichotic listening studies and, more recently, on the work of Matthews (1991), Smith, Pennington, and others (1990), and Wolff (1990). Kimura and McGlone's remediation process uses earphones and the neurological impress method to focus reception. So far, the medical model remediation of dyslexics has emphasized the sound processing but not the sense processing. In normal readers, both are completed in parallel.

Educational remediation of poor readers focuses on reading, spelling, or language deficits. The Frenald technique has been around the longest and is probably the most widely used. This approach is a kinesthetic-sensory method that involves the learner's sense modalities in learning word forms. The techique consists of four stages in which the student progresses from tracing, saying, and seeing each word (in the air or on sandpaper) to a point where the student sees, says, and writes words on his or her own.

One debate among educators seems to be whether to teach to students' strengths or to remediate weaknesses. Hynd (1987) believes that strength-oriented teaching may widen the gap between the abilities and deficits; deficit remediations assume that dysfunctions are correctable. And while these debates are going on, some teachers are asking exactly how one teaches to strengths or remediates individual weaknesses in a classroom of 35 students. Remedial reading teachers are asking the same question when they have 5 to 7 students for 30-minute increments, interrupted by testing schedules, assemblies, and programs. As a result, educators are remediating with modified alphabets, color coding, motor and perceptual training, programmed materials, small incremental learning steps with immediate feedback, computer programs, and mechanical aids. All are attempting to find strategies and materials that will work with dyslexic and remedial students.

## Summary

Depending on the definition, remedial readers can be identified by medical or educational terms. The content teacher is in one of the best situations for observing some of the reading and emotional behaviors remedial readers demonstrate in response to their frustrations. Regardless of the symptoms or severity, content teachers should define dyslexic readers as those who demonstrate the inability to read successfully despite normal intelligence and adequate instruction. The cause of dyslexia is not agreed upon but it results in a disruption in the computation of either the sound and/or the sense of language. Teachers should define learning-disabled or minimal brain-damaged children according to behaviors demonstrated in class and on standardized tests. When all language-processing and other learning functions appear to be adequate for classroom tasks, teachers should begin to look for educational deficits and learning preferences. Only when the student has been carefully studied is he or she likely to receive appropriate instruction.

# Talented and Gifted

## Identification

The understanding that all students have talents and gifts dictates the purpose of talented and gifted programs: to cultivate student differences. A great deal of federal funding has gone toward making the learning disabled more competent while the talented and gifted have been neglected. Karlin (1984) states that the gifted receive the least amount of instructional time and read below capacity level in most cases. They are frequently identified by their ability to comprehend abstract materials and their constant curiosity. Talented and gifted students in the classroom need a variety of reference materials and different creative assignments to keep their interests alive. Although it does not seem possible for the content teacher to structure specific assignments for these students, the perspective is incorrect. Such students should be encouraged to define their own problems and then read to find the answers. Open-ended assignments work best for them.

These types of assignments, which require self-reliance, are not time consuming for teachers.

Principles of effective instruction for talented and gifted students require the following:

**1.** Provide instruction when needed. The author once had a talented and gifted senior drop out of school, stating, "I would stay in school if teachers were people I wanted to get to know." If this attitude prevails, students should be provided with instruction when needed by mentors or other teachers.

**2.** Provide exercises of value and at ability level. Many talented and gifted students do not want to be in appropriate programs because they are given more of the same work found in regular classes. If you don't like ironing but you are good at it, it doesn't make sense to take courses where you are given even more ironing.

**3.** Provide materials in areas where the students are interested. These students can lead teachers and others into unusual areas of study.

**4.** Provide discussions that promote various points of view. Debates are excellent for these students.

**5.** Provide the students with freedom to select some of their own materials. An excellent instructor of talented and gifted, Robert Godwin, told his students they would spend a portion of class studying what they needed to study for the curriculum. Once finished, they would spend the rest of the class studying what they wanted to explore.

Judy Thornton and Donna Bruner, sixth-grade teachers, demonstrated how little influence instruction by television or printed media has on learning by the talented and gifted. Both teachers divided their students into three ability groups according to their California Achievement Test scores. Each group was given three stories to read and three videos of the stories to watch. In compiling the data after examining the influence of video versus reading on comprehension, both teachers found apparent learning differences. High-level readers (or talented and gifted) scored equally high whether the selection was seen on video, read silently, or read orally. Their test-taking skills increased as the study progressed, demonstrating talented and gifted students' ability to become more critical viewers as well as better readers. The middle group of average readers seemed to have better comprehension with the use of a video. The low-level readers showed significant improvement in their reading skills when first given video stories. When video precedes a reading selection, the middle and low-level readers show great improvement in comprehension skills, whereas the high-level readers showed no significant change. In order to help middle and low-level readers, teachers should use videos as part of the reading curriculum. High-level readers may not gain reading comprehension skills but they enjoy diversification in teaching methods

## Summary

Talented and gifted students must have their differences encouraged. Topics and material must be very carefully selected because simply being in a talented and gifted program provides self-confidence that extends long after the experience. Care must also be taken to develop interesting projects. Students should be taught the procedures of how to define problems and learn how to read and think about their solutions. Do we want problems dealing with environmental pollution, population explosion, and technological impact on values addressed by bureaucrats? If teachers see only children from one race or one socioethnic background, they should be aware that they have a talented and gifted program that reflects the characteristics of the selectors, not a talented and gifted program that encourages excellence and diversity.

# English as a Second Language (ESL)

## Identification

Anyone who has listened to a conversation in another, unintelligible language understands the feelings of ESL students. Without fluency in the native language of the country, immigrants often confine themselves to particular areas, foreign students do not get to know those they have come to learn about, and adults and students alike feel isolated. So, while identifying ESL students is not difficult, breaking the classroom isolation they experience is most difficult. Without an ESL program, international students find themselves wandering the halls of high schools, wearing nametags, carrying school maps, and failing all their courses.

### Case 1—Hidake

The first year Hidake came to the United States, he was sent to an expensive boarding school. He failed all of his classes and decided that Americans didn't like Japanese because no one talked to him. That was because no one *could* talk to him. The second year, Hidake arrived with a bleached streak in the front of his hair and a braid in the back, four designer letter jackets, an earring, and the largest collection of American hard rock tapes ever owned by a teenager in the city. He spent the second year walking around campus with his headphones on, trying to look "American." The school made him cut his braid, take out his earring, and repeat all his classes. Because he had been in the United States for two years, he could not qualify for admission to a Japanese university and he certainly could not pass the entrance exams to an American university. It was at this point that the author was hired to teach English to Hidake.

*Case 2—Aybars*

Aybars was 33 years old and taught elementary school in a remote Turkish village. When his wife had triplets, he had to make more money, which could be done by teaching English. For a year, every day after work, he translated *War and Peace* word by word and listened to BBC on the only radio in the village. When Aybars was selected to come to the ESL instruction in Istanbul, he spent a week without talking, as he had never had a conversation in English.

*Case 3—Maria*

Maria was sent to learn English in the United States because her father wanted her to speak with American tourists who frequented his business. At age 13, Maria was enrolled in the junior high that was closest to where her aunt lived. It didn't matter what grades she got in classes as long as she learned how to speak English.

English is the language of commerce, education, and sometimes economic survival. In Egypt, a secretary who is fluent in English can triple the salary she would get without her language skills. As a result of these pressures, American teachers are working as ESL instructors throughout the world and in their own subject classrooms in the states. In many cases, content teachers' training has been limited in training them how to diagnose and develop ESL students.

## Identifying English competency levels

The first question that should be asked of an ESL student is how much schooling the individual received in his or her native country. After spending five months trying to teach a Kuwaiti rudimentary English skills, someone had the good sense to ask how far she had gotten in school in Kuwait. She had failed junior high twice. Likewise, a Mexican adult who went through the third grade in Mexico came to the United States at age 18 and read on the fourth-grade level in English. He is self-taught and doing well, considering his formal educational level.

For younger children, the second step is to test readiness by using drawings. The reading readiness-writing model identified in Chapter Three can be used to determine how ready the child is to begin to learn to read. No student who is in stages 1–4 in writing should begin to learn to read English. For older students, translate an informal reading test into their language—if possible. From the scores on that test, the teacher will be able to determine reading level in the native language and English. Test for hearing capacity with the informal reading test. Hearing capacity is the difference between test scores on passages that are read to the student and those that the student reads. The discrepancy will indicate how quickly the student will progress. Steven Krashen, an ESL educator, believes that the monitoring theory of language learning best explains progress. The language learner must have listening skills in the language to be learned in order to be able to self-correct second language production.

Once reading level is determined, appropriate material can then be obtained. For example, when Mary went to Egypt at age 11, she was told she could attend the French Lysee if she learned French within the year. Her mother bought her first-grade French textbooks, which Mary read on her own in the back of the classroom. She was admitted to the school after her mathematics scores indicated she had the intelligence to be successful in the school. She attributed personal determination and having the appropriate textbooks for her success in learning French. The same conditions apply to every successful ESL student.

## Suggestions for ESL programs

If you are a history teacher, what do you do when a 14-year-old Rumanian enrolls in your class? According to Collier (1987), it can be projected that at least 4–8 years may be required for all ages of limited English proficient students to reach national grade-level norms of native speakers, in all subject areas of language and academic achievement (as measured on standardized tests). Students who entered school at ages 8–11 were the quickest achievers, requiring 2–5 years to reach the 50th percentile in all subject areas. This does not mean that ESL students are slow. Mary, the student just discussed, was much faster than most because of her age, previous language experiences, and intelligence. She also tested out of her freshman year at Harvard.

The best immediate strategy is to assign the student to a cooperative learning group or to a student helper. Social interactions among students facilitate communication and play—a vital role in the students construction of meaning. Cooperative learning enables the ESL student to gain knowledge of the structure of the English language in a safe and nonthreatening environment. The individual also learns to express himself or herself orally and in written form.

Grading should consist of gain scores on writing, reading, and listening comprehension in English and concept understanding communicated in pictures. The picture technique was discovered by the author when teaching ESL students from Japan, France, and Iran in the same classroom. After reading a short story on Geronimo, the students could answer all the questions about who, what, where, and when. After that, students were asked to draw an interpretive map of how they thought the battle had gone between Geronimo and the soldiers. Imagine our surprise when we saw that Medhat drew Geronimo with a turban like a Sikh. The comprehension of the entire story had been distorted for him by his interpretation of Indians as coming from India. This experience indicates how context provides different meaning and interpretation for children from different racial and ethnic groups. The teacher had to work with the students until the class experienced shared meanings of the readings.

As a teacher of history or any other subject, the instructor should view students as culturally different people with similarities as hu-

*"It's time to identify my talented and gifted, remedial, and bilingual students!"*

man beings. Each year, 8000 kindergarten, first-, second-, and third-grade students in Midland, Texas, visit the Carver Center where an appreciation of cultural diversity is the only message. They spend three days a year learning customs and shared similarities with people throughout the world: Kenya, Italy, New Zealand, the Southwest, Colonial America, and Egypt in one year. The message they are to learn is that people from all over the world are more alike than they are different.

A second objective should be to provide an environment that encourages children to experience people as unique parts of a community. If students are not willing or able to help ESL students in the classroom, then the teacher can use reciprocal teaching. Karen Mills reports her success with using reciprocal teaching with two bilingual second-graders.

Eladio was extremely excited at the prospect of helping me learn Spanish. He has been at the bottom of the class, with retention highly promblematic until we began this experiment. He has blossomed! He will now ask questions and volunteer in class, which was something he had not done to any degree before. He is also willing to guess at answers, which was unheard of prior to our working together. He was very eager to give me stickers and praise when we were working together and was also very happy when I used some of the Spanish words when talking to the class. I was also able to use some of the words to help him with his reading.

Asusena was also very excited at being a teacher. Her self-confidence improved but not to the degree experienced by Eladio. Frequently, she would raise her hand to volunteer but would seldom answer when called on. She would look down and be silent. She is more willing, now, to speak out, even if she is not absolutely certain of an answer. A big problem we have with Asusena is her frequent absences when she accompanies her family to Mexico. Neither her mother nor father speak English, and Spanish is the only language spoken at home. This has resulted in pronounced "language problems" as she constantly struggles to listen, translate, speak, and learn.

Both self-concepts did improve with this idea of reciprocal teaching in even the brief time that we were able to work together. The objective to improve self-concept (and reduce social isolation) was moderately successful with Asusena and highly successful with Eladio.

This project was unlike any I have done before. Working with the two children underscored my belief that teachers must encourage students to take risks in a safe environment. It also reminded me that bilingual youngsters have an exceedingly difficult time learning new ideas and concepts in an unfamiliar language. The continual "switching" activities can cause tremendous confusion and, as a result, a feeling of inadequacy on the part of the student. Much care needs to be taken in order to help build these youngsters' self-concepts in the face of a daily barrage of negative occurrences. My efforts to learn underscored the importance of taking risks, making mistakes, and learning from every opportunity while maintaining a positive image of myself. This positive attitude did "rub off" on my two little teachers.

Some additional activities Karen did with her ESL students in her regular classroom were to write a big book, keep a Spanish language journal, and film a skit.

Probably the most successful ESL experience occurs when the students use language experience. Combined with cooperative learning, the author found students in other classes stealing copies of language experience textbooks. The language level, content, and genuine understanding of the difficulties of learning English is easily captured in this technique. To quote an Egyptian ESL student, "Why do we want to learn about telephone installers and Toshido delivering pizza in Egypt?" With many more student statements like that, the published ESL series we had been using was carefully reexamined. The result was the development of culture-specific textbooks. Content teachers who have ESL students enrolled in their classes might be eager to use ESL series textbooks, for they are sequenced, come with tests and workbooks, and enable students to learn English by reading elementary school basals.

ESL students are a reflection to the rest of the world of this country's foreign policy statements. These students share with relatives and friends what they learn about our country from our language and the degree of kindness we show them as they struggle to learn new customs, course content, and educational processes in a second language.

## Summary

The most important aspect of working with any type of special reading student, be it remedial reader, dyslexic, ESL, or talented and gifted, is that the educator must remember that each student is a unique individual with his or her own special needs and circumstances. If a specific program is not working for a student, then the teacher should not hesitate to try a new or unique program just for the one student. Teachers must remember that a student's needs in reading instruction is the most important variable in designing any program.

## Application Exercises and Teaching Activities

### Application Exercises

1. You are communicating with a parent about his or her dyslexic child. Combine the educational and medical terms into a list that will enable you to discuss the student's behavior with intelligence.

2. The following child is 12 years old and is described as his mother sees his behavior. What would you do for this child in your classroom?

*Mother's Description*

Matt has the ability to read word by word and many times seems to comprehend intricate details from a passage, but he does not have the ability to organize his thoughts for comprehending the main idea or sequence of story-line events. Matt's dyslexia has been categorized as "stylistic" but he really is a combination of several dyslexic characteristics. Matt's inability to "hear" and distinguish phonetically makes visual and graphic learning a more effective strategy for his instruction. Matt has improved comprehension skills recently with the implementation of a home-study guide notebook in which he writes words he considers key vocabulary words. He needs continued encouragement to become an independent thinker who can sequence those words, find main ideas, or determine how important details are. Using a highlighter has helped him to visually "see" main ideas. Matt has great difficulty in comprehending directions orally and graphically. We have encouraged him to always look at the teacher when she is giving directions. Another help has been for Matt to use the notion of imagining that he is underlining the most important part of the directions, such as, "Circle the names of the. . . ." Many times he appears distracted while listening and needs encouragement or can be motivated by the teacher asking him to listen for a specific event, etc.

Much can be learned quickly about Matt's reading problems by using a "naturalistic" testing approach. In a small group or a one-to-one setting, try having Matt read a high-interest article, such as an article about Nolan Ryan in *Sports Illustrated for Kids.* Matt puts incorrect emphasis on punctuation, reads word by word, and mispronounces "easy" words. He does love to try to read with excitement and interest, which has been a source of untimely amusement for his classmates. After reading a portion of an article, Matt usually has very limited retention of facts, events, or main idea.

**3.** Discuss whether the following student is remedial as a result of dyslexia, educational deficiency, or learning preference.

*Tutor's Description*

It is difficult to say just how Eric got through thirteen years of school with a reading ability of only the fifth grade. It seems as though Eric has not built up a sufficient vocabulary. He was able to read many words on the Slosson but had no understanding of what they meant. With a poor vocabulary, such as Eric's, it is difficult to get much comprehension. On the Informal Reading Inventory, his most frequent miscue was repetition by substitutions and insertions. Eric needs to develop a larger sight vocabulary, which could best be done through wide reading. Since he is, in most cases, able to get unknown words right because of his good use of word-analysis skills, it would be safe to assume that he would be saying these unknown words correctly and thus improve his word recognition ability. Although he made a number of repetitions, it was evident that he did so only to use the context of an unknown word or to correct a word that was miscalled. For this reason it would probably not be necessary to work on the repetitions as errors, as they are only symptomatic of other problems.

Eric has not done well in high school and his SAT score was too low for admission to college, but his skill in football was good enough that he was allowed entry to college with two letters of recommendation. He is required to attend study hall each night, Sunday though Friday, from 7:30 to 9:00 nine P.M. The football team has hired tutors in some subjects; however, Eric needs to have his own tutor to help him with each of his subjects. If Eric is to stay in college, he will need a great deal of help. He is failing all of his classes at the present time.

**4.** Mrs. Branch has sixth-grade remedial readers and eighth-grade honors readers in her class. Assuming Mrs. Branch has the projected three dyslexics that exist in most remedial classes, what seems to be her main behavioral problem?

*Interviewer's Description*

The biggest problem in teaching reading is the students themselves. Many of them want or crave my attention just to have someone to talk to. Their emotional needs are what interferes with their progress in reading.

The next biggest problem is having enough time to do things. I have tons of paperwork to grade, students who want my attention, and a need to develop and plan more activities. With an aide and two volunteer helpers, things still demand more time than I have in my day.

I would like to be able to find out about other reading tests and reading material on the market. I am limited to using what my school district wants. I also have no time to investigate other materials on my own initiative.

I give what time I can to listen to my students and devise activities for them. The aide and the two volunteers grade as much of the paperwork as they can handle. The school district itself is trying to decrease its class sizes.

The emotional needs of the students concern me the most. Whenever possible, I go from desk to desk to watch a student at work and to lay a hand on his or her shoulder with a squeeze and a smile. This often helps the student more than words.

By the time a student enters eighth grade, games and activities in reading are no longer appealing. Remedial readers in the eighth grade and above have usually given up on themselves unless someone can really work with them and get through to them. A Big Brother and a Big Sister Program could be used with great success to help these students.

# Teaching Activities:
# Objectives of Reading Instruction Programs

I. Developmental Reading
    A. The mechanics of reading
        1. Development of a large sight vocabulary
        2. Development of skill in identifying unfamiliar words, through the use of
            a. Context clues
            b. Phonics
            c. Structural analysis
            d. Dictionary
        3. Development of good eye-movement habits
        4. Development of good postural habits while reading
        5. Development of oral reading skills
            a. Phrasing and expression
            b. Volume, pitch, and enunciation
        6. Development of speed and fluency in silent reading
    B. Reading comprehension
        1. Acquisition of a rich, extensive, and accurate vocabulary
        2. Learning to interpret thought units of increasing size
        3. a. The phrase
            b. The sentence
            c. The paragraph
        4. Learning to read for specific purposes
            a. Finding and understanding main ideas
            b. Locating answers to specific questions
            c. Noting and recalling details
            d. Grasping and sequence of events
            e. Anticipating outcomes
            f. Following directions
            g. Grasping the author's plan and intent
            h. Evaluating and criticizing what one reads
            i. Remembering what one reads
        5. Coordinating rate with comprehension
II. Functional Reading
    A. Learning to locate information
        1. Mastering alphabetical order
        2. Using an index
        3. Using an encyclopedia
        4. Using other reference works
    B. Developing functional comprehension skills
        1. Learning specialized vocabularies
        2. Applying comprehension skills in content areas
            a. Learning to read textbooks in content subjects
            b. Learning to read independently in content subjects

# Reading Skills: Approximate Level of Introduction

**Word-Recognition Skills**

| | *Grade* |
|---|---|
| 1. Picture clues | 1 |
| 2. Contextual clues | 1 |
| 3. Configuration clues | 1 |
| 4. Phonetic analysis | |
|     Rhyming words | 1 |
|     Consonants | |
|         Initial consonants | 1 |
|         Final consonants | 1 |
|         Digraphs | 2 |
|         Initial blends | 2 |
|         Final blends | 2 |
|         Hard and soft sounds | 2 |
|         Silent letters | 3 |
|     Vowels | |
|         Long | 1 |
|         Short | 1 |
|         Double | 2 |
|         Similar sounds | 2 |
|         Modified by "r" | 2 |
|         Diphthongs | 2 |
| 5. Structural analysis | |
|     Root words | 1 |
|     Inflectional forms | 1 |
|     Contractions | 2 |
|     Compound words | 2 |
|     Possessives | 2 |
|     Prefixes | 3 |
|     Suffixes | 3 |
|     Syllables | 3 |

**Vocabulary-Building Skills**

| | |
|---|---|
| 1. Sight vocabulary | 1 |
| 2. Rhyming words | 1 |
| 3. Antonyms (opposite meanings) | 1 / 2 |
| 4. Synonyms (similar meanings) | 2 |
| 5. Homonyms (similar sound) | |
| 6. Developing and extending common, specialized, and technical vocabulary | 3 |
| 7. Extending word meaning through use of the dictionary | 3 |

**Comprehension Skills**

| | |
|---|---|
| 1. Forming sensory images | 1 |
| 2. Understanding a sentence is a unit of thought | 1 |
| 3. Rereading to recall | 1 |
| 4. Finding the main idea | 1 |
| 5. Relating ideas to experiences | 1 |
| 6. Anticipating endings | 1 |
| 7. Reading for information | 2 |
| 8. Making inferences | 2 |
| 9. Summarizing to remember | 2 |
| 10. Following directions | 2 |
| 11. Fact and fancy | 2 |
| 12. Contrasting and comparing | 2 |
| 13. Rereading to recall ideas or facts, or to verify | 2 |
| 14. Forming vivid impressions | 3 |
| 15. Recognizing cause and effect | 3 |
| 16. Paraphrasing stories or parts of stories | 3 |
| 17. Interpreting motives | 4 |
| 18. Anticipating outcomes through logical inference | 4 |
| 19. Selecting pertinent facts | 4 |
| 20. Rephrasing ideas for recall | 4 |
| 21. Generalizations from facts | 4 |
| 22. Implied ideas | 4 |
| 23. Evaluating content of selections | 4 |
| 24. Interpreting influences— ethical, moral, spiritual | 4 |

**Location Skills**

| | |
|---|---|
| 1. Using table of contents | 1 |
| 2. Title page | 2 |
| 3. Alphabet in sequence | 2 |
| 4. Picture dictionary | 2 |
| 5. Supplementary books to locate information | 2 |
| 6. Using maps and globes | 2 |
|     Direction-cardinal | 3 |
|     Symbols | 3 |

|  |  |  |
|---|---|---|
|  | Interpret simple legend | 3 |
|  | Color | 3 |
|  | Location | 3 |
|  | Grid | 4 |
|  | Scale | 3 |
|  | Use and interpretation | 4 |
| 7. | Using alphabet in sequential and random order | 3 |
| 8. | Locating paragraphs | 3 |
| 9. | Skimming for key words | 3 |
| 10. | Using word books | 3 |
| 11. | Index | 3 |
| 12. | Sources to locate information | |
|  | Glossary | 4 |
|  | Dictionary | 4 |
|  | Encyclopedia | 4 |
|  | Charts and graphs, time lines | 4 |
| 13. | Dictionary skills | |
|  | Alphabetizing | 4 |
|  | Guide words | 4 |
|  | Definition selection | 4 |
|  | Syllables and accent marks | 4 |
|  | Long and short diacritical marks | 4 |
| 14. | Using library file cards Simple Dewey Decimal system | 4 |
| 15. | Skimming for key words and main ideas | 4 |

## Organizational Skills

|  |  |  |
|---|---|---|
| 1. | Telling story in sequence | 1 |
| 2. | Following sequence of directions | 1 |
| 3. | Classify words into categories | 2 |
| 4. | Arranging sentences in logical order | 2 |
| 5. | Summarizing | 2 |
| 6. | Organizing material with teacher | 2 |
| 7. | Story sequence | 2 |
| 8. | Main idea of paragraph | 3 |
| 9. | Simple outlining with teacher | 3 |
| 10. | Summarizing a story or parts of stories | 3 |
| 11. | Classifying into like categories | 3 |
| 12. | Recalling time sequence in a story | 4 |
| 13. | Finding the main topic of paragraphs | 4 |
| 14. | Beginning outlining—two and three headings | 4 |
| 15. | Summarizing material read | 4 |

## Evaluation Skills

*Retention or Study Skills*

|  |  |  |
|---|---|---|
| 1. | SQ3R or PQRST | 4 |

# Dyslexia Behavioral Checklist

*Introduction*

This handout has behaviors listed that can be noted through observation of a student socially and those behaviors related to school and other classroom activities. A list of information relevant from other school sources and the family would help in observing and gathering data on the student.

   This instrument was not prepared to be used as a diagnostic instrument of dyslexia. It is designed to serve as a basis whereby a decision would be made as to whether a student should be referred for further testing to ascertain his or her problem toward learning.

   It is important to remember that dyslexic symptoms occur in various degrees and are not all present at any given one time. One reversal does not mean dyslexia. A pattern of errors is important to establish before any judgments are made. The instrument should be administered, the errors recorded, and the patterns formed and described. This information should next go to the school counselor. A decision is then made as to whether further testing is necessary.

*School and Family Information*

1. IQ test scores
2. Results of reading achievement tests and the findings on an infomal reading inventory
3. Results of past remedial reading programs
4. Results of family history data (evidence indicates that dyslexia is hereditary)

*Observable Behaviors*

1. General immaturity.
2. Emotional problems; may have a low self-concept.
3. Sensory modalities show no impairment.
4. Tends to ambidextrous or mixed in motor preference. There also may be a lack of motor coordination.
5. Confusion in judgment of time, seasons, and months of the year.
6. Confusion of direction, size, and distance.
7. Difficulty in articulation and poor oral vocabulary when speaking.

*Observable Behaviors in School Work*

1. Inability to pronounce an unfamiliar word with a tendency to guess wildly at its phonetic structure. Difficulty in associating the sounds with the visual symbols of letters. May be seen in reading as well as spelling.

2. Failure to realize the differences between words that are somewhat similar in spelling or in sound (example: *on* and *no*).
3. Unable to detect the difference in the auditory properties of words or letters.
4. Difficulty in keeping track of the correct place while reading.
5. Unable to switch accurately or smoothly from the extreme right-hand point of one line of print to the beginning of the next line on the left.
6. Lip movement and subdued vocalizing of sounds while attempting to read silently.
7. Failure to read with complete understanding.
8. Incorrect pronunciation of vowels (example: *bag* for *bug*). Incorrect pronunciation of consonants (example: *bold* for *bolt*).
9. Rotations of letters, which constitute an important error and may entail mirror-opposite letters. (example: *did* for *bid* and *dad* for *bad*). Whole words may be reversed (example: *was* instead of *saw*). Short sequences of words may be read in the wrong order (example: *did he* for *he did*).
10. Inappropriate phonemes may be interpolated (example: *trick* instead of *tick*), or phonemes may be dropped (example: *tick* instead of *trick*).
11. Substitutes one word for another (example: *was* for *lived; the* for *an; this* for *that; here* for *there*).
12. Words may be repeated in a persistent manner (example: *the cat the cat*).
13. Words, inappropriate or otherwise, may be added (example: *once upon a time* may become *here was for once* or *there was*).
14. Omission of one or several words (example: *A dog* instead of *A fierce dog*).
15. Faulty placement of stress on polysyllabic words, especially as the student gets older.

*Handwriting*

1. Messy handwriting.
2. Many words illegible.
3. Malalignment.
4. Intrusion of block letters or capitals into the middle of a word.
5. Omissions or repetitions of words and letters.
6. Rotation of letters.
7. Odd punctuation marks.
8. Misspellings that do not occur in partial or complete reversal of groups of letters (example: *not* could be spelled as *ont, ton,* or *tno*).

9. Incorrect positioning as related to rotation (example: E = ш; N = ƨ; S = ω).

10. Unusual manner of joining adjacent letters. Linkages may be either too short or too long. One letter may fuse with the next to form a strange merger, difficult to identify out of context.

11. Serial confusion is present, rather than simple reversal. When writing numbers with many digits from dictation, confusion results as to the correct placement of commas.

# WISC-R Intelligence
# Test Which is Frequently Used to Identify LD and/or Dyslexics

# WISC-R RECORD FORM

Wechsler Intelligence Scale
for Children–Revised

NAME _____ SEX _____

ADDRESS _____

PARENT'S NAME _____

PLACE OF TESTING _____

REFERRED BY _____

## TABLE OF SCALED SCORE EQUIVALENTS*

| Scaled Score | Information | Digit Span | Vocabulary | Arithmetic | Comprehension | Similarities | Picture Completion | Picture Arrangement | Block Design | Object Assembly | Digit Symbol | Scaled Score |
|---|---|---|---|---|---|---|---|---|---|---|---|---|
| 19 | — | 28 | 70 | — | 32 | — | — | — | 51 | — | 93 | 19 |
| 18 | 29 | 27 | 69 | — | 31 | 28 | — | — | — | 41 | 91-92 | 18 |
| 17 | — | 26 | 68 | 19 | — | — | 20 | 20 | 50 | — | 89-90 | 17 |
| 16 | 28 | 25 | 66-67 | — | 30 | 27 | — | — | 49 | 40 | 84-88 | 16 |
| 15 | 27 | 24 | 65 | 18 | 29 | 26 | — | 19 | 47-48 | 39 | 79-83 | 15 |
| 14 | 26 | 22-23 | 63-64 | 17 | 27-28 | 25 | 19 | — | 44-46 | 38 | 75-78 | 14 |
| 13 | 25 | 20-21 | 60-62 | 16 | 26 | 24 | — | 18 | 42-43 | 37 | 70-74 | 13 |
| 12 | 23-24 | 18-19 | 55-59 | 15 | 25 | 23 | 18 | 17 | 38-41 | 35-36 | 66-69 | 12 |
| 11 | 22 | 17 | 52-54 | 13-14 | 23-24 | 22 | 17 | 15-16 | 35-37 | 34 | 62-65 | 11 |
| 10 | 19-21 | 15-16 | 47-51 | 12 | 21-22 | 20-21 | 16 | 14 | 31-34 | 32-33 | 57-61 | 10 |
| 9 | 17-18 | 14 | 43-46 | 11 | 19-20 | 18-19 | 15 | 13 | 27-30 | 30-31 | 53-56 | 9 |
| 8 | 15-16 | 12-13 | 37-42 | 10 | 17-18 | 16-17 | 14 | 11-12 | 23-26 | 28-29 | 48-52 | 8 |
| 7 | 13-14 | 11 | 29-36 | 8-9 | 14-16 | 14-15 | 13 | 8-10 | 20-22 | 24-27 | 44-47 | 7 |
| 6 | 9-12 | 9-10 | 20-28 | 6-7 | 11-13 | 11-13 | 11-12 | 5-7 | 14-19 | 21-23 | 37-43 | 6 |
| 5 | 6-8 | 8 | 14-19 | 5 | 8-10 | 7-10 | 8-10 | 3-4 | 8-13 | 16-20 | 30-36 | 5 |
| 4 | 5 | 7 | 11-13 | 4 | 6-7 | 5-6 | 5-7 | 2 | 3-7 | 13-15 | 23-29 | 4 |
| 3 | 4 | 6 | 9-10 | 3 | 4-5 | 2-4 | 3-4 | — | 2 | 9-12 | 16-22 | 3 |
| 2 | 3 | 3-5 | 6-8 | 1-2 | 2-3 | 1 | 2 | 1 | 1 | 6-8 | 8-15 | 2 |
| 1 | 0-2 | 0-2 | 0-5 | 0 | 0-1 | 0 | 0-1 | 0 | 0 | 0-5 | 0-7 | 1 |

(RAW SCORE — VERBAL TESTS: Information, Digit Span, Vocabulary, Arithmetic, Comprehension, Similarities; PERFORMANCE TESTS: Picture Completion, Picture Arrangement, Block Design, Object Assembly, Digit Symbol)

*Clinicians who wish to draw a profile may do so by locating the subject's raw scores on the table above and drawing a line to connect them. See Chapter 4 in the Manual for a discussion of the significance of differences between scores on the tests.

|  | Year | Month | Day |
|---|---|---|---|
| Date Tested | ____ | ____ | ____ |
| Date of Birth | ____ | ____ | ____ |
| Age | ____ | ____ | ____ |

### SUMMARY

|  | Raw Score | Scaled Score |
|---|---|---|
| **VERBAL TESTS** | | |
| Information | ____ | ____ |
| Digit Span | ____ | ____ |
| Vocabulary | ____ | ____ |
| Arithmetic | ____ | ____ |
| Comprehension | ____ | ____ |
| Similarities | ____ | ____ |
| **Verbal Score** | | ____ |
| **PERFORMANCE TESTS** | | |
| Picture Completion | ____ | ____ |
| Picture Arrangement | ____ | ____ |
| Block Design | ____ | ____ |
| Object Assembly | ____ | ____ |
| Digit Symbol | ____ | ____ |
| **Performance Score** | | ____ |

|  | Sum of Scaled Scores | IQ |
|---|---|---|
| VERBAL | ____ | ____ |
| PERFORMANCE | ____ | ____ |
| FULL SCALE | ____ | ____ |

THE PSYCHOLOGICAL CORPORATION
HARCOURT BRACE JOVANOVICH, INC.

9-991829

# Sample Remediation Activities

*Grounding**

Focusing the child's attention on a reading page is called grounding. Grounding to the reading pages before reading silently or orally allows children to skim the pages, focus visually on words, and become familiar with material on the pages before they read. Grounding can be done by:

1. Discussing the picture:
   a. What's happening?
   b. What time of day is it?
   c. What will happen next?
   d. How do you feel?
   e. What colors do you see?
   f. How many children do you see?
2. Asking the children to quickly find:
   a. A specific word.
   b. A period.
   c. A question mark.
   d. The first word on the page.
   e. The last word on the page.
3. Asking the children to *quickly* point to a word that:
   a. Begins with the sound of _____ .
   b. Ends with the sound of _____ .
   c. Means _____ .
   d. Means the opposite of _____ .
   e. Is the name of a girl, boy, animal, etc.
   f. Is a color word.
   g. Tells what time of day it is.
   h. Tells how the _____ feel.
4. Asking the children to read orally.

*Multiple Word Meanings*

On index cards write words with multiple meanings. On other index cards write definitions or illustrate the words with pictures. Give several word cards to the student. Have him or her pronounce each word. Then spread the cards out in front of the student. Begin reading the meanings or describing the pictures for one of the words. When the student knows which word you are defining, he or she should say the word aloud and show you the corresponding picture card. Continue until all words and meanings are matched. Repeat for review. This game may also be played in small groups. This is a good activity for visual learners.

---

* Reprinted from *Unicorns Are Real* by B. Vitale © 1986 B. L. Winch and Associates/ Jalmar Press. Used with permission from B. L. Winch/Jalmar Press.

## Mind Maps

Initial concepts are jotted around a central focus. The mind map (also called semantic map or graphic organizer) is a vocabulary relationship pattern which allows additional information to be easily inserted. The pattern should include pictures and symbols as well as words.

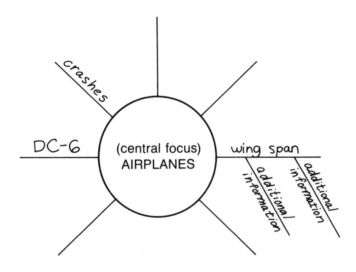

## Story Maps

Story maps help students more clearly perceive the organization of their reading material. They serve several functions; for example, they may be a prereading activity to organize known information, they may be used as a visual device for summarizing, and they may be a review of story structure. Also see page 149.

## Predicting with Visual Cues

Predict what the people in the following cartoons are saying.

# CHAPTER NINE

# *Television, Computers, and Reading Instruction*

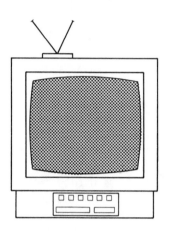

- Impact on Students

- Programs

- Activities for Classroom

## Television and Reading Instruction

T. S. Eliot explained the splintered imagery in his writing as an attempt to bring the various experiences in western culture into a unified vision. He obviously wrote before television. Even at the time of Eliot's death in 1965, schools were still responsible for the education of children in those areas not under the jurisdiction of the family or church. Television was controlled with evening segments called family viewing time. "The Ed Sullivan Variety Show," "The Ted Mack Hour," "Leave It to Beaver," "The Mickey Mouse Club," "The Wonderful World of Disney," "Lassie," "Dr. Hudson's Secret Journal," and "Topper" were aired between 6:00–8:00 P.M. before most children went to bed. In the 1990s, television is deregulated and it is difficult to find a show during that same time period that portrays average family life, much less a show that is suitable for family viewing.

### *Effects of television on children*

Statistics show that the impact television has on children is great. Television has become the second parent and perhaps the first educator. In Edward Palmer's (1988) *Television and America's Children: A Crisis of Neglect,* television is cited as a babysitter for millions of children. It is on an average of eight hours a day in most homes, and by the time an 18-year-old graduates from high school, he or she has spent more time in front of a TV than in school. For teenagers, time spent watching TV is second only to sleeping. A Nielsen survey (1979) showed that TV is even replacing sleeping, in that nearly 3 million children ages 6–11 were found to be still watching TV between 10:00 and 11:00 P.M. About 380,000 of these watch past midnight. How many of these homes have cable and R-rated shows? Whatever the content, the process of watching TV promotes passivism and conspicuous consumerism, and bombards youngsters with visual images that control their thinking. Social scientists say that viewers are conditioned to sequences of 30-minute gratification and many have troubled interpersonal relationships in life outside TV. Vance Packard (1983) is uneasy with children having unsupervised access to television for the following reasons:

> I would be concerned that TV was turning my children into materialistic cynics, distrustful of adults. The typical youngster finishing high school has been the target of several thousand hours of commercials on TV. This selling barrage does more than influence children's brand preferences. It helps shape their concept of life.
>
> I would wonder whether heavy viewing was making my children passive and less imaginative. Preschool kids play less if they are heavy viewers and that is bad. Play is important for growing children. It helps stretch their imaginations and ease anxieties. Interacting with playmates not only improves verbal skills but also teaches children how to have arguments and still be friends. I'd hate to have kids without those talents. (Packard, 1983)

Television has been accused of raising the crime rate, dropping students' test scores, crippling the imagination, undermining national literacy, and layering American homes with an attention-numbing narcotic. TV has definitely contributed to the desensitization of children to violence and provided models of violent behavior for high-risk children and adults. For example, NBC telecasted "Doomsday Flight," ignoring pleas by airline pilots not to do so. A made-for-TV special, it represented a factual extortion attempt by bomb threat against an airliner in flight. After the show, the Federal Aviation Agency recorded a dramatic increase in phone-in bomb threats to airlines. The connection between television and violence has been made for adults and children.

The connection to television and reading has also been made. When children are watching TV, they could be doing other things, including reading and homework. For most children, the more TV they watch, the worse they do in school. Research has identified three hours of daily viewing as the maximum number of hours before schoolwork suffers. Benefits have also been established for children with limited experiences whose reading comprehension improves with up to three hours of TV viewing, as it builds background that helps in understanding reading passages.

The motivation for programming today is money. A minute of

network prime-time advertising during what used to be known as "family viewing hours" could pay the salary of seven or eight teachers for a whole year. If watching 9,230 scenes of sexual contact a year (89 percent occurring outside marriage) encourages viewers to watch TV, an increase in sexual scenes is guaranteed. Not only is TV providing models and shaping lifelong habits and behavior in children but it has control over the images that shape thinking. Little girls and boys must have designer jeans, which they equate with personal excellence. Shopping with 2-year-olds has become an experience in beginning reading when they beg for products they have seen advertised on cartoons. As recommended in *Advertising Age* (1982), "If you truly want big sales, use the child as your assistant salesman. He sells, he nags, until he breaks down the resistance of his mother or father."

When teaching in public schools, video playback machines and films are the rewards. Teachers may show a video of the book they have assigned to students, or, better yet, let the students make their own videos. With the possible exception of "Sesame Street" and some educational television, the bulk of students' viewing time is spent watching commercially popular programs that aim only to entertain. Children regard TV primarily as an entertainment medium and books as an information-gathering medium. Herein lies the secret for education. No school is going to be able to turn off the economic driving force of commercial television. No school is going to be able to control television watching behavior that is the domain of the home. But children do learn images of our society, not from T. S. Eliot's collage of written images but from television. To follow Iyer's (1990) logic, TV requires a different literacy.

> Unlike books, television tells us when to stop and think. The flow of messages from the instant it is turned on fills every niche in our consciousness, crowding out knowledge and understanding. Although knowledge is steady and cumulative, information is random and miscellaneous. If today's computer-literate young truly do have the capacity to process images faster than their parents, they enjoy an unparalleled opportunity—as long as they learn to process words as well. They could become the first generation in history to be bilingual, in this sense fluent on screen as well as off. (Iyer, 1990)

### What can teachers do with television in the classroom?

If media changes in children's lives cannot be controlled by teachers, what is their role regarding literacy or reading and utilizing the medium in the classroom? The relationship is clear. Teachers must use television to unify the vision of our country and not to have it shape the passive consciousness of our young.

An uncritical acceptance of the stereotypes presented on most TV series has many people worried that children are also receiving subtle attitudes about the proper roles of men and women in our society. A more varied portrayal of characters can occur only if the viewing public demands it. This will happen only if children learn to view TV with a critical eye and make their criticisms known to the television industry. By seeing the content of commercially popular TV shows as the material for critical reading and writing skills, teachers may be performing a social service more valuable than any other they could make. When analyzing the characters on TV shows, women are generally presented as passive and governed by emotion. For the most part, the elderly are seen as unhappy, and blacks and minorities continue to be stereotyped. One might ask why Chung Lee on "Falcon Crest" was not elevated to a more interesting character in the 10 years that the show aired.

Stereotyping is also communicated to other countries. The author lived in Egypt from 1980 to 1983. The only American television shows allowed on Egyptian television were "Little House on the Prairie" and "Dallas." These two shows formed the Egyptian perspective of what America was like—good and honest in the past with a solid family life, and greedy, selfish, and sexual (even with edited versions with all kisses taken out) in the present. What is lacking in Egypt and in our schools is the use of TV as a vehicle for teaching critical thinking about the meaning of what the media characterizes in American life.

Television can become a motivating bridge between entertainment and learning. Giving a TV assignment might be interpreted as more enjoyable because entertainment is associated with the medium. TV can also provide reinforcement for classroom instruction. Some newspapers print the scripts of TV specials so students can study them in class and then watch the show. Students creating their own videotapes of commercials, interview shows, or documentaries can be extension activities and motivational for those students who find school boring.

At Oxford Hills High School in South Paris, Maine, Schlich (1973) reports that hard-core, remedial students were trained to use TV videotape equipment and told to use their knowledge of commercial TV programs to create their own programs. They were encouraged to use the popular formats of the soap opera and situation comedy for the production of written scripts, cue cards, and other written studio directions. No attempt was made to lead them to books, but Schlich reports that the project soon became so successful that students were voluntarily checking out books in order to find additional information for the production of their program scripts. Results showed an average gain of one full year on the Metropolitan Achievement Test for the TV group, and their social skills were also improved. These students, who had developed a definite distaste for reading prior to the experiment, were soon readily reading of their own accord. This study demonstrates how it is possible to transfer students' enthusiasm for one medium to another because of the motivational involvement in the project of producing their own shows.

When teachers consider the impact all the hours of TV watching must have on children, they can utilize all the audio and visual experiences into motivational class assignments. Hamilton's (1975) study of suburban seventh-graders also found that TV programs motivate reading. These junior high school students became avid readers when supplied with a steady diet of "TV tie-ins," which are books with a story line adapted from an original commercial TV program. These books far surpassed the traditional children's classics in popularity, and in the traditionally low-reading categories of boys, low IQ students, and low socioeconomic students, the preference was even more dramatic. Dalzell (1976) reported similar results in a Philadelphia TV-script-reading program.

By using the actual scripts from popular programs as primary reading materials, Schlich (1973) was able to raise his students' reading scores on standardized reading achievement tests by an average of a year and a half. Some remedial high school students were able to gain two or three grade levels in one year of the program. The scripts-reading program has since spread to dozens of cities and its potential is limited only by the lack of imagination of the local leaders called on to support the program. These programs channel the incidental learning that results from watching commercial TV and the motivation associated with entertainment rather than education. This motivation could also be extended to instructional TV and probably accounts for some of the appeal computers have for students.

Television in the schools has also come to the attention of industry. For example, in Midland, Texas, Whittle Corporation has provided the school system with a fixed satellite dish programmed into Channel One. They provided all of the cabling for the schools and 19-inch TVs for all sixth- through twelfth-grade classrooms. In exchange, 92 percent of the students are expected to watch Channel One everyday, which has 10 minutes of current news and 2 minutes of commericals made especially for adolescents. The news can be previewed before it is released to the school. Some of the schools are using the televisions for school announcements in addition to news. A jack on the monitor allows classes to select programs relevant to a particular subject area. Two other channels, one with educational programs and one for staff in-service programs, are a part of this delivery system.

However, some states, including California and New York, have banned Channel One in the classroom in response to the commercials. Whatever the choice of the school district, commercial TV has started to enter the classroom. Some 12,000 schools have signed up for CNN Newsroom, a daily 15-minute commercial-free newscast from Ted Turner's Cable News Network. The Discovery Channel also has a new program called "Assignment Discovery" and the Christian Science Monitor has "World Classroom" with ad-free services (Charren, 1990).

And finally, television can be used to teach language and reading skills. Gattegno (1964) saw the reluctance of teachers to use TV in the classroom as one of different cultures stressing different sorts of powers of the senses, different modes of processing information. Print-oriented teachers may lack sufficient appreciation of TV's swift integration of impressions to feel confident enough to use the medium as a teaching tool. Becker (1972) urges teachers to watch popular commercial programs that their students watch with the aim of tying some aspect of these programs to the instructional program. The popular educational consideration is satisfied when teachers take students from where they are in viewing to understanding new material, and thus proceed from the known to the unknown.

Borton (1971) took this idea even further with a dual audio TV system that broadcasts a second audio track to be listened to during commercial breaks and directly after the program. Teachers may add clarification and supplementary information to the concepts that are never fully explained in the course of most commercial programs. By clarifying key vocabulary and concepts and by suggesting connection to similar content in books, teachers can increase the depth of understanding that children have about the things they see on TV.

Critical thinking cannot occur about shows or stereotyping if the flow of action is not in some way slowed and made understandable to children. Such a system of additional explanatory information is necessary if children are to learn how to evaluate critically the material that they encounter daily on TV. Borton (1971) sees little learning coming from TV watching because the viewers have not been taught to translate this information into their own terms of how to determine how or if it can be of use to their lives. It all seems to rush over them like a rapid tide. A common critique voiced by many teachers is a fear that the repetitive, instantaneous nature of TV has led to an uncritical, passive acceptance by youngsters of whatever is presented on commercial channels. Teachers must take responsibility for some of their students' responses to TV as a part of their education. E. B. White wrote in 1938:

> I believe television is going to be the test of the modern world. And that in this new opportunity to see beyond the range of our vision we shall discover either a new and unbearable disturbance of the general peace or a saving radiance in the sky. (White, 1977)

### Techniques for developing reading skills with television

Developing a gradual improvement of the ability of children to choose to watch programs of higher educational or aesthetic value can very efficiently fit with the objectives of educational programs. The following activities are suggested for classroom use because they will take care of discipline problems that occur when students cannot read the book. Remedial readers can participate in whole-class instruction with the TV. Furthermore, if students are remedial or ESL and must work on their own, these critical thinking reading activities (and those in the Teaching Activities section) can be used as independent assignments. A teacher can use these activities with any TV program shown in class, in the library or media center, or at home. Additional TV resources for remedial and "defined minimum" students have been identified by the Office of Instructional Technology in South Carolina.

**Evaluation Skills.** To develop evaluation skills it is necessary to establish some means of involving the students in the actual process of critically thinking about something that is important to them. Students who show an interest in television shows can be urged to join a "TV Club." This group would be primarily interested in two objectives—reviewing TV shows with a critical eye and alerting students and parents to upcoming programs of high educational or aesthetic value. A weekly newsletter or a daily or weekly announcement would serve as a means of communication for this group. The TV Club could also discuss upcoming weekend shows during class time on Friday. Club members could also do some research about special movies or programs. Both technical and biographical aspects of programming could be investigated.

Another group of activities would be to compile the results from in-school opinion surveys about TV viewing habits or popularity ratings of current commercial prime-time shows. The TV Club could then draw conclusions from the data and report it to interested groups—the students, PTA, or television networks. The conclusions could be distributed to classrooms for use in writing activities.

A "TV Review Board" could be staffed with students who establish a set of criteria for rating TV shows. Since TV is deregulated, the students could assume the role abandoned by the federal government. They could develop an informal guide or questionnaire for student use. The questions could include evaluation of whether the plot and the characters were believable when compared to people and events students know. Such criteria could include a checklist for classifying shows according to originality, believability, historical accuracy, and bias of presentation.

**Analysis Skills.** For evaluation to be worthwhile, students need to practice analyzing types of TV programs to determine the techniques that constitute popular formats. Activities in story-elements analysis could easily fit into language arts, reading, and English objectives at any level above fourth grade. Using a videotaped half-hour segment of "Star Trek," for example, the teacher could ask students to list elements such as camera angles, makeup techniques, or costuming differences, or even to compare the differences between the old TV shows and movie releases about the *Enterprise*. This type of analysis of parts could be used with any show. Students would learn that TV is a business that uses certain plot formulas in an endless number of variations.

Character analysis can also be useful. The actions of talk-show hosts could be examined to determine the hosts' values and how they influence their ways of interviewing. The consistency of actions could be charted in different situations. Awkward situations could be compared and contrasted with how friends, parents, or the students themselves would deal with similar events. Such qualities as consistency and purposefulness could be discussed by using these TV personalities as introductory aids to the task of leading students to read, write, and think about their own values.

Another useful analysis activity would be the comparison of differences in characters as they are portrayed in books and on TV. Students could then think about the different impact that characters have on students in the two different media. By noticing additions, deletions, or shifts in emphasis, children can begin to see that each medium uses a different approach but is able to present information in valid and emotionally satisfying manners. The literary treatment of a TV show could be read after the students see the show, which will demonstrate the more detailed perspective available in books. Students could also be encouraged to read critiques on shows to understand differing viewpoints on the same experience. Students might then write their own critiques of the show.

**Literal Skills.**    Television lends itself to developing students' literal comprehension skills. One area of activity is vocabulary acquisition. Word banks could be the basis for comparison, contrast, sequencing, classification, and interpretation activities. One type would be words that are most commonly heard on certain types of shows. A separate list of specialized words for detective, medical, science fiction, and sport shows could be compiled by class members who watch these shows. Another approach would be to have students write down all the words they do not know that are used in a certain TV show. Parents and siblings could get involved in helping the student with this homework assignment.

With vocabulary skills encouraged, students could then begin to practice writing and thinking skills that incorporate a number of interpretation and application skills. Prediction skills could be developed by providing incomplete plots and allowing the class to work in groups to see who can create the most plausible ending. Writing short, creative scripts based on the premise of characters from different shows meeting and interacting would involve the use of interpretive and synthesis skills.

Many games could be modeled after TV game shows. "Wheel of Fortune" was so popular with viewers in Florida that the evening news had to be moved when it was in conflict with the show. Like "Wheel of Fortune," many games could be made in which the student has to match characters to vocabulary lists or to spell words learned on TV. Playing "Jeopardy" even raised SAT scores of students when a class was developed to improve vocabulary (Cochran & Montanado, 1978).

These various activities allude to the many possibilities that TV presents to teachers. For remedial students, such activities could form the bulk of the program, for it has been demonstrated that students who are in remedial classes spend more time watching TV than other group of students. For this reason, TV will have a naturally high motivational potential for many poor readers. Using TV as the content to develop thinking skills seems to be one way to lead these students to reading and books. Possibly using two media in conjunction with each other will be useful for students who have rejected reading but have not rejected the latest soap opera or cops-and-robbers show. The ultimate goal of children to read books must first involve a detour through TV. Learning to obtain meaning from TV is learning to read visual imagery and visual manipulation. To quote Proefriedt, a TV educator,

> For teachers to ignore the electronic acculturation of America is to turn over our hopes for a better quality of life for our people to those who are much more interested in manipulation for personal gain than education. (Proefriedt, 1978)

### Summary

Television has been a factor in the development of passive and socially incompetent children. TV addicts are bombarded with commercial and stereotypical images, violence, and aggression. The 30-minute segments of many programs teach children that most problems can be resolved in a short period of time and reduce their tolerance to frustration of any duration. Television is used by parents as babysitters, aiding in the neglect of children. But more importantly, the process of watching thousands of hours of programming establishes lifelong habits of immediate gratification, desensitization to violence, and passivity.

Teachers must move into the educational vacuum where incidental but not direct instruction takes place. A number of activities have been described that could be used for direct instruction in any classroom. An additional 22 activities follow in the Teaching Activities at the end of the chapter.

# Computers and Reading Instruction

Computers, like television, have become an influence in children's lives and promise to be even more of an influence in their futures. As computers become more intrusive in the curriculum, the role of the teacher will change from pedagogic to management; from information disseminator to facilitator of students' learning at an individualized pace; from designer of curriculum to provider of situations where subject matter is applied, synthesized, analyzed, and evaluated. The computer will not replace the teacher but some will feel uncomfortable as they find their present functions redefined.

It is exciting to be at the forefront of the computer revolution—learning new skills and new vocabularies, using both humanistic and mechanistic approaches to reach students, finding better ways to be more efficient and enabling teachers to spend more time with students (Darter, 1990). But many teachers are novices when they encounter something very new and very different. As MecKlenburger (1989) states, "Unfamiliar tools and techniques require careful, thorough, sensitive, timely and ongoing staff development."

### GOALS OF EDUCATION

*Reprinted with permission from Copley News Service.*

As novices, teachers must expect that first encounters with computers will mean shock then confusion—confusion about capabilities and roles, and confusion about the alien experts. Attempts at control will then occur. Resources such as others' ideas and examples will be tapped. If teachers are successful at tapping into these available resources and are able to exert control over this strange and alien technology, the teachers will, in all likelihood, continue to willingly allow themselves to be further socialized into this new culture. If they fail to gain control because they do not understand or feel self-images are being diminished, they will get angry, withdraw, and become cultural dropouts (Hass, 1990). Change can be difficult to experience. The excitement will diminish if change is not approached in the right manner.

When teachers attempt to get information about the best program or equipment from computer experts, they are likely to encounter people interested in development. Experts are always aware that something much better than what is currently on the market is coming in a few months that will be twice as good and half as expensive. And when the program or equipment comes, the "bugs" have not been worked out of it. Thus, both the people in the computer field and those attempting to use its products are in a continual state of updating, waiting, and debugging. At some point, educators have to begin shaping the educational software field in the same effective fashion as the producers of computer games have done. The purpose of this section is to give teachers an understanding of terminology and some practical considerations necessary for using computers in the content classroom.

Computer terminology most frequently heard relates to computer-assisted instruction (CAI), computer-managed instruction (CMI), and record-keeping and writing functions. Each major heading has subareas with related terminology.

1. Computer-assisted instruction (CAI), which is directly instructional:
   a. Tutorial programs that do the actual teaching and assume the role of the teacher in presenting material for students to learn
   b. Problem solving (like LOGO) that allows the student not only to solve problems but to generate and define problems to be solved
   c. Educational games that are designed to be fun as well as to encourage appropriate learning
   d. Drill and practice activities that provide the equivalent of workbook and homework activities to follow up instruction by tutorials or teachers
2. Computer-managed instruction (CMI), which deals with the management of instructional activities by linking them together, monitoring at single or groups of computer stations:
   a. Diagnostic packages that identify a student's strengths and weaknesses in a particular content area and then prescribe instructional activities
   b. Programs that allow teachers to monitor all student work at the same time
3. Record keeping and writing functions:
   a. Grade tabulation and recording packages
   b. Attendance programs
   c. Writing packages (word processing)
   d. Programs that provide writing capabilities for teachers and students for papers, letters, study guides, graphics, and certificates
   e. Authoring programs where teachers can write their own tests, tutorials, and simple instructional sequences; monitor and track children's performances; administer pre- and posttests; grade and correct tests automatically

Once the terminology is familiar, teachers must then determine where and how they want to use computers in the classroom. Most teachers say they do not use them because of a lack of knowledge or in-services, a lack of funding for computers, and a low quantity and quality of available educational programs. The lack of availability of computers exists in spite of the more than 1.2 million computers in U.S. schools in 1989 and the estimates that computers are installed in 96 percent of all public schools (with the most rapid increase in elementary and special education classrooms) (Watkins, 1989). Furthermore, computers are less likely to be found in school districts with lower socioeconomic bases. If and when teachers have access to a computer, they must answer the following questions:

**1.** How can I be sure that computers can be used to improve student learning?

**2.** How can computer programs be integrated into existing content and reading programs?

**3.** Do I agree with criticisms of using computers in the classroom?

Teachers know how to ask these questions but often the criticism of computers and the lack of understanding of answers given in technical terminology makes teachers' transition to computer use difficult. Some of the most frequent teacher concerns are answered below.

### How can I be sure that computers can be used to improve student learning?

Developmental psychologists believe learning is a result of interaction with the environment. In that case, the computer forces an interaction that can maximize student attention, present material in new ways, provide immediate feedback, and be infinitely patient. The environment is much more invigorated when motor and sensory functions of students are actively engaged by computers (Darter & Phelps, 1990; Dees, 1990). Computers demand interaction and thus become the environment in which the student experiences learning.

Behavioral psychologists believe that learning is taught by the environment in a reward-punishment format. Habit hierarchies are developed through the reinforcement of small increments. Drill-and-practice computer programs follow this learning theory. The student works with small increments or skills one step at a time. Most computer programs are of this type, as it is the easiest to program and therefore less expensive to produce (Snyder & Palmer, 1986; Futrell & Geisert, 1984, Kinzer, 1986). For example, these programs can help beginning readers by teaching letters and letter/sound relationships. Most programs require that students identify pictures, then letters, and then match them up. Features can be added to drill-and-practice programs like graphics, color, animation, and speech synthesizers. The benefit of these programs is that they provide immediate feedback or reward to the student on the correctness of answers, which is not physically possible for teachers without computer-assisted instruction.

Learning theory aside, research has consistently indicated that students who are actively involved in the reading process do better in reading improvement (Cronin & Hines, 1990; Darter & Phelps, 1990). For example, Reitsma (1988) investigated reading achievement on three groups: a guided reading group, a listening-while-reading-along group which had a tape of a story that they followed in their text, and an independent reading with computer assistance. The independent computer group and the guided reading group achieved well. Students were actively engaged in reading in both methods. Hassel (1987) found that students generally learn more efficiently and spend more time on computer-assisted lessons and reported an increase in interest and motivation with CAI.

Computers are a motivational tool that supports learning. Just as the television was introduced for private home use and moved into the classroom as an instructional medium, so too has the computer. It is a medium of instruction that can be used to aid in producing a motivational and risk-free environment.

The use of graphics and sound to present instruction sustains students' interest and enriches the quality of their task involvement, making the computer environment motivating for young children. Dees (1990) found that computers are easily accepted by older children because they allow also students to be in control and proceed at their own rate. With the objectivity of the computer, students can learn without the judgments and criticisms that may come from interactions with adults or peers. "A computer does not have built-in prejudices and can determine appropriate instruction without worrying if the student is ahead or behind" (Bitter, 1989). The control and immediate feedback of successes help students to form more positive self-concepts about themselves and their ability to learn.

### How can computer programs be integrated into existing content and reading programs?

Integrating computers into the existing curriculum is certainly a concern for teachers. As long ago as 1987, there were 608 reading and 736 language arts programs (Balajthy, 1987). How to survey all of these programs and then select the one that is most functional in a specific classroom is a challenge. Furthermore, those people who assist teachers in selecting programs are frequently computer instructors provided by the business community. Working in business and industry, it is possible that many have not been in the classroom for years. Teachers who are becoming socialized into computer terminology and technology are not likely to read trade journals that review educational software as a second source of program selection. In short, teachers trying to determine which programs to use often follow the advice of those who conduct in-services and who are representatives of the computer industry. Furthermore, the elevation of computer teachers to status positions alienates classroom teachers from computers by making them feel ignorant (Hass, 1990).

Still, the question of integration remains. The first issue is the changing role of the teacher in CAI. Teachers want to select a program that identifies their responsibilities. This may be an inappropriate consideration because whatever the program, the teachers' function becomes that of manager and integrator rather than an information disseminator. A description of a philosophy for teacher-student-computer program integration comes from Damarin (1986):

> The computer may help students become literate, but the teacher must help them understand they are literate and the meaning of literacy for them. The computer may help students develop problem-solving strategies, but the teacher must help the students to understand they are problem solvers and to have confidence in their solutions. The computer may be charged with the sequencing and pacing of students' instruction, but the teacher must help the students to learn that ultimately, they are in charge of, and responsible for, the computer.

Integration also involves the careful selection of programs with care given to complement the reading approach. Some say that teachers do not know how to use the existing technology to support education. One case in point could be the reading programs classified as games, simulations, and thinking skills (see Figure 9–1). These programs teach comprehension skills; however, they may not appear to be instructional in the step-by-step skill acquisition approach to reading used by many educators and most reading textbooks. Games are interactive software that encourage readers to apply their prior knowledge, set goals, and integrate new material. Adventure games and simulations also encourage students to discover cause-effect relationships and promote social interactions when used as cooperative learning activities. Some of these games require higher-level reading skills of prediction or synthesis, evaluation, and hypotheses testing.

**Figure 9–1**  *Software Categories*

1. Drill and Practice: This is the most widely used type of computer program. It is similar to the use of flashcards or worksheets. These programs use repetition to reinforce a skill that has already been introduced to the students. (Examples:  Reader Rabbit, Magic Spells)
2. Teaching/Tutorial: These programs attempt to teach the student about a subject in the same way a teacher would do on a one-to-one basis. (Examples:  Word Attack Plus, Learning Improvement Series)
3. Learning Games: These programs differ from the low-level drill-and-practice exercises because they require the student to integrate information and use problem-solving skills. They motivate interest in learning. (Example:  Grammar Examiner)
4. Simulations: Simulations are models of the world and create an imaginary environment for the student. Often this type of program presents a series of problems posed to a character who is under the child's control (Examples:  Where in the World Is Carmen Sandiego?, Oregon Trail)
5. Teacher Aids: These programs are designed to help teachers create learning materials or tests for classroom use. (Example:  Microtest)

Snyder and Palmer (1986) consider most games to serve three purposes: to incorporate cultural values, attitudes, and beliefs; to provide an environment for participants to experience, discuss, and change rules for social interaction; and to promote the development of contextually based skills. Such programs are sometimes called *interactive fiction.* Interactive fiction also promotes discussions and gives evidence that the reading is meaningful to students. They make predictions, paraphrase text, build vocabulary, and participate in other comprehension processes and higher-level thinking skills. Such computer games, simulations, and interactive fiction must be carefully chosen to support the philosophy, themes, and orientation of the teacher, and could either complement or conflict with the reading approach utilized.

Computers and database programs can help implement and integrate with individualized reading programs. They can manage, sort, organize, and retrieve an enormous amount of information, which is important in assessing reading. Open-ended computer programs such as LOGO and word processing have been shown to be the most effective programs with individualized instruction because they allow for individual differences, creativity, problem-solving, and thinking skills, with no limits on time allotment for mastery.

Word-processing programs not only integrate well into existing programs but they can become the program itself. In the area of writing, the computer has many benefits that ease the writing process. According to Grabe and Grabe (1985), the computer can be used for several writing activities in primary classrooms, beginning with language experience and moving students into writing their own stories. Smith (1985) states that teachers often tend to record children's language slightly differently than the students dictate because of the efforts to write it on chart paper.

Revising and recopying may also be avoided because of the editing capabilities of word-processing programs. Students can also write their own stories or papers by either choosing a topic or writing on a teacher-assigned topic. They type their rough draft and make revisions where needed. The computer word-processing function allows the writer to quickly and easily type over what has been typed, to insert new text within the old, to erase sections as large or small as needed, and to print a final copy that is both legible and professional.

Student sequencing of stories is another use of word processing that integrates with existing curriculum. It helps show the students the beginning, middle, and ending concepts of stories. One program presents a blank title page and a sequence of pictures that tell a story in a general manner (Grabe & Grabe, 1985). The teacher helps an individual or a group through the pictures to discuss what might have happened. A title is given to the story, which works on main idea or summarizing. The text is then given to each illustration to develop the story. Students are provided with copies of their own stories.

Word processing has also become a reading program in the case of the software program called Writing to Read (WTR). Writing to Read is an IBM program for children in kindergarten and first grade who use computers with voice output to encourage writing and hence reading development (Whitmer, 1987). The WTR program provides a computerized beginning reading program and daily language-experience/student-generated writing activities, and can be used with ESL and special-education secondary students. WTR's philosophy is that what you can write, you can read. Reading is developed from writing on the word processor. (One teacher's experience with this program is presented in the Case Studies section of this chapter.)

Schaeffer (1987) found that virtually all word-processing software programs had the following outstanding features: (1) the writer can instantly see on the monitor what he or she is typing; (2) it is possible to edit at any point of the writing process; (3) it provides a long-term storage of children's stories on a disk or tape; and (4) stories can be reproduced on a printer for the child. Whitmer (1987) states that the word processor also provides other features that relate to motor, visual, and auditory learning. When children are typing, they are working on motor development. When it comes time to read the text, visual learning is being used. In the case of children working on voice-synthesized computers, the story is read back to the children, enabling them to use auditory learning to edit their stories. In short, computers can be used for tools, tutors, exploring language, media, thinking strategies, and new modes of communication.

### Do I agree with criticisms of using computers in the classroom?

A socialization process is occurring between computers and users. Jacobsen (1987) surveyed the sources educators are utilizing in their decisions related to computers. In October 1986, 100 randomly chosen K–6 teachers in both public and private schools were sent questionnaires, 60 of which were returned and tabulated. Results indicated the bulk of information being presented to the educational community is coming from within that community itself. The instructor was the major source of information. Promotional materials and catalogs from dealers and manufacturers were another source of influence. Very few educators who were using computers in their classrooms were reading computer periodicals or magazines. In fact, the responding rate dropped dramatically when teachers were asked what publications they personally felt to be very valuable in helping them gain information on computers. Regular use of periodicals in which promotional materials appear did not seem to be extensive. Jacobsen concluded that persuasion factors are at play in training and workshop environments.

More studies are needed to determine what sources educators are using on which to base their decision about computers. Are the criteria educationally based, economically based, or perhaps not based on anything at all? Elkins (1986) feels that the norms of the culture are uncritically accepted by many people. It is possible that the attitudes regarding computers being fostered in educators are from sources other than teachers' interactions with actual computers.

Some of the concerns that are associated with computers are the lack of appropriate software, the lack of social interaction, and the failure to consider student learning styles. First, the lack of software is a problem that needs to be dealt with because the drill-only type of programs do not provide practice in reading comprehension. In addition, much software is too sophisticated for primary grades.

Many researchers are afraid of the effects that computer instruction will have on the social interactions among students and between students and teachers (Vermett, Orr, & Hall, 1986). However, other studies indicate that computer-aided instruction actually strengthens social skills through team planning and cooperative learning (Swick, 1989).

Many feel that computers keep genuine learning from occurring and do not allow for a process where ideas can be tested and new thoughts can evolve. The tightly controlled presentation of literacy skills by a computer program allows little or no time for reflection on its social or ethical implications and will, in the long run, create children with lifelong disabilities. Learning to read is a complex task that cannot be characterized as rational, logical, or sequential (Balajthy, 1987). Computer instruction, with its rule-oriented configuration, limits intellectual exploration. Computer instruction teaches absolute truths; it does not answer questions, it does not discuss, and it does not exchange ideas (Karger, 1988). It focuses on drill and practice and it is not used to full capacities by students and educators (Snyder & Palmer, 1986; Balajthy, 1989; Isaak & Hamilton, 1989).

# Summary

Today's schools are a blend of tried and true technology and strategies, many of which date back to the nineteenth century. They include lectures, grading, testing, field trips, busing, textbooks, workbooks, and chalkboards. All these aids were at one time new and innovative (MecKlenburger, 1989). By incorporating the tools of the information age (computers, televisons, video cameras, satellite dishes, calculators), schools are simply adopting a different mix of technology. Administrators play an essential role in the effective use of electronic technology. Without their efforts, new technology is unlikely to take hold. This new technology requires the same careful considerations, attention, and maintenance just as do chairs, desks, chalkboards, buses, PA systems, and athletic equipment. It is necessary for administrators to understand both the capabilities and limitations of technology. Only then can they adequately plan and budget for, carefully purchase, properly install, dutifully maintain, adequately schedule appropriately distribute, and systematically replace the electronic technology best suited for their needs (Balajthy, 1989).

# Application Exercises and Teaching Activities

## Application Exercises

1. How would television or computers help with the instruction in the following classroom?

Denise Abernathy is a reading resource teacher. In addition to all the "regular teacher" duties, it is also her responsibility to:

1. Teach each student in accordance with the individualized education plan and according to each one's particular learning disability
2. Develop individualized learning plans
3. Complete individual testing of goals on all students every three months and update their individualized plans
4. Schedule evaluation meetings and generate all paperwork for them
5. Keep all conference logs and documentation up to date
6. Organize each student's folder and keep profiles current
7. Coordinate communication between the regular classroom teacher and special-education teacher at least every three weeks and mail progress reports to parents
8. Make lesson plans for students in each subject area (any particular student may have as many as four lesson plans a day)
9. Juggle schedules for PE, lunch, other special classes (e.g., speech, physical therapy, staff meetings, counselor, diagnostician) and library for all students.

# Teaching Activities:
# Television Reading Activities

1. *Reading skill area:* Consonant clusters
   *Materials:* Any TV show; paper and pencil
   *Activity:* Copy 10 words you read from the TV. Circle all of the consonants clusters.
   *Number of students:* Class, group, or individual

2. *Reading skill area:* Understanding the use of different letter sizes
   *Materials:* Any three TV advertisements; paper
   *Activity:* Study and take notes on the different sizes or print used in the ads. Discuss the uses in class.
   *Number of students:* Class, group, or individual

3. *Reading skill area:* Phrase meaning
   *Materials:* Any TV program; paper
   *Activity:* List five phrases you read on the TV. Discuss the literal vs. the contextual meaning.
   *Number of students:* Class, group, or individual

4. *Reading skill area:* Recalling information
   *Materials:* Any TV advertisement; paper
   *Activity:* Write the name of your ad on one sheet of paper. On another sheet, list all of the facts about the ad, but not the name or product. Classmates try to guess the ad from the clues given.
   *Number of students:* Class or group

5. *Reading skill area:* Understanding characters
   *Materials:* Any movie or story-type show; paper
   *Activity:* Take notes on everyone or everything that gives you information on the main character or your favorite character.
   *Number of students:* Class, group, or individual

6. *Reading skill area:* Word meaning
   *Materials:* Several TV advertisements; paper
   *Activity:* As you watch the ads, select four words that could be used differently due to multiple meanings. (Example: Dash dog food, the 50-yard dash, and dash meaning a short line)
   *Number of students:* Class, group, or individual

7. *Reading skill area:* Outlining
   *Materials:* Any TV movie; paper
   *Activity:* Make a simple outline of a movie or show you see on TV. Notice how the movie breaks for ads at key moments of the plot.
   *Number of students:* Class, group, or individual

8. *Reading skill area:* Research
   *Materials:* Any TV ad, especially ads on cars and medicines; paper

*Activity:* Write down any research information you get from the ads. Notice if they give you actual data or if they just say "research proves." Discuss in class.
*Number of students:* Class, group, or individual

9. *Reading skill area:* Making a report and note taking from a lecture
*Materials:* Any factual TV show, such as "Underwater Adventures" or "Wild Kingdom"; paper.
*Activity:* Take notes from the information given in the show. Write a summary of the program and present it to the class. Be sure to note source of direct quotes and specific factual information.
*Number of students:* Class, group, or individual

10. *Reading skill area:* Note taking from print
*Materials:* Several TV ads; paper
*Activity:* Take notes on words or phrases from the actual products that are advertised that the commercial does not say out loud. Notice what words the announcer does say and what words are seen in print only. Discuss in class.
*Number of students:* Small group

11. *Reading skill area:* Dictionary definitions
*Materials:* Any TV show; dictionary; paper
*Activity:* Write down three long words you read on TV but are not sure of the precise meaning. Note how the words were used in the TV show. Look them up in the dictionary and use in "password" game.
*Number of students:* Reading or English class divided into small groups of four students per group.

12. *Reading skill area:* Alphabetical order
*Materials:* Any TV show; paper
*Activity:* Copy 10–20 words that you read on the TV screen and then put these words in alphabetical order. Use words that are in your favorite TV show.
*Number of students:* Class or remedial group

13. *Reading skill area:* Charts
*Materials:* TV weather report; paper
*Activity:* Report and discuss symbols or pictures used on the TV weather chart. (One student or a small group could maintain a daily weather chart in the classroom.)
*Number of students:* Class, group, or individual

14. *Reading skill area:* Abbreviations
*Materials:* Any TV ads; paper
*Activity:* Watch 10–20 TV ads. Copy all abbreviations and symbols used in the ads. Discuss the meaning and prepare a list of all of the abbreviations that the class finds in TV ads.
*Number of students:* Class, group, or individual

15. *Reading skill area:* Adjectives
*Materials:* Any TV ads; paper

*Activity:* Watch 10–20 ads, Copy all of the adjectives that are printed on the screen to sell the product to the viewer. Rewrite one ad using antonyms of the adjectives and note opposite effect.
*Number of students:* Class, group, or individual

16. *Reading skill area:* Association, picture to word
    *Materials:* Any TV ad or show; paper
    *Activity:* Write down all words that you read in 60 minutes that are also "pictured" on the TV screen.
    *Number of students:* Class, group, or individual

17. *Reading skill area:* Dialogue
    *Materials:* Several TV commercials that have dialogue; paper
    *Activity:* Take notes on the dialogue used in commercials. Get into groups and select a product and write your own commercials.
    *Number of students:* Entire class divided into groups of 2–4 students

18. *Reading skill area:* Conclusions and summary
    *Materials:* Any TV story-type show; paper
    *Activity:* Certain words or phrases that you hear in the show lead the viewer to a conclusion. Make a list of these words and discuss in class.
    *Number of students:* Secondary English or creative writing class

19. *Reading skill area:* Classification
    *Materials:* Several TV commercials; paper
    *Activity:* Divide all of the words that you read in commercials into categories, such as glad words, scare words, words that create a mood or feeling, statistics or figures, names of famous people, and humorous words. You may add any other categories you feel that you need. Discuss your words in class with other students and see if they agree with you.
    *Number of students:* Class, group, or individual

20. *Reading skill area:* Cause and effect
    *Materials:* TV commercial or show; paper
    *Activity:* List words used in ads that show a cause and effect. (Example: "Congested nasal passage due to cold" [cause], headache, sinus pain, etc. [effect]). Or note situation in a TV show that indicates cause and effect.
    *Number of students:* Class, group, or individual

21. Encourage students to write fan letters to favorite video personalities.

22. Working with a collected sequence of scripts, students can try to guess what the ending of a plot situation will be and write a version that satisfies them.

23. Obtain current scripts of daytime shows. With scripts in hand, the children can watch the show daily. Beforehand, they can look up all the unfamiliar words.

24. A TV interest center should include materials for a wide range of abilities from coloring books about TV characters to "Twenty Questions" or quizzes about favorite stars.

# CHAPTER TEN

## *Overview of Reading Program Organization*

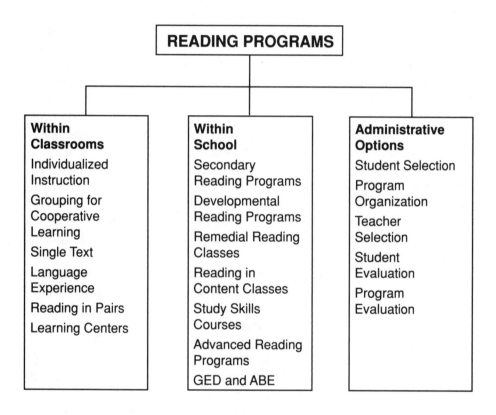

```
                    ┌─────────────────────┐
                    │  READING PROGRAMS   │
                    └─────────────────────┘
```

| Within Classrooms | Within School | Administrative Options |
|---|---|---|
| Individualized Instruction | Secondary Reading Programs | Student Selection |
| Grouping for Cooperative Learning | Developmental Reading Programs | Program Organization |
| Single Text | Remedial Reading Classes | Teacher Selection |
| Language Experience | Reading in Content Classes | Student Evaluation |
| Reading in Pairs | Study Skills Courses | Program Evaluation |
| Learning Centers | Advanced Reading Programs | |
| | GED and ABE | |

What can a teacher do with students who cannot read as well as they should? The options available to teachers for helping these students are usually decided by the available resources and how teachers have organized their own classrooms. The relationships between reading programs in the schools and the content teacher are generally mandated by law or district policies. Once they become aware of students' reading problems, teachers must then begin a search for support, resources, and information. The easiest way to begin the search is to look within their own classroom and to reorganize their classes. The second procedure is to place the remedial student in the type of reading program available in the school. The third option is to begin a reading program at the school.

No matter which option the teacher selects, she or he must be knowledgeable as to how to put a reading program together. The structural components of any reading program consist of placement and diagnosis, information delivery and organization, and evaluation or grading.

# Classroom Organization

### Individualized classroom remediation

Individualized reading has been used for over 40 years to describe reading remediation in which skill development is based on completing independent study activities designed especially for the student. The components consist of a checklist of behaviors the student must demonstrate to be placed at a certain level, a checklist of activities to be completed at the student's own pace, and evaluation procedures. Individualized instruction allows time for student (and parent) conferences with the teacher and student selection of materials. For example, the checklist may define a weakness in syllabification. A student who enjoys hiking or sports can practice the skill in material with content about hiking or sports. If such content does not exist in the skill books or in the classroom, then the student is given an option of several skill books to study. Examples of individualized checklists using multiple skill books may be found at the end of the chapter in the Teaching Activities section.

When it comes time to grade the student on the individualized plan, the teacher can either consider the completed checklist as adequate or give exercises in the books as tests with a level of competency set at 80 or 90 percent. Other teachers have made up tests or administer standardized tests that they give after the student has obtained 80 or 90 percent mastery on at least five exercises out of a skill book or workbook. The Teaching Activities section shows how individualized evaluation is compartmentalized in a secondary remedial reading classroom. Similar forms can be found in every school district and vary somewhat from region to region. The examples included in this chapter can serve as models for teachers to use in constructing their own forms.

The Teaching Activities section gives an example of how complex individualized instruction can become for the teacher and the student. Mrs. Sharon Salloway, originator of the Reading/Language Arts Weekly Assessment, changes categories of evaluation as her students master the skills she identifies. She uses this individualized form for her entire class. Any junior high or secondary content teacher could take the same form and make it into an individualized contract for one student or an entire class.

The involvement of students in selecting the material used to develop their reading skills is motivational for younger and older students. The single factor to remember in developing an individualized program is that *individualized* does not mean *isolated*. Individualization means developing material and the presentation of that material in a way that matches a student's learning needs. The word *individualization* comes from the specialization of the learning process, not the isolation of the student from teacher and other children. The child's checklist or program should include activities that involve other children, such as book sharing or reciprocal teaching and alone time with the teacher. Individualized instruction's self-paced process works well with students who are self-starters or who may have learning needs that are not being met in whole-class instructional processes. However, individualized instruction should never consist of a series of activities a child does alone.

## Cooperative learning

All content classrooms can also use grouping as a means of remediation for individual students. Grouping can be done in various ways for the same purpose, which is to improve reading skills. Cooperative learning is a method of forming groups for content delivery to students. Although many have written on the advantages of cooperative learning/teaching, Martens (1989) says it very well when she states that teachers must teach children to work in groups and provide basic rules before successful group work can be accomplished. She recommends four children in a group with specifically assigned roles: questioner, doer, prober, and summarizer. The teacher starts with a simple task to complete, using previously mastered skills. In this manner, students are able to internalize the learning process and use the skill more effectively each time. The teacher circulates in the room to spot problems. Regardless of the techniques used within the group, grouping format itself can be selected based on the teacher's instructional purpose.

One format, skill grouping, places three to five students together who need work on the same skill. Students are given assignments to work on a task in order to practice or reinforce reading skills needed by all. The teacher may or may not be present with each group but the assignment is designed by the teacher. The difficulty of this grouping approach is that the teacher must prepare for four, five, or six groups, which is somewhat overwhelming unless she or he uses published material, prepared programs, and games.

A second remediation grouping occurs when students are allowed to work on certain assignments with friends. This method works well with remedial students, as their peers can often explain classwork more clearly and enjoyably. They also will support each other regardless of skill level, and cooperation rather than competition is reinforced in the classroom. Time limits and group grades for assignments keep friendship groups on task.

Interest grouping, a third format, could help remediation of slower students if skill development is included in the assignments. When units are being taught in content areas such as science, interest groups may be allowed to read supplementary material on different topics. Of course, it is possible to have material on different reading levels but covering the same subject matter in the class. However, most teachers are pleased just to have enough copies of content books without concern about the reading levels of multiple copies. This is where the teacher might want to have a set of other science, mathematics, history, or English textbooks in the class. If the reading level of some supplementary books is below that of the class average, interest groups might be able to read on all levels. This type of grouping would be the beginning of research groups in preparation for report writing in later grades. A sample of material on the same subject but written on different levels is found in Figure 10–1. In this instance, students might be grouped according to interest in fungi or the solar system. The books listed are all on the first- through third-grade reading levels in order to demonstrate that secondary content can be found written on elementary readability levels.

A fourth arrangement, ability grouping, is used when teachers or counselors place students in classes based on the scores on state tests, textbook competency tests, or standardized ability tests. The classroom teacher then uses test scores administered outside of the classroom to place students in ability groups. The classroom teacher then uses test scores administered outside of the classroom to place students in ability groups. The dangers of this type of grouping are documented in the following student's experience as told by a parent:

> My daughter, Amy, is 11 years old and is presently in the fifth grade. She is placed in the medium-high group. Ability grouping in her school is set up into 10 levels: SPACE (the highest, gifted class), high-high, medium-high, low-high, high-medium, medium-medium, low-medium, high-low, medium-low, and self-contained). Amy was grouped in the high-high group from first to third grades and maintained an A average on the honor roll.
>
> Upon entering the fourth grade the children faced a new challenge—SPACE. Children had to be invited into the SPACE program with a formal invitation through the mail. Although Amy was recommended for the program, only 20–25 students are selected by the SPACE teacher. Amy was not one of those selected and she was

**Figure 10–1**    *Different Levels of Subject Matter*

*Books and Films on Fungi*
Webster, V. (1982). *Plant experiences.* Chicago: Children's Press, 10–13.
    (1st-grade reading level)
16mm Motion Picture Films (1960). *Fungi.*
Video Tapes Circulation (1978). *Fungi, the one hundred thousand.*

*Books and Films on Solar System*
Arvetis, C. (1983). *What is a rainbow?* Middletown, CT: Field
    Publications. (1st-grade reading level)
Lewellen, J. (1981). *Moon, sun and stars.* Chicago: Children's Press,
    7–11. (1st-grade reading level)
16mm Motion Picture Films (1975). *Learning about solar energy.*
16mm Motion Picture Films (1976). *Universe.*
Video Tapes Reproduction (1985). *The solar sea.*

greatly confused and frustrated. She was convinced she was "dumb." After talking to her teacher and asking for her assistance in convincing Amy she was not dumb, Amy's opinion did not change but she convinced herself she would make the best of it.

Amy is now in a high-medium group because her math SRA score dropped last year to 88 percent. Her math was at 4.6 grade level in January of her fourth grade, so she was dropped from the high-high group. You can now understand my interest and frustration with ability grouping.

The high groups at Amy's school have to read 600 pages in six weeks of a fourth-grade reader or above, while the low classes have to read 400 pages in six weeks at the second-grade level or above. This is very disillusioning for Amy. She feels punished for knowing how to read on her grade level. (She does not enjoy reading.) Yesterday, her class was told they only needed to read 500 pages because they were not in the high-high group. Amy got mad because she thought they were telling her that she was dumb again, and she's going to read 700 pages.

Grouping for reading remediation is an excellent strategy. Whether teachers prefer friendship, interest, skill, or ability grouping, they will find that cooperation and enthusiasm increase in their classroom. Evaluating students' performances as a group member should also be done formally rather than informally. The form in Figure 10–2 can be used as a starting place for secondary teachers. As they answer the questions in the flowchart, they can determine where they want to place their students. The best approach to grouping is a variety of teaming approaches that suit both the teacher and the students. Simply asking the students to write down four or five names of people they want to work with controls for personality conflicts that might occur if the teacher did the teaming.

The essential purpose of grouping is to provide differentiated instruction based on each pupil's needs and abilities. The teacher must consider such things as: How many groups can I manage effectively? How much time for each group do I have? What amount of space and what types and amounts of material will be available for use? Any form of grouping must always provide for flexibility. Over 30 years ago, Smith (1963) found that classes involving subgrouping for reading instruction achieve substantially better results than classes with undifferentiated instruction. Supporters of cooperative learning would not disagree today.

## Single-text classroom organization

Some teachers use a single textbook, which places all students in the same book. Most textbooks supply a teacher's manual with suggested activities. The same approach is possible for remedial readers in content classes. There are remedial secondary and elementary reading basals with workbooks, teacher's manuals, and recommended correlated supplementary material. If not available in the school district,

**Figure 10–2**   *Teachers Plan for Skill-Based Program*

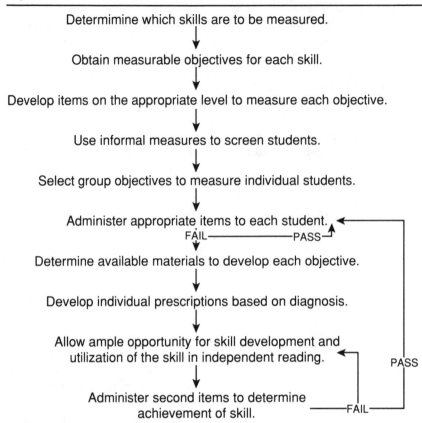

they are available at the state and federally funded educational service centers. Should a math, history, or English teacher have a few students who cannot read the assigned textbook, or even the easier versions that are sometimes available, the students can be placed in a single text on their grade level. The student then moves through the graded textbook series as skills develop. Vocabulary and comprehension difficulty are controlled so that there is no reading variability within the books and new skills are not introduced haphazardly.

Rather than place remedial readers in a separate remedial basal, another alternative is to keep students in the same text as everyone else and then make assignments in the basal book where they are appropriately placed for outside classroom work. This strategy enables students to appear as if they are keeping up with the class. Using a comprehensive textbook approach conspicuously labels children as remedial readers unless the second alternative is used.

### Language experience

Teachers with self-contained classrooms can also use language experience for remedial students. Language experience merely transcribes spoken language into written language. What the children can say, they can read. The transcription is the problem for most teachers who do not have the time to sit with one child and write an experience or story down as the student tells it.

The best solution for this problem is to use a tape recorder and have a parent or student volunteer, a teacher's aide, or a school support person transcribe the tapes into books for students to read. Steps for any content teacher to use in making language experience books are listed here.

1. Select an experience, subject area, concept, movie, or feeling that the student wants to describe.
2. Give the student a tape recorder (or a volunteer) so that the spoken words can be recorded (or written). Select a quiet place for this activity.
3. Have the transcribed or written experience laminated or in some way preserved for the student to read.
4. The student becomes responsible for all the words in the experience material as far as spelling, reading, and pronunciation.
5. The language experience material becomes a textbook that is interesting, relevant, and personal.

One language experience story composed by a 39-year-old school board president follows. It indicates the variety of material possible to develop with this strategy. ESL, nonreaders, and remedial readers are all motivated through this instructional procedure. In this manner, speech is translated into written form and the student can easily read what has just been spoken. Success is very quick and student motivation to continue to develop reading skills is increased. Once transcriptions are finished, the student might illustrate the book. The result will be a student-written book, readable for remedial students, that may be placed in the library or classroom.

### My Day at the Ranch

I go to the ranch to feed my cows. First I load the pick-up with hay. Then I go to the ranch. I open the gate. I go find the cows. Then I drop the hay on the ground. I undo the wire around the hay. All the cows come and eat the hay. Then I leave.

When I feed my cows at the feedlots, I do the same. But I put the feed in a trough. My girls sometimes help me feed. But most of the time I feed their animals. My girls are in FFA, which they think stands for Father Feeds Animals. I do not mind, because I love them and they love me.

The interesting content, enjoyment from reading student-written material, and relevancy of this remedial approach are benefits from using this remedial strategy. It has been used in probation camps, ESL classes, and content classes with special-education students.

*Reading in pairs*

The components of reading in pairs are that teachers pair students according to similar abilities, personalities, and learning styles. The teachers then choose reading activities and materials that match the reading abilities of the children and make materials easily available. After designing a checklist for children to follow, teachers then train students in the rules and behavior necessary in this laboratory-like organization. Students are expected to get their reading material and checklist from a designated place and go to a special place in the room. They follow their checklist, marking activities off as they are completed. They must share with their partners and replace material when they are finished.

Reading activities found in classrooms that use this organizational pattern might include the following, which are described by Susan Peery and Britt Leach.

**1.** *Word Rings:* Words the students do not know are taken from their story. The rings are checked each week. For each word that a child reads correctly, he or she receives a stamp on that word card. When a word card has four stamps, it is removed from the ring and placed in a word box. These words then serve as a student's personal dictionary.

**2.** *Workjobs:* These individualized learning centers reinforce reading and language skills.

**3.** *Reading Games for Two or More Players:* These games serve to reinforce vocabulary and comprehension, as well as sharing, cooperation, and patience.

**4.** *Writing Center:* This ongoing center consists of mailboxes, picture dictionaries, assorted writing paper, envelopes, and story starters—some of which pertain to stories that have been read.

**5.** *Listening Center:* This center involves planned selection as well as self-selection. It can be used by individuals or small groups.

**6.** *Activity Tubs:* These include a task card and materials needed for a particular activity. The activity pertains to the story that has just been read.

**7.** *Special Reading Places:* Each pair chooses its own special place. Special places may also be created to go along with certain stories.

**8.** *Rotating Committees:* Children are placed in small groups to accomplish given tasks within a four- or five-day period.

**9.** *D.E.A.R.-Daily:* Students choose who they want to read with, where they want to read, and what they want to read.

**10.** *Journals:* Children write in spiral notebooks daily, beginning with the date.

**11.** *Outside Reading:* Students read books at home for school.

## Learning centers

Learning centers are areas of the classroom where specific activities take place. Usually no more than one or two students work in a learning center at the same time. Some classrooms use only learning centers to deliver content. In that case, specific centers can be assigned to those who are having trouble reading. In most cases, however, learning centers are a part of the classroom organization and can be easily adapted to fit individual needs.

Nan Bowen uses centers in her reading instruction in the following manner: First, she appoints three skill groups, which are color coded into red, green, and yellow. Her skill group selection is based on ability test scores. Each color is represented under a number on a large class schedule. When the yellow group is at the reading table, then the green group knows they have to go to learning centers. The red group does seatwork at the same time. The centers are established around reading, math, and science skills. The centers could just as easily be established around different aspects of a mathematics, art, history, English, or music problem. Nan has 10 centers in reading that can be used at the same time. Centers consist of puzzles working on visual acuity, a rocking chair where a student sits and reads a book, a center that has spelling words, and a writing center with an activity like "Invent a car for the year 2020 and draw a picture of it." The learning centers are changed every two weeks. Each student does an activity from the learning center every day. No child stays at a center more than one day.

Other teachers use centers for reading and content instruction with different systems of moving students through centers. Some place students at a center for the entire week. Others have centers one or two days a week and have nothing else going on during "center time." At one federally funded drop-out program, students stay at the center until they master all of the content presented at that location.

The construction of reading centers also varies. Some teachers do no more than put published material in a specific location, provide directions, and call it a center. Others put learning center material in plastic buckets, baskets, bags, or file folders, and tell students to take their center wherever they want to work. Others have computers, filmstrips, and editing materials that they call a center.

The disadvantages of center instruction are mainly overcoming the insecurity of using them and the thought of putting all the centers together. But once they are structured and developed, centers are usable for a long time. Also, the advantages of centers often outweigh the disadvantages. They are very useful with children who finish early and those who do not understand material when it is presented to the whole group. Centers can contain activities the teachers think are valuable but they cannot find the time to implement in the time allotted for reading. And finally, centers are a good way to prevent monotony for students.

# Schoolwide Reading Programs

## Secondary reading programs

Until recently, the public has assumed that by the time children reach high school, they can read. This assumption is false, as demonstrated by a number of national studies (which do not even survey the number of students who drop out of high school because they cannot read). Sources of the high school reading problems have been attributed to lack of supervision of children after school, increasing poverty, increasing number of single women with children who live in poverty, and the lack of direct instruction. Schools can do little about the poverty and number of single parents, but they can directly teach reading.

The first step is to educate reading specialists who can teach someone over the age of 12. Strategies and materials that work with remedial elementary students are inadequate with secondary students who probably failed the material the first time they worked with it. The second step is to educate secondary content teachers about diagnostic and remedial strategies useful in different subject fields.

## Developmental reading programs

Recognition of the importance of reading in content instruction as well as necessary teacher training have resulted in reading programs that are required in some junior highs, regardless of a student's reading ability. These are called developmental reading programs and they may use a basal reading series, work on critical comprehension skills, or develop vocabulary expansion.

The material for developmental reading courses would include both printed matter and multimedia materials. Printed material includes basic textbooks, detailed teacher's editions and manuals, supplementary workbooks, source books, and perhaps paperback books like lab manuals. Multimedia material include films, motion pictures, records, charts, tapes, materials for controlled readers and computers, word games, and other devices to assist the teacher in implementing the reading program. The teacher in developmental programs does not need to rely on only the textbook, but should use a variety of materials. But because there is no agreed upon model for such programs, the specific description of how these are conducted is defined by the individual schools. An attempt to describe some secondary reading programs in one geographic region is detailed later in this chapter.

### Remedial reading classes

Remedial reading classes are generally limited to between 10 and 12 students. Bilingual, remedial, and special-education students could all be in this class. Structure can vary from a programmed approach to a language experience methodology. The important difference is that these students are reading at least two grades below the grade level where they should be placed. Reading specialists should be teaching these clinics and classes.

### Reading in content classes

Reading in content classes are either mandated by the school or the curriculum is written so that one segment of all English and/or content classes is devoted to reading instruction. The English teacher is the one who teaches reading. It has been assumed that because the English teacher has studied literature and linguistics, she or he is knowledgeable about reading instruction. This is often not the case, as many English certification programs do not include a course in reading instruction. In a few cases, reading can be a mandated part of a content course. This more than likely occurs on the junior high level when the specific teacher has expertise in reading.

### Study skills courses

Study skills courses are either a semester or a year in duration. In a study skills course, students can learn how to speed read, take notes, listen more effectively, expand vocabulary, take tests, and manage their time through schedules and study strategies. All students may take these courses or they are sometimes limited to advanced, college-bound students.

### Advanced reading programs

Advanced reading programs can be anything from preparation to take the ACT and SAT exams to vocabulary-enhancement courses. They can be honors courses or limited to high school seniors. Generally, there are not more than one or two sections of these courses in a high school.

### General education development and adult basic education programs

According to the National Commission on Civil Disorders, 39.9 percent of our nonwhite population and 14.8 percent of our white population over the age of 25 are functional illiterates. That means that over 18 million people, or a population percentage of 10.5, cannot read. It is difficult to estimate the exact costs to our society and economy of total and functional illiteracy. If the cost for remediating 80 percent of these persons is $1,000 per individual ($3.2 billion) and the cost for remediating the remaining 20 percent is $4,000 per individual (another $3.2 billion), the total remediation costs amount to $6.4 billion. But the increased productivity over the course of the lifetime of the individuals involved would amount to at least $10,000 per person. This adds up to $40 billion. Subtracting the remediation costs then yields a profit of $33.6 billion. Clearly, total and functional illiteracy is costing the country a great deal—both in terms of frustration and dollars.

The General Educational Development (GED) and Adult Basic Education (ABE) programs are serving secondary students. These are both externally funded programs. The GED is a means for high school drop-outs to get a high school equivalency diploma. These programs are mentioned here because many must have a reading component to raise students' reading levels so that they can read the programmed material of the course. Adult Basic Education programs teach illiterate adults how to read. The reason this tutorial program is mentioned here is that many use school buildings at night and in the afternoon to conduct their programs. Begun in 1966 under the Federal Adult Education Act, the Adult Basic Education program and materials include reading, math, and English. Many use this program for a transitional step to taking the GED exam. The tuition is free because of government funding. Most penal institutions and city high schools have this program available under the state division of Adult and Continuing Education.

The curriculum consists of low-level vocabulary and high-interest reading materials about real-life happenings. Most ABE units use the Sequential Competency System (SCS), which allows for a great deal of individual flexibility. Six components make up the system: reading skills checklist, competency of the student, pretesting, prescriptions of needs, cross-references of materials, and mastery checks (Drabeck, 1980).

For too many years, adult reading programs have been called a profession in search of an identity. Myths surrounding the adult reading teacher have included characteristics as teachers having inadequate training and having little knowledge of the classroom. Consequently, adult reading teachers have not had the status that is given to secondary or elementary reading teachers.

The last 20 years have brought improvement and professional status to the adult reading teacher. Some reasons for this growth are media, surveys, reports, finances, educational reforms, community colleges, learning centers, and college campus credit courses. These factors contribute to the evident progress in the field of adult reading (Cranny, 1983).

# Administration of Reading Programs in One Geographic Location

## *How are students selected?*

There is no single way students are selected for either remedial or regular reading classes. No standard of what makes a reader remedial is uniformly found. In most cases, a standardized test is administered. Either the district, school, or teacher establishes the cut-off point. For example, remedial students are identified in the following manner in two junior high schools: They are given a standardized achievement test (California Achievement Test) and a state achievement test. Those who score in the bottom one-fourth of the CAT and below 70 percent in the state-developed test are placed in remedial reading. At three other schools, the students are given the state-mandated dyslexia test and the Stanford Reading Achievement Test. At an alternative school, students are placed by administering a test that accompanies a self-paced, integrated curriculum delivered by computer. And finally, an elementary school can have a plethora of tests. For example, test scores on the Gates McGinnitie, the San Diego Quick Assessment Test, the Troll Listening Test, and a K–6 checklist could place a child in remedial reading. Also, exit scores after 9–15 months in a remedial reading program and teacher referral would result in remedial reading placement.

## *How are remedial reading programs organized?*

Once placed in a program, a student may find he or she is in what is called a skill-based, whole language, or eclectic format. In a skill format, the skill is either identified and independently remediated or students are placed in books and reading groups that introduce skills as determined by the authors. Two such series would be *Focus* (Scott, Foresman) and *Insights* (Holt, Rinehart and Winston). These would become the curriculum for the remedial class. Independent skill selection and remediation requires a wide variety of texts and supplementary books and a curriculum guide that identifies the page where a specific skill is taught in a number of different books. The teacher's knowledge of books in her or his room may omit the need for a curriculum guide.

A third method for addressing skill-based curriculum is the use of computer programs. Many self-contained programs operate with their own tests and sequenced content, much as the book skill series. Computer programs are expensive but are often purchased by a school system for use with alternative and elementary schools. Educational Development Laboratory (EDL) and IBM both have series that go from illiteracy to advanced reading skills.

Whole-language approaches use children's or adolescents' literature as the basis of instruction. A variety of activities constructed by the teacher reflect the needs of the students and the nature of the piece. For example, one seventh-grade remedial reading class reads *The Line Witch, Blue Dolphin,* and other books and stories that the teacher finds appropriate. Reading instruction occurs in the context of literature instruction.

## How are teachers selected to teach remedial reading?

The appropriate answer would be that teachers with appropriate education courses in reading and certification are remedial reading teachers. In reality, this is not the case, as expediency, rapport with children, and school politics often make the teacher selections. In an informal survey of two high schools, two junior highs in the same city, a small and large rural school district, two alternative schools, and five elementary schools, reading teachers were selected because they had master's degrees in reading, they had elementary certification with reading courses, or they were the English, Speech, or Spanish teachers. Their response to reading as a result of this selection process reflects their prior training. Some are comfortable with the assignment; others are frustrated. A questionnaire sent to teachers at one elementary school described the range of curriculum and the variety of backgrounds. Their backgrounds, programs, and attitudes about teaching reading are described in the Teaching Activities section.

## How are students evaluated?

Test scores on either teacher-made or standardized tests usually determine progress. In the basal, pre- and posttests come with the program, which are handy and sometimes appropriate measures of reading improvement. Some teachers use competency tests with pretests and set mastery levels; others use the WRAT (Wide Range Achievement Test) or the SRA (Stanford Reading Achievement Test). Teachers also use tests that they construct.

In reading programs, evaluation of students is based on established criteria and determining the behaviors that indicate the criteria have been met. Generally, this evaluation process does not use a teacher-made objective test. Thus, grades for remedial reading students in content classes are often unfavorable and inaccurate indicators of what the students have mastered in the remedial reading class. It is necessary, therefore, for the teacher of remedial readers to devise an evaluation system that results in a grade that is based on behavior that is achievable for his or her remedial reader. The procedure for evaluating one or more remedial readers in a regular classroom should be defined differently.

First, the student should be involved in determining how he or she wishes to be evaluated. The evaluation should be based on improvement documented in the deficiency areas identified at the beginning of the class. Behavior that demonstrates gains in these characteristics can be in attitude and reading behavior. For example, a student who now finishes reading would demonstrate both the attitude of perseverance and the desire to complete work, in addition to specific reading behaviors. In establishing this evaluation process, the student and the teacher determine each area of concern. The teacher then asks how the student will demonstrate competency. After each item, the teacher will write the evaluation procedure and give the student a copy. The emphasis is on the individual's remediation needs. The evaluation should be established prior to the instruction. Although the process is initially time consuming, with practice it becomes quicker, as both the student and the teacher cooperate on establishing criteria and behavior that will determine competency. Weekly reading assessment formats are in the Teaching Activities section.

## *How are reading programs evaluated?*

Even the best program will look inadequate if it is not properly evaluated. When evaluating reading programs, most educators think in terms of reporting individual or group reading scores. More specifically, they may categorize scores on vocabulary, comprehension, or rate. Problems then occur when an administrator asks for a cost-effectiveness report or a researcher asks for a justification of a particular method of instruction. These inquiries cannot be answered by providing individual or group reading scores. The program implementor then becomes aware of the fact that evaluation has many dimensions. Although reading scores are a significant aspect of a reading program, they may not answer all questions.

The evaluation process, then, becomes a means of communicating with all concerned with the program. Unfortunately, a reading program's effectiveness is not always judged from the same perspective. Differing evaluation criteria are often the cause of a negative review or a principal's lack of interest in a program. The program implementor needs to determine who will be evaluating the program and what that individual(s) will consider as significant factors before beginning data collection. The main objective of every evaluation system is to provide defensible evidence that the reading program is effective—from a variety of perspectives.

Depending on the type of testing used—criterion referenced, norm referenced, or products or behavior—the evaluation process will look different. A criterion-referenced test will have a percentage score; a standardized test score will have an improvement score, provided there was a pre- and posttesting of the students; and a unit completion will demonstrate a skill. Evaluation must be made on an objective basis with a criterion or a standard established before the student is evaluated. For example, a criterion for evaluating the value of a reading program could be skill level attainment, usefulness of information, or percentage gain. Reference is always made from a personal framework but, like self-evaluations, must be quantitatively measured.

# Summary

Reading programs demonstrate many varieties in classroom organization. They can be individualized, use different cooperative learning formats, or use single textbooks and/or learning centers. These organization patterns exist mainly on the elementary level but can also be found in secondary and alternative educational programs. Schoolwide reading programs can be developmental, advanced, remedial, study skill, or integrated into content classes. Alternative programs are usually federally funded and directed at secondary-age or adult students. And finally, the administration of reading programs is as varied as their formats and forms. The principles of good administration, however, are just as important to reading programs as they are to budget management. The effectiveness of the reading program to a large extent is responsible for the productivity of the population.

Although teachers and school districts are aware of the importance of content reading programs, teachers often feel poorly equipped to teach reading. They also view themselves as the primary source of knowledge, and since they must provide instruction in ever-expanding course content, they do not feel they also have the time to teach reading.

Teachers' attitudes may be reflected in the lack of help in reading for students. In a national survey of content reading programs in U.S. schools, approximately 63 percent of the schools have not developed content reading programs (Gee, Olson, & Forester, 1989). Teachers, however, cannot be held responsible as the only factor that is important in establishing content reading programs. They must be given time to plan, supportive administration, someone to coordinate the programs, budgets to provide support time, in-service education, and needed materials.

# Application Exercises and Teaching Activities

## Application Exercises

**1.** Determine the type, organization, grade level, student selection, and evaluation process of the actual programs described. (Each reading teacher was interviewed by a reading student.)

*School 1*

Ms. Harris has two reading classes. One is a developmental reading class and the other is an advanced reading class. She is also an English teacher. She informed me that the English and reading programs more or less tie in together. All of the remedial programs are in special education.

There are three reading teachers at this school. Each class is made up of 20–25 students. The classes are listed as English electives and they can be chosen on a trimester basis. The developmental classes are for any student who reads on grade level or slightly below grade level. To get into the advanced class, a student must take the Nelson Denny Adult Reading Test.

Ms. Harris sets up her reading classes on a contract basis. Each contract is made up of students' interests, career goals, and of course their own level of reading. All contracts are individualized. This is done by Ms. Harris every week. She said it is a lot of work but it is worth it because it proves to be rewarding for the students. The students work on what they want to but the contract must be completed. Ms. Harris informed me that the developmental classes are in such demand that a mini-course is given at 7:30 A.M. to accommodate as many as possible.

As far as grading, the students do earn a letter grade for the trimester. Ms. Harris explained as follows: Students check their own work. The students label their work and if they make a score of less than 70 they have to let her know so she can help them. She gives every student 100 points at the beginning of the week. They can lose points by being absent, which they can make up either before or after school. They also lose points by not following instructions and not showing the teacher their work.

The reading lab is actually fairly small in size. The equipment is adequate. There are many different types of reading kits that cover different subjects. Some kits I found interesting were the reading kits for preparing students for college. There were reading tapes and all the other machines we have talked about this semester. In my opinion and the teacher's opinion, the lab was very adequate and the students in the class I observed seemed to be enjoying their work.

To me, the program seemed to be a pretty good one. It is very well organized. The part I like best in this developmental program was the fact that the program is centered around the students' interest. I think this is probably the main reason why their test results are so good. Each teacher seemed to have his or her own strategy and I found this to be interesting also.

The problems that Ms. Harris did talk about were few. She was satisfied with the way things were going. Her main complaint was that trimesters only give a teacher enough time to get to know the student and find out what their real reading problems are and then it is over. She said that time is a big factor in working effectively with students and in helping them develop the skills they need.

### School 2

I am a believer in learning from others' mistakes; therefore, I decided to interview a reading teacher and try to examine problems, as well as strong points, and propose a few solutions. The teacher I interviewed has taught reading for two years in a small rural school. She has students in her class from first through fourth grades. The testing of her students was as follows:

1. There was no formal testing done.
2. IQ tests were scored and available for her use; however, she did not do anything with those scores.
3. In the spelling book she used, there were sentences with the spelling words left out. She used these to assess spelling, concepts, sentence understanding skills, and vocabulary.
4. She had the students read out loud from their texts as well as papers they had written.

Next, we discussed grouping. This was done very subjectively:

1. Reading placement came from the informal measures stated above.
2. Each group used a different test.
3. The group was named after colors or birds.

The teacher stated that the children are not grouped by grade level in any way during reading. They progress to a new group when they can read aloud and master the questions at the end of each story in the book. (She remembers making exceptions to this.) The texts she uses are those adopted for the school. She likes these texts, stating that they provide extra reading materials in various areas of interest. For the most part, she purchased or brought these texts from home. All the students are free to use any book of their choice.

This teacher feels pleased with the way her students are spending time. Reading lessons progress smoothly. Considering the setting she is in, she feels she is providing good techniques for good reading skills.

*School 3*

The teacher has a teaching certificate with an English major; 18 hours of graduate courses, working toward a master's degree for Reading Specialist; and taught reading in seventh and eighth grades for 16 years.

The program has EDL machinery with text and skills books; each story covers vocabulary, cause-effect, main idea, and so on; each story covers a reference and study or literary skill; and each story covers a different comprehensive skill. Instructional aids include computers and audiotape instruction when using the computer. The students are provided with opportunities to use their own creativity on the computer by typing and writing their own stories or paragraphs; this also helps in the correction of writing. The class is organized around the skills from the EDL program.

The teacher has one day of in-service support, usually with a guest speaker at the beginning of the school year. Sometimes there is one more day of voluntary in-service in the summer. The teacher has not talked to the reading supervisor since school started and it is now February.

General information is that every junior high has at least two reading teachers. Students switch classes at the end of the semester—from lab to developmental reading. All reading programs at the junior high are remedial programs. To be placed in remedial reading in seventh grade, the student has to be reading 5.7 or below on the Iowa test as a sixth-grader. To be placed in eighth-grade remedial reading, each seventh-grader in the reading program is given the Iowa test and must do well not to have to take reading in the eighth grade. Failing a grade or repeatedly having bad grades could make it so that a student is recommended for reading.

In the high school, one teacher teaches reading from the lowest students to the highest students who elect to take reading; she also teaches reading to those students who failed to master the state-mandated competency test. The highest students take reading as an elective and practice speed reading.

# Teaching Activities: Basic Reading Skills

| | 19__ Blue Ink | 19__ Red Ink | 19__ Black Ink | | 19__ Blue Ink | 19__ Red Ink | 19__ Black Ink |
|---|---|---|---|---|---|---|---|
| **I. VOCABULARY** | | | | **Long Vowels** (circle) <br><br> a  e  i  o  u | | | |
| A. The student recognizes and knows the meaning of: | | | | **Short Vowels** (circle) <br><br> a  e  i  o  u | | | |
| 1. 220 Dolch Words <br> 2. 95 common nouns | | | | **Digraphs** (circle) <br><br> gh  ph  sh  th  ch <br><br> wh  gu | | | |
| B. The student can use a new word in a sentence. | | | | **Letters used as consonants and vowels** (circle) <br><br> y  w | | | |
| C. The student can define a word in a sentence according to its 2nd or 3rd meaning. | | | | **Two sounds of** (circle) <br><br> c  g | | | |
| **II. WORD ATTACK SKILLS** | | | | **Vowel combinations** (circle) <br><br> $\overline{oo}$  ŏo  oi  oy  er  ir <br><br> ur  ay  or  igh  ind <br><br> au  aw  ou  ow  ar  är | | | |
| **Consonants** (Circle ones mastered) <br><br> z  x  v  s  q  n  l  j <br><br> g  d  f  h  k  m  p  r <br><br> t  w  y  b | | | | **Silent letters** (circle) <br><br> wr  kn  gh  ph  ck | | | |
| **Blends** (Circle ones mastered) <br><br> gl  bl  cl  tr  br <br><br> gr  sp  st  pr  pl <br><br> dr  fl  fr  sl  sm <br><br> sn  sw  tw  sc  str <br><br> spr  spl  thr | | | | | | | |

| | 19___ 19___ Blue Ink | 19___ 19___ Red Ink | 19___ 19___ Black Ink | | 19___ 19___ Blue Ink | 19___ 19___ Red Ink | 19___ 19___ Black Ink |
|---|---|---|---|---|---|---|---|
| **III. RECALL** | | | | 3. Student can record in his own words the answers to the two questions | | | |
| A. Longer story. | | | | | | | |
| 1. Select a name for a selection | | | | C. Get specific information from charts and graphs | | | |
| 2. Five character traits | | | | D. Use parts of book | | | |
| 3. Find answer to specific question | | | | 1. Table of contents | | | |
| 4. Distinguish between reality and nonreality | | | | 2. Index | | | |
| 5. Determine cause and effect | | | | 3. Glossary | | | |
| B. Sequence events from a story. | | | | E. Library | | | |
| 1. Three statements | | | | 1. Card catalog | | | |
| 2. Four statements | | | | 2. Find book by using Dewey System | | | |
| 3. Five statements | | | | | | | |
| C. Distinguish between fact and opinion. | | | | **V. ORAL-SILENT READING** | | | |
| **IV. STUDY SKILLS** | | | | (Diagnostic observations) | | | |
| A. Dictionary. | | | | A. Oral reading | | | |
| 1. Find word | | | | 1. Slow, fumbling | | | |
| 2. Select appropriate meaning of a word | | | | 2. Dependent upon content clues | | | |
| B. Encyclopedia (appropriate level) | | | | 3. Uses phonics | | | |
| 1. Find topic | | | | a. letter by letter | | | |
| 2. Find and read answers to two directed questions | | | | b. in larger units | | | |
| | | | | c. slowly | | | |
| | | | | d. easily | | | |

# Evaluation Checklist of Reading Skills

|  | Intro-duced | Under-stands | Mastery |
|---|---|---|---|
| **WORD RECOGNITION SKILLS:** | | | |
| Does he use phonics? Yes ___ No ___ | | | |
| What areas does he have trouble with? | | | |
| (list in pencil) _____ | | | |
| _____ | | | |
| _____ | | | |
| **VOCABULARY BUILDING SKILLS:** | ___ | ___ | ___ |
| Does he gain meaning with structural analysis? | ___ | ___ | ___ |
| Does he use dictionary skills? | ___ | ___ | ___ |
| Does he use pronunciation key? | ___ | ___ | ___ |
| Does he use diacritical marks? | ___ | ___ | ___ |
| Does he use appropriate meaning form context? | ___ | ___ | ___ |
| Does he use notes? | ___ | ___ | ___ |
| Does he use meaning of roots, prefixes, suffixes, etc.? | ___ | ___ | ___ |
| Does he use main and subordinate entries? | ___ | ___ | ___ |
| Does he use cross-references? | ___ | ___ | ___ |
| **COMPREHENSION SKILLS:** | ___ | ___ | ___ |
| Does he follow instructions? | ___ | ___ | ___ |
| Does he understand sequence? | ___ | ___ | ___ |
| Does he compare? | ___ | ___ | ___ |
| Does he find main idea of story? | ___ | ___ | ___ |
| Does he observe details? | ___ | ___ | ___ |
| Does he summarize? | ___ | ___ | ___ |
| Does he outline? | ___ | ___ | ___ |
| Does he find and use questions? | ___ | ___ | ___ |
| Does he understand maps and graphs? | ___ | ___ | ___ |
| Does he find part of a story for specific purpose? | ___ | ___ | ___ |
| **INTERPRETATION SKILLS:** | ___ | ___ | ___ |
| Does he draw conclusions from ideas? | ___ | ___ | ___ |
| Does he use imagination? | ___ | ___ | ___ |
| Does he recognize story plots? | ___ | ___ | ___ |
| Does he identify with story characters? | ___ | ___ | ___ |
| Does he weigh facts and opinions? | ___ | ___ | ___ |
| Does he evaluate content in terms of author's purpose? | ___ | ___ | ___ |
| **STUDY SKILLS:** | ___ | ___ | ___ |
| Does he use table of contents? | ___ | ___ | ___ |
| Does he use a study method? | ___ | ___ | ___ |
| Does he use the glossary? | ___ | ___ | ___ |
| Does he use the dictionary? | ___ | ___ | ___ |
| Does he use an index? | ___ | ___ | ___ |
| Does he use the encyclopedia and other references? | ___ | ___ | ___ |
| Does he use the library? (card catalog) | ___ | ___ | ___ |
| Does he use the bibiliography? | ___ | ___ | ___ |
| Does he understand footnotes? | ___ | ___ | ___ |

# Evaluation Student Contract

Name _____    Work must be completed by _____

*Kit Materials:*
RFU General _____    SRA Kit 3a: power card:color _____
RFU Senior _____        3a: rate card:color _____
Rdg. Dev. Kit C _____    SRA Kit 4a: power card:color _____
SPA College Rdg. Prog. _____        4a: rate card:color _____

*Machine Reading:*
Controlled Reader MM-EA, G,H,I,J,K,L,M    Flash-X:G,H,I,J,K,L   Lesson _____
                    @ _____    Phrase Flasher _____
Craig Reader          _____    Tach-X          Mon-Tues-Wed-Thurs-Fri

Audio Tapes-Listen & Think series: F,G,H,I,JKL,MN series No. ____

| *Vocabulary Materials:* | Vocabulary Builder _____ |
|---|---|
| Graflex:   Bergen-Evans _____ | A Systematic Guide to Voc. Dev. _____ |
|              Wordcraft 3 _____ | Word Clues G,H,I,J,K,L: Lesson _____ |
|              Wordcraft 2 _____ | Basic Vocabulary Skills _____ |
| Vocabulab III: color _____ | Dev. Your Vocabulary _____ |
| Word Attack _____ | McGraw-Hill Voc. 1,2,3,4,5 _____ |
| Vocabulary for College:A,B,C,D _____ | Words Are Important _____ |
| Word Power Made Easy _____ | Vocabulary Workshop _____ |
|  | A Zest for Words _____ |

*Comprehension Materials:*      (Timed)
Design for Good Reading A,B,C,D _____    Systems for Study _____
Guide to Effective Reading _____    Read, Underline, Review _____
Reading at Efficient Rates _____    Library Skills _____
Reading Skills for Young Adults _____    Skimming & Scanning Improvement _____
Art of Efficient Rates _____    Reading to Understand Science _____
Efficient Reading _____    Reading for Significant Facts _____
Be a Better Reader I,II,III,IV,V,VI _____    Reading for the Main Idea _____
                              (Other)    Reading to Discover Organization _____
Tactics in Reading I,II,III _____    Critical Reading Improvement _____
Reading for Concepts A,B,C,D,E,F,G,H ___    Preface to Critical Reading _____
Quest Academic Skills _____    English: Practice for Mastery _____
How to Become a Better Reader _____    Rapid Reading _____
Basic Reading Skills _____    Language Exercises _____
Better Work Habits _____    Functional English _____
How to Read Your Newspaper _____    Paragraph Problems _____
How to Read the Social Sciences _____    Problem Solving Improvement _____
How to Read the Sciences _____    Writing Skills I _____
How to Read the Humanities _____    Writing Skills II _____
How to Read a Short Story _____    Fundamentals of Elem. Algebra _____
The Reading Line: Social Studies, Math,    Fundamentals of Inter. Algebra _____
    Science, English, Language & Lit, Vo-    Algebra _____
    cational, Technical, Business _____    Working with Numbers _____
Getting It Together _____    Read Better-Learn More: A,B,C _____

Skills in Spelling _____  How to Get Into College & Stay There ____
Gateways to Correct Spelling _____  How to Study _____
Correct Spelling Made Easy _____  College Survival _____
Basic Spelling Skills _____  Improving College Study Skills _____
Programmed Spelling Demons _____  How to Develop a College Level Voc. ____
Spelling 1500 _____  Dev. Speed Reading Course _____
Other: _____  88 Passages to Develop Read. Comp. ____
_____  100 Passages to Develop Read. Comp. ____

Comments: _____

_____

_____

_____

_____

|  | Rate | Scores |
|---|---|---|
| Machine Readings | _____ | |
| | _____ | |
| | _____ | |
| Timed Readings | _____ | |

# Reading Weekly Assessment

| Reading: | Possible Points | Points Earned | Comments |
|---|---|---|---|
| Enthusiasm/uses silent reading time to read independently/ completes homework reading assignments | 20 | | |
| Uses beginning/ending consonants to decode words | 20 | | |
| Identifies main idea: Who, did what, when, where, why | 20 | | |
| Vocabulary (reads charts in room) | 20 | | |
| Oral reading/reads with expression/knows all words in assigned stories | 20 | | |
| Total Reading: | | | |
| Language Arts: | | | |
| Recognizes introduced patterns at beginning of words | 25 | | |
| Correctly uses capital letters and punctuation marks | 25 | | |
| Correctly forms introduced upper/lowercase letters | 50 | | |
| Total Language Arts: | | | |

# Evaluation Progress Chart

Name _____ Grade _____ Reading Grade Level _____

Mental Age _____ Reading Age _____ Chronological Age _____

| Skills | Beginning Evaluation (Yes or No) | Date Improvement Noted | Ending Evaluation (Yes or No) |
|---|---|---|---|
|  |  |  |  |
| COMPREHENSION |  |  |  |
| 1. Good oral Vocab. |  |  |  |
| 2. Good sight Vocab. |  |  |  |
| 3. Uses context clues for meaning |  |  |  |
| 4. Reads for main ideas |  |  |  |
| 5. Reads for details |  |  |  |
| 6. Reads to learn |  |  |  |
| 7. Reads critically |  |  |  |
| 8. Knows technical vocabulary |  |  |  |
| WORD ATTACK |  |  |  |
| 1. Associates sound with total word |  |  |  |
| 2. Knows the names of letters |  |  |  |
| 3. Associates sound with beginning consonant |  |  |  |
| 4. Associates sound with medial vowel |  |  |  |
| 5. Uses configuration clues |  |  |  |
| 6. Uses structural clues |  |  |  |
| 7. Handles consonant blends or digraphs (speech consonants) |  |  |  |
| 8. Has no difficulty with long vowels |  |  |  |
| 9. Has no difficulty with syllabication |  |  |  |

| | Beginning Evaluation (Yes or No) | Date Improvement Noted | Ending Evaluation (Yes or No) |
|---|---|---|---|
| ORAL READING<br>1. Has appropriate eye-voice span | | | |
| 2. Phrases correctly | | | |
| 3. Does not make constant repetitions | | | |
| 4. Enunciates well | | | |
| 5. Pronounces well | | | |
| 6. Has no inadequacies in pitch and volume | | | |
| STUDY SKILLS<br>1. Has adequate dictionary skills | | | |
| 2. Has adequate reference or locating skills | | | |
| 3. Uses indexes, glossaries, maps, etc., effectively | | | |
| 4. Uses library resources effectively | | | |
| 5. Organizes data | | | |
| RATE OF COMPREHENSION<br>1. Makes left-to-right movements | | | |
| 2. Does not regress frequently | | | |
| 3. Does not vocalize | | | |
| 4. Can skim or scan | | | |
| 5. Adjusts rate to materials | | | |

# Reading Background of Teachers at One Elementary School

| QUESTIONS | 1 | 2 | 3 | 4 | 5 | 6 | 7 | 8 | 9 | 10 | 11 | 12 | 13 | 14 | 15 | 16 | 17 |
|---|---|---|---|---|---|---|---|---|---|---|---|---|---|---|---|---|---|
| What do you teach? | PE | 3rd | K | K | 2nd | Magnet Reading | 1st | 4th | K | LD Resources 1–3 | 5th | 4th | 2nd | 2nd Bilingual | Chapter 1 Reading | N/A | Comp Lab |
| Years teaching? | 1 | 13 | 11 | 5 | 9 | 24 | 2 | First Year | 3 | 13 | 13 | 1 | 13 | 11 | 13 | 13 | 22 |
| Bachelor's? | Yes | Yes | Yes | Yes | Yes | Yes | Yes | Yes | Yes | Yes + 24 hrs. | Yes | Yes | Yes | Yes | Yes | Yes | Yes |
| Master's? | No | Yes | No | No | No | No | No | No | No | No | No | Yes | Yes | Yes | Yes | Yes | Yes |
| Hours beyond master's? | 0 | 0 | 0 | 0 | 0 | 0 | 0 | 0 | 0 | 0 | 0 | 0 | 0 | Yes | 3 | 36 | 30 |
| Major/Specialization | PE/Minor—Health | El. Ed. | K/Art | El. Ed. Reading Kinder. | English | English El. Ed. | History | History | El. Ed. Kinder—Edorse. | Math, Lang. & Learning Disabil. | Special Ed. | PE/El. Ed. | English, Counseling | Spanish | Reading | English Spec. Ed. Mid-Mgmt. | Spanish Spec. Ed. |
| College hours in reading? —Undergrad. | | 3 | 6 | 24 | 12 | 12 | 0 | 6 | 6 | 12 | 15 | 6 | 3 | 12 | Yes | 3 | 3 |
| —Graduate | | 0 | 0 | 0 | 9 | 4 | 12 | 0 | 0 | 9 | 9 | 12 | 0 | 9 | Yes | 0 | 3 |
| Current reading program used? —Basal | | Yes | No | No | Yes | Yes | Yes | No | No | Yes (some) | Yes | Yes | Yes | No | No | No | No |
| —CIRC | | Yes | No | No | No | Yes | No | Yes | No | No | Yes | Yes | No | Yes | Yes | No | No |
| —Other | | Insights | Whole Lang. | Whole Lang. | Insights | Gonzales | None | None | Writing to Read Whole Lang. Wright Group Materials | Focus | Insights | Children Lit. | Insights | Focus | Whole Lang., Gonzales | N/A | ILA |
| Do you like the program? | | Yes | Yes | Yes | Yes | Yes | No | Yes | Yes | Yes | Some Parts | Yes | No | Yes | Yes | N/A | No |

# Difficulties in Teaching Reading

*Teacher: In your opinion, what is the most difficult thing about teaching reading?*

Teachers' Responses

1. —
2. The different levels to organize and prepare for—the use of peer teaching to give teacher extra time for children at risk or handicapped children (VH children).
3. Having enough materials to keep up with the kids.
4. Parents who do not read to their children, or encourage reading, make it difficult for children who want to read.
5. (Most people seem to do what they think, but is it the correct way?) Organizing different groups within the classroom is sometimes difficult. Also, what do you do on a daily basis without getting bored?
6. Motivation of students.
7. New vocabulary.
8. I think reading is hard to teach as a subject. In my opinion it should be taught throughout the other subject areas and not as a subject itself.
9. Focusing the kindergartner's attention. Convincing parents to read to their child and provide materials for reading at home.
10. Getting my students to stay on task and *follow* when other students are reading.
11. Motivation.
12. Most students have limited experiences necessary.
13. No real consensus of program.
14. Having enough time to teach both English and Spanish reading.
15. Having to try to explain to negative whole-language people what my objectives are and the smile on my face because I have so much fun in my job.
16. The varying levels of ability.
17. Teaching students to predict outcome.
18. Children's lack of experience; not enough time to teach everything we want to cover; teaching in 2 languages.
19. Teaching is a whole-language program in a heavily based skills curriculum.
20. —
21. Saturating the children with letters and their sounds, and teaching them to read.
22. Main idea.
23. Not enough time for all the activities I want to do.
24. Materials, staying up on current methods—trying to integrate into all subjects.

25. Children who have not been taught to listen are always behind when it's time to teach a new skill.
26. —
27. —
28. I feel that the skills such as main idea and context clues are very difficult. In the beginning, I felt that getting children to love reading was the most difficult. But, with the new approach I am using, my kids *love* reading.
29. Kids who will not do the work.
30. —
31. The different levels of all the students.

# REFERENCES

## Chapter One

Beck, I. (1989, May). Reading and reasoning. *The Reading Teacher, 42,* 676–684.

Burmeister, L. (1978). *Reading strategies for middle and secondary school teachers.* Reading, MA: Addison-Wesley.

Cairns, J. C., & Floriani, B. P. (1982, January). Assessing combining forms in science. *Science & Children, 19*(4), 58–59.

Costanzo, N. (1981, January). Introducing abstraction to junior high students. *Art Education, 34*(1), 37–38.

Duffy, B., Guild, P., Freeley, M., Perrin, J., Wilderson, R., & Butler, K. (1990, January). *Restructuring for individual differences: Using learning styles in all aspects of education.* Paper presented at the Association of Curriculum Developers, San Antonio.

Dupuis, M., & Snyder, S. (1983, January). Develop concepts through vocabulary: A strategy for reading specialists to use with content teachers. *Journal of Reading, 26*(4), 297–305.

Dynneson, T., & Gross, R. (1983). *What should we be teaching in the social studies?* Bloomington, IN: Phi Delta Kappa Educational Foundation.

Eisner, E. (1982, January). The relationship between theory and practice in art education. *Art Education, 34*(2).

Engle, M. (1981, March). Some helpful hints for teaching arts seriously. *Art Education, 35.*

Glasser, W. (1986). *Control theory in the classroom.* New York: Harper and Row.

Gross, R., & Dynneson, T. (1986, November/December). A century of encounter. *Social Education, 50*(4).

Gross, R. E., & Allen, D. (1963, May). Time for a national effort to develop the social studies curriculum. *Phi Delta Kappan, 360.*

Guthrie, J. T., & Kirsch, I. S. (1984). The emergent perspective on literacy. *Phi Delta Kappan, 66,* 351–355.

Hafner, L. E., Stakenas, R. (1990). A study of social studies reading achievement & reading interests of 8th graders. RIESEP90.

Hanna, P. (1963, April). Revising the social studies: What is needed. *Social Education, 27.*

Hess, C. (1981, March). Teacher talk/Handwriting—Self confidence—Visual expression. *Art Education, 34*(2).

Hickday, G. (1990, March). Reading and social studies: The critical connection. *Social Education, 54*(3), 175–176.

Hoff, G. (1982, March). The visual narrative: Kids, comic books and creativity. *Art Education, 35*(2).

Hubbard, G. (1989, November). Poetic insights into visual arts. *Arts and Activities, 106*(3), 46–47.

Jefferson, B. (1981). Teaching art from the inside out. *Art Education, 32*(2).

Kuhn, T. (1962). *The structure of scientific revolution.* Chicago: University of Chicago Press.

Losa, J. W., and others (1983, February). *Readability grade levels of selected Navy technical school curricula: Focus on the trained person.* Naval Training Analysis and Evaluation Group, Orlando.

Lundstrum, J. (1978). *Teaching reading in the social studies.* Urbana, IL: Eric Clearninghouse.

Maddon, L. (1988, November). Impacting reading attitudes of poor readers through cooperative reading. *Reading Teacher, 42.*

McKenna, M., & Robinson, R. (1990, November). Content literacy: A definition and implications. *Journal of Reading, 34*(3).

Mikulecky, L. (1990). Literacy for what purpose. In R. L. Venezky, D. A. Wagner, & B. S. Ciliberti (Eds.), *Toward defining literacy* (pp. 24–34). Newark, DE: International Reading Association.

Miller, P. (1982, November). Reading demands in a high-technology industry. *Journal of Reading, 26*(2), 109–115.

Miller, S. D. (1986). Listening maps for musical tours. *Music Education Journal, 73,* 28–31.

Neuman, F., & Archibals, D. (1988). *Beyond standarized testing.* Madison, WI: National Association of Secondary School Principals.

Peragallo, A. (1981, July). Incorporating reading skills into art lessons. *Art Educator, 34*(4).

Rush, J. (1981). Integrated arts: Obstacles and opportunities. *Art Education, 34*(6).

Stewart, R. (1990). Factors influencing pre-service teachers' resistance to content area reading instruction. *Reading Research and Instruction, 29*(4).

Stieglitz, E. (1983). Effects of a content reading course on teacher attitudes and practices: A four year study. *Journal of Reading, 26*(8), 690–696.

Taylor, D. (1989). Toward a unified theory of literacy learning and instructional practicies. *Phi Delta Kappan, 71,* 181–193.

Thomas, R. (1884). Music school and the basic curriculum. *Music Teachers, 63*(12).

Wilder, S. (1981, January). Rainbow riding. *Art Education, 34*(1).

Zarnowski, M. (1988, November). Learning about fictionalized biographies: A reading and writing approach. *The Reading Teacher, 42*(2), 136–144.

## Chapter Two

Cairns, J. C. (1982, January). *Science and Children, 19*(4), 58–59.

Carrell, P. (1987, June). Readability in ESL. *Reading in a Foreign Language, 4*(1), 21–40.

Chall, J. (1981, August). *Readability: Conceptions and misconceptions.* Paper given at the Council of Teachers of English Conference, Urbana, IL.

Coleman, J., & Liau, T. (1975). Q computer readability formula designed for machine scoring. *Journal of Applied Psychology, 60,* 283–284.

Crandall, J., & Charrow, V. (1990, September). *Linguistic aspects of legal language.* Evaluation Report, U.S. District of Columbia.

Drummond, D., & Kraig, B. (1988). *World history.* Glenview, IL: Scott, Foresman.

Dynneson, T., & Gross, R. (1986, November-December). A century of encounter. *Social Education, 50*(4).

Early, M., Canfield, M., Karlin, R., & Schottma, S. (1975). *Moving forward, skills in reading.* New York: Harcourt Brace Jovanovich.

Flesch, R. (1950, December). A new readability yardstick. *Journal of Applied Psychology, 34,* 384–390.

Fry, E. (1986, April). *The varied uses of readability measurement.* Paper presented at the Annual meeting of the International Reading Association, Philadelphia.

Fuchs, L., and others (1984, Winter). Inaccuracy among readability formulas: Implications for the measurement of reading proficiency and selection of instructional material. *Diagnostique, 9*(2), 86–95.

Green, G. M. and others (1980). *Problems and techniques of text analysis.* Technical Report No. 168. Cambridge, MA: Center for the Study of Reading.

Gross, R. E., & Dynneson, T. (1983). *What should we be teaching in the social studies!* Bloomington, IN: Phi Delta Kappa Educational Foundation.

Gunning, R. (1968). *The technique of clear writing.* New York: McGraw-Hill.

Hanna, P. (1963, April). Revising the social studies: What is needed? *Social Education, 27,* 190–196.

Hilgendorf, P. (1980, April). *Readability levels of second grade hi-low reading materials.* Master's thesis, Kean College, Union, NJ.

Hill, W., & Erwin, R. (1984). The readability of content textbooks used in middle and junior high schools. *Reading Psychology, 5,*(1/2), 15–17.

Idson, L. (1988, January/February). Johnny can't read: Does the fault lie with the book, the teacher, or Johnny? *Remedial and Special Education, 9*(35), 8–25, 35.

Kincaid, P. and others (1975, February). *Derivation of new readability formulas.* Research Branch Report 8-75, CNTT Naval Air Station, Memphis.

Kincaid, P., and others (1980, March). *Development and testing of a computer readability editing system (CRES).* Final Report, Naval Training and Evaluation Groups TEAG-R-83.

Langan, Y. (1980, May). *Readability levels of first and second grade basal texts.* Master's thesis, Kean College, Union, NJ.

Langer, J., & Nicolich, M. (1980, May). *Prior knowledge and its effect on comprehension.* Paper presented at the Annual Meeting of the International Reading Association, St. Louis.

Loftin, R. (1988). *Our country's communities.* Morristown, NJ: Silver, Burdett and Ginn.

Nelson-Herber, J. (1985). Readability: Some cautions for the content area teacher. In H. J. Harker (Ed.), *Classroom strategies for secondary reading* (2nd ed.). Newark, DE: International Reading Association.

Noe, D., & Standall, T. (1984, March). Readability: Old cautions for the new technology. *The Reading Teacher, 37*(7), 673–674.

O'Hear, M., & Ramsey, R., (1990). *A comparison of readability scores and student perceptives of reading ease.* RIEDEC90.

Olson, A. (1984). *Readability formulas—fact or fiction.* Research Report 143.

Perera, K. (1980). The assessment of linguistic difficulty in reading materials. *Educational Review, 32*(2).

Powers, R. D., and others (1958, April). A recalculation of four readability formulas. *Journal of Educational Psychology, 49*(105).

Robbins, J. (1980). Choosing the right basal readers. *Curriculum Review, 19*(5), 395–399.

Roe, B., Stodt, B., & Burns, P. (1987). *Content area reading.* Boston: Houghton Mifflin.

Rogers, J. (1987). Readability as a source of perceived failure in adult literacy instruction. *Lifelong Learning, 10*(4), 26–29.

Sloan, B. (1980, October). *Readability levels of fourth and fifth and sixth grade basal readers.* Master's thesis, Kean College, Union, NJ.

Squire, L. R. (1987). *Memory and the brain.* New York: Oxford University Press.

Stansell, J., & Deflord, D. (1981, October). When is reading not a problem? *Journal of Reading, 25*(1), 14–20.

Staufer, R., and others (1978). *Diagnosis and correction and prevention of reading disability.* New York: Harper and Row.

Talesayon, V. (1983, October). Feedback based readability formulas for science and mathematics curricula materials. *Journal of Science and Mathematics Education in Southeast Asia, 6*(2), 5–10.

Wright, D. F., & New, B. (1978). *Introduction to algebra.* Boston: Prindle, Weber, and Schmidt.

Wright, J., & Spiegel, D. (1984, April). Teacher to teachers: How important is textbook readability to biology teachers. *American Biology Teacher, 26*(4), 221–225.

## *Chapter Three*

Afflerbach, P. (1990, Winter). The influence of prior knowledge on expert readers main idea construction strategies. *Reading Research Quarterly, 25*(1), 31–41.

Bauman J. (1988). *Reading assessment: An instructional decision making process.* Columbus, OH: Merrill.

Brown, J. & Bennett, J. (1988). *Nelson Denny Adult Reading Test.* Chicago: Riverside.

Brown, J., Bennett, M., & Hanna G. (1981). *Nelson Denny Adult Reading Test.* Chicago: Riverside.

Burns, P., & Roe, B. (1988). *Informal Reading Test.* Boston: Houghton Mifflin.

Cadenhead, K. (1987, February). Reading level: A metaphor that shapes practice. *Phi Delta Kappan, 68*(6), 43.

Conoley, J., & Dramer, J. (1989). *Oscar Burro's Institute Mental Measurement Yearbooks, Tenth Mental Measurement Yearbook.* Highland Park, IL: Gryphon.

Davey, B. (1989, May). Assessing comprehension: Selected interactions of task and reader. *The Reading Teacher, 42*(9).

Housson, S. (1990, May 7). Research Specialist, Texas Education Agency, personal communication.

Johnson, M. (1987). *Informal reading inventories* (2nd ed.). Newark, DE: International Reading Association.

Maeroff, G. I. (1991, Dec) Assessing alternative assessment. *Phi Delta Kappan, 73*(4), 272–275.

Miller, S. (1990) Relations among oral reading, silent reading and listening comprehension of students at differing competency levels. *Reading Research and Instruction, 29,* 2.

Morris, D. (1990). Educators give TEAM exam a passing grade. *Midland Reporter Telegram,* May 6.

Pearson, P. D. (1985, April). Changing the face of reading comprehension instruction. *The Reading Teacher, 38*(8), 724–739.

Pearson, P. D., Taylor, B., & Harris, L. (1988). *Reading difficulties: Instruction and assessment.* New York: Random House.

Ranking, E. F. (1970). The cloze procedure—Its validation and utility. In R. Farr (Ed.), *Measurement and evaluation of reading.* New York: Harcourt Brace & World.

Sivaroli, N. (1965). *Classroom reading inventory.* Dubuque, IA: Wm. C. Brown.

Taylor, B., Harris, L., & Pearson, P. D. (1988). *Reading difficulties: Instruction and assessment.* New York: Random House.

Tierney, R. J., Carter, M. A., & Desai, L. E. (1991) *Portfolio assessment in the reading-writing classroom.* Norwood: Christopher Gordon.

Thelen, J. (1990, April-May). Commentary: What's "dreadfully inadequate in reading." *Reading Today, 2.*

Valencia, S., & Pearson, P. D. (1987, April). Reading assessment: Time for a change. *Reading Teacher, 40*(8), 726–732.

Wittrock, M. C. (1987, April). Process oriented measures of comprehension. *Reading Teacher, 40*(8), 734–737.

Wixson, K. (1987, April). New directions in statewide reading. *Reading Teacher, 40*(8), 749–754.

## Chapter Four

Chall, J. (1989). The great phonics debate? *Phi Delta Kappan, 71,* 158.

Cunningham, P. M. (1987, January). Are your vocabulary words lunules or lupulins? *Journal of Reading, 40*(5).

Duffy, G. G. (1987, January). Teaching reading skills as strategies. *Reading Teacher, 40*(5).

Earle, R. (1973, April). The elusive factor in reading competence. *Journal of Reading, 16*(7), 550–555.

Gates, A. (1953). *Teaching reading.* Department of Classroom Teachers, American Educational Research Association of the National Education Association.

Greene, B. (1990, June). Content area reading and vocabulary development. *Reading Psychology, 11*(2), 167–172.

Hafner, L. E. (1978). *Developmental reading in middle and secondary schools: Foundations, strategies, and skills for teaching.* New York: Macmillan.

Herman, W. (1979, Summer). Reading in the social studies: Needed research. *Journal of Social Studies Research, 3*(2).

Irwin, J. (1986) *Understanding and teaching cohesion comprehension.* Newark, DE: International Reading Association.

Johnson, D., Heimlich, J., & Pittleman, S. (1986, April). Semantic mapping: Classroom applications. *The Reading Teacher, 39*(2).

Konopak, B., & Williams, N. (1988, March). Using the keyword method to help young readers learn content materials. *The Reading Teacher, 41*(7), 682–687.

Lomas, R., & Shanahan, T. (1988, Summer). The reading writing relationship: Seven principles. *Reading Teacher, 41*(10).

Lundstrum, J., & Taylor, B. (1978). *Teaching reading in social studies.* Urbana, IL: ERIC Clearninghouse Publishers.

Manzo, A., & Manzo, U. (1990). *Content areas reading: A heuristic approach.* Columbus, OH: Merrill.

McIntosh, M. E. (1985, April). What do practitioners need to know about inference research? *Reading Teacher, 41*()8).

Melting pot, year 2,000. (1990) *Time*, April 9.

Nicholson, T., & Hill, M. (1984). Experts and novices: A study of reading in the high school classroom. *Reading Research Quarterly 19*(4).

Olson, A., & Ames, W. (1972). *Teaching reading skills in secondary school.* Scranton, PA: Intext Educational Publication.

Pearson, P. E., & Johnson, D. D. (1984). *Teaching reading vocabulary.* New York: Holt, Reinhart and Winston.

Reutzel, D. R. (1985, January). Story maps improve comprehension. *Reading Teacher, 28*(4).

Rupley, W. H., & Blari, T. R. (1987, January). Assignment and supervision of reading seatwork: Looking in on 12 primary teachers. *Reading Teacher, 40*(4), 391.

Ryder, R. J. (1986, October). Teaching vocabulary through external context clues. *Journal of Reading, 30*(1), 701–705.

Schatz-Kress, E., & Baldwin, S. (1986, Fall). Context clues are unreliable predictors of word meaning. *Reading Research Quarterly, 21*(4), 439.

Scheu, J., Tanner, D., & Au, K. H. (1986, October). Designing seatwork to improve students' reading comprehension ability. *Reading Teacher, 40*(1), 32–34.

Schmidt, M. B. (1986, October). The shape of content: Four semantic map structures for expository paragraphs. *Reading Teacher, 40*(1).

Simpson, M. (1986). PORPE: A writing strategy for studying and learning in the content areas. *Journal of Reading, 29.*

Smith, C. (1990, March). Vocabulary development in content area reading. *Reading Teacher, 43*(7).

Thelen, J. (1990, April-May). Commentary: What's "dreadfully inadequate in reading." *Reading Today, 2.*

Wysolki, K., & Jenkins, J. R. (1987). Deriving word meanings through morphological generalization. *Reading Research Quarterly, 22*(1), 66–81.

## *Chapter Five*

Barrett, T. (1972). *A taxonomy of reading comprehension.* [Reading 360 Monograph]. Lexington, MA: Ginn.

Bartlett, F. (1932). *Remembering.* Cambridge: Cambridge University Press.

Baumann, J. F., & Schmitt, M. C. (1986, March). The what, why, how and when of comprehension instruction. *Reading Teacher, 39*(1), 640–648.

Beck, I. (1989, May). Reading and reasoning. *Reading Teacher, 42*(9), 676–682.

Belkin, G., & Gray, J. (1977). *Educational psychology: An introduction* (pp. 66–68). Dubuque, IA: Wm. C. Brown.

Bloom, B. C. (1956). *Taxonomy of educational objectives: Cognitive domain.* New York: David McKay.

Bower, G. (1973). How to remember. *Psychology Today, 7,* 82–90.

Bristow, P. S. (1985, December). Are poor readers passive readers? Some evidence, possible explanations, and potential solutions. *Reading Teacher, 29*(3).

Britton, B. K., & Glynn, S. M. (Eds.). (1987). *Executive control processes in reading.* Hillsdale, NJ: Lawrence Erlbaum.

Boyles, N. (1988, July/August). The new improved critical reading. *Learning 7,* 49–51.

Cohen, M. P., Giorno, B, Harlan, J., McComack, A., & Staver, J. (1984). *Science.* Glenview, IL: Scott Foresman.

Collins, C. (1987). Fixing incorrect answers in recitation. *Reading Teacher,* *40*(6).

Cook, L., & Mayer, R. (1983). Reading strategies training for meaningful learning from prose. In M. Prosley & J. R. Levin (Eds.), *Cognitive strategy research: Educational applications* (pp. 87–131). New York: Springer-Verlag.

Cooper, J. D. (1986). *Improving reading comprehension.* Boston: Houghton Mifflin.

Crano, W. D., & Johnson, C. D. (1991, Winter). Facilitating reading comprehension through spatial skills training. *Journal of Experimental Education, 59*(2), 113–127.

Davis, I. (1980). Assessing readability checklist approach. *Journal of Reading, 24,* 129–130.

Durkin, D. (1979). What classroom observations reveal about reading comprehension instruction. *Reading Research Quarterly, 14*(4), 481–533.

Durkin, D. (1981). Reading comprehension instruction in five basal reader series. *Reading Research Quarterly, 16*(4), 515–544.

Durkin, D. (1984). Is there a match between what elementary teachers do and what basal readers manuals recommend? *Reading Teacher, 37,* 734–744.

Durkin, D. (1986, January). Reading methodology textbooks: Are they helping teachers teach comprehension? *Reading Teacher, 39*(5), 410.

Dyck, M., & Sundbye, N. (1988, Summer). The effects of text explicitness on story understanding and recall by learning disabled children. *Learning Disabilities Research, 3*(2), 68–77.

Eisner, E. (1990, February). *What's worth teaching?* Paper presented at National Conference of the Association of Supervision and Curriculum Development, San Antonio.

Epstein, H. (1970). *A strategy for education.* New York: Oxford University Press.

Epstein, H. (1984, February). Brain growth and cognitive developmental response to Richard Queen. *Educational Leadership, 41*(5), 72–75.

Escoe, A. (1981, May). *Schooling and scheming.* Paper presented at International Reading Association, New Orleans.

Farr, R. (1989, October). *Reading for the English teacher.* Paper presented at the Texas Council of Teachers of English, Midland, Texas.

Farr, R., & Carey, P. (1986). *Reading as communication: An interactive approach.* Columbus OH: Merrill.

Frager, A. M., & Thompson, L. C. (1985, October). Conflict resolution. *Journal of Reading, 29*(1), 58–63.

Fredericks, A. D. (1986, October). Mental imagery activities to improve comprehension. *Reading Teacher, 40*(1), 78–84.

French, J. (1986). *Reading and study skills in secondary school: A source book.* New York: Garland.

Gates, A. (1917). Recitation as a factor in memorizing. *Archives of psychology, 40.*

Gray, M. (1969). Research and elementary school critical reading instruction. *Reading Teacher, 22,* 477–479.

Gray, W. (1960). The major aspects of reading. In I. H. Robinson (Ed.), *Development of reading abilities* [Supplementary Edition Monograph #9]. Chicago: University of Chicago Press.

Gusak, F. (1967). Teacher questioning and reading. *Reading Teacher, 21,* 227–234.

Gusak, F. (1985). *Diagnostic reading instruction.* New York: Harper and Row.

Hahn, A. L. (1985, October). Teaching remedial students to be strategic readers and better comprehenders. *Reading Teacher, 38*(14).

Herber, H. (1978). *Teaching reading in content areas.* Englewood Cliffs, NJ: Prentice Hall.

Hillerich, R. L. (1979). Reading comprehension. *Reporting on Reading, 5,* 103.

Hollingsworth, P. (1988). Get a "grip" on comprehension. *Reading Horizons, 29,* 71–79.

Hudgins, B. B. (1977). *Learning and thinking: A primer for teachers.* Itasca, IL: Peacock.

Indrisano, R. (1982). *Independent application of SEARCH in reading and language arts.* Columbus, OH: Ginn.

Jewell, M., & Zintz, M. (1990). *Learning to read and write naturally* (2nd ed.). Dubuque, IA: Kendall/Hunt.

Just, M., & Carpenter, P. (1987). *The psychology of reading and language comprehension.* Boston: Allyn and Bacon.

Klein, M. (1988). *Teaching reading comprehension and vocabulary.* Englewood Cliffs, NJ: Prentice Hall.

Kolb, B., & Whishaw, I. (1990). *Fundamentals of human neuropsychology* (3rd ed.). New York: W. H. Freeman and Company.

Langer, J. A. (1982). Facilitating text processing: The elaboration of prior knowledge. In J. Langer & M. Trika Smaith Burke (Eds.), *Reader meets author: Bridging the gap* (pp. 149–162). Newark, DE: International Reading Association.

Langer, J. A., & Nicolich, M. (1980, May 5–9). *Prior knowledge and its effect on comprehension.* Paper presented at the Annual Meeting of the International Reading Association, St. Louis.

Linn, M. C., & Clancy, M. J. (1990, April). Designing instruction to take advantage of recent advances in understanding cognition. *Academic Computing, 18*(8), 17–19.

Manzo, A., & Manzo, U. (1990). *Content area reading: A heuristic approach.* Columbus, OH: Merrill.

Mayer, R. (1989). Models for understanding. *Review of Educational Research, 59*(1).

Nelson-Herber, J., & Herber, H. (1984). A positive approach to assessment and correction of reading difficulties in middle and secondary schools. In *J. Flood (Ed.), Promoting reading comprehension* (pp. 232–242). Newark, DE: International Reading Association.

Nessel, D. (1987, February). Reading comprehension: Asking the right questions. *Phi Delta Kappan, 68*(6), 35.

Pearson, P. D. (1985, April). Changing the face of reading comprehension. *Reading Teacher, 38*(8), 724–739.

Pearson, P. D., & Johnson, D. (1978). *Making judgments about the written word: Teaching reading comprehension* (pp. 133–152). New York: Holt, Rinehart and Winston.

Pogrov, S. (1990). *A three-phase approach to solving the at-risk problem.* Paper presented at Association for Supervision and Curriculum Development, San Antonio.

Pyrczak, R. (1976, Fall). Reducing reading illiteracy by improving reading materials. *Reading Improvement, 13,* 159–162.

Rayner, K., & Pollatsek, W. (1989). *Psychology of reading.* Englewood Cliffs, NJ: Prentice Hall.

Reutzel, D. R., & Hollingsworth, P. M. (1988). Highlighting key vocabulary:

A generative-reciprocal procedure for teaching selected inference types. *Reading Research Quarterly, 23*(3), 358–378.

Reutzel, D. R., & Hollingsworth, P. M. (1991). Reading comprehension skills, Testing the distinctiveness hypothesis. *Reading Research Instruction, 30*(2), 32–46.

Richardson, J., & Morgan, R. (1990). *Reading to learn in the content areas.* Belmont, CA: Wadsworth.

Roberts, T. (1988). Development of pre-instructional versus previous experience: Effects on factual and inferential comprehension. *Reading Psychology, 9*(2), 141–157.

Robinson, H. A. (1978). *Teaching reading and study strategies: The content areas* (2nd ed.). Boston: Allyn and Bacon.

Sanders, N. (1966). *Classroom questions—What kinds?* New York: Harper and Row.

Schmitt, M. C., & Baumann, J. F. (1986, October). How to incorporate comprehension monitoring strategies into basal reader instruction. *Reading Teacher, 40*(1), 28–32.

Smith, R. J., & Dauer, V. L. (1984). A comprehension-monitoring strategy for reading content area materials. *Journal of Reading, 28,* 144–147.

Squire, L. K. (1987). *Memory and the brain.* New York: Oxford University Press.

Stevens, R. J., Slavin, R. E., & Farnish, A. M. (1991, March). The effects of cooperative learning and direct instruction in reading comprehension strategies on main idea identification. *Journal of Educational Psychology, 83*(1), 8–16.

Thatcher, R. W., Walker, R. A., & Guidice, S. (1987). Human cerebral hemisphere development at different rates and ages. *Sciences, 236,* 110–113.

Trabasso, T. (1981). On the making of inferences during reading and their assessment. In *Comprehension teaching: Research in review.* Newark, DE: International Reading Association.

Vacca, R., & Vacca, J. (1989). *Content area reading.* Glenview, IL: Scott, Foresman.

Wendler, D., Samuels, J. S., and Moore, V. (1989, Fall). Comprehension instruction of award-winning teachers, teachers with master's degrees, and other teachers. *Reading Research Quarterly, 24,* 382–398.

Whitener, E. (1989). A meta-analytic review of the effect of learning on the interaction between prior achievement and instructional support. *Review of Educational Research, 59*(1).

## Chapter Six

Anrig, G. R. (1984, March). *Schools and higher education in a period of reform: Strengthening standards and performance.* Paper presented at National Conference of Higher Education, San Francisco.

Arlo, R. (1969). *The relative effectiveness of inductive and expository teaching of principles of general semantics upon the critical reading ability of 9th grade students.* (Educational Reproduction Service No. 046 923).

Association of American Publishers. (1981). *Book and materials selection for school libraries and classrooms: Procedures, challenges, and responses.* Washington, DC: Author.

Atwood, B. (1975, November). Critical reading: A social experience. *Learning, 18,* 34–40.

Baumann, J. F., & Schmitt, M. C. (1986, March). The what, why, how, and when of comprehension instruction. *Reading Teacher 39*(1), 640–648.

Berger, A. (1971). Increasing reading rate with paperbacks. *Reading Improvement, 9*, 78–84.

Boyan, C. (1972, March). Critical reading: What is it? Where is it? *Reading Teacher, 25*(6), 51.

Boyles, N. N. (1988, July/August). The new improved critical reading. *Learning, 88*.

Bristow, P. S. (1985, December). Are poor readers passive readers? Some evidence, possible explanations, and potential solutions. *Reading Teacher, 29*(3).

Carton, K. (1990, October). Collaborative writing of mathematics problems. *Mathematics Teacher, 83*(7).

Caskey, H. J. (1970, April). Guidelines for teaching comprehension. *Reading Teacher, 23*(7).

Cooper, J. D. (1986). *Improving reading comprehension.* New York: Houghton Mifflin.

Cornish, R. L. (1967, November). You can challenge the gifted child. *Grade Teacher, LXXXV*, 141–144.

Culp, C., Eisman, L., & Hoffman, M. (1988). *World of music.* Morriston, NJ: Silver Burdett and Ginn.

D'Angello, E. (1972) Critical thinking in reading. *Elementary English, 48*, 946–950.

Davis, N. (1967, November). *How to work with the academically talented in the social studies.* (Educational Document Reproductive Services Number 083 005).

Denberg, R., & Jones, C. (1967, March). Critical reading in a developmental reading course, *Journal of Reading, 30*(6) 399–403.

Downing, F. M. (1974). An investigation of critical thinking while reading in grades thirteen and fourteen. (Educational Document Reproductive Services Number 110 946).

Duquette, R. (1974). Critical reading—Can it be taught? *Elementary English, 48*, 946–950.

Durr, W. (1970, January). Let's not neglect the gifted. *Instructor, LXXIX*, 58.

Dynneson, T., & Gross, R. (1983). *What should we be teaching in the social studies?* Bloomington, IN: Phi Delta Kappa, Educational Foundation.

Frager, A. M., & Thompson, L. C. (1985). Conflict: The key to critical reading instruction. *Journal of Reading, 28*, 676–683.

Fredericks, A. D. (1986, October). Mental imagery activities to improve comprehension, *Reading Teacher, 40*(1), 78–84.

Gentile, L., & McMillan, M. (1989). Reading style or coping style: A response to Stahl and Carbo. *Reading Research and Instruction, 29*(1).

Gray, M. (1969). Research and elementary school critical reading instruction. *Reading Teacher, 22*, 470–479.

Hahn, A. L. (1985, October). Teaching remedial students to be stragtegic readers and better comprehenders. *Reading Teacher, 39*(1), 72–77.

Hollingsworth, P., & Reutzel, R. (1985, Fall). Get a grip on comprehension. *Reading Horizons*, 71–78.

Holmes, B. C., & Ammon, R. I. (1985). Teaching content with trade books: A strategy. *Childhood Education, 61*(5), 366–390.

Jacobs, L. B. (1989). Reading, writing, reminiscing. *Teaching K–8, 34*(35).

Jenkinson, M. D. (1965). *Reading and inquiry* (pp. 112–114). Newark, DE: International Reading Association.

Karlin, R. (1984). *Teaching reading in high school: Improving reading in content area.* New York: Harper and Row.

Konopak, B., Martin, S., & Martin, M. (1990). Using a writing strategy to enhance sixth-grade students comprehension of content material. *Journal of Reading Behavior, 22*(1).

Krebs, J. P. (1987, October). Connections: Writing about family. *English Journal, 76*(6), 58.

Lee, D. M. (1969). What is reading? *The Reading Teacher, 22*, 403–407.

Lyman, B. G., & Collins, M. D. (1990, Spring). Critical reading: A redefinition. *Reading Research and Instruction, 29*(3), 56–63.

Manzo, A., & Manzo, U. (1990). *Reading in the content area: A heuristic approach.* Columbus, OH: Merrill.

McManus, G., & Kirby, D. (1988, March). Using peer group instruction to teach writing, *English Journal, 78*(3), 14–19.

Newman, F., et al. (1988). *Higher order thinking in high school social studies: An analysis of classrooms, teachers, students and leadership.* Washington, DC: Office of Educational Research.

Niemi, P. (1990). Recent explorations into the etiology of reading difficulties: Insights from language and cognition. *International Journal of Disability, Development & Education, 37*(1), 17–28.

Oakhill, J., and others (1986, September). On the nature of the differences between skilled and less-skilled comprehenders. *Journal of Research in Reading, 9*(2), 86–91.

Odom, N. (1971, April). A dozen assignments from the newspaper. *Journal of Reading, 14*, 475–476.

Rapheal, T. (1981, Winter). The effects of known reading difference on meta-comprehension and comprehension. *Journal of Reading Behavior, 13*(4), 323–334.

Rapheal, T. (1984, January). Teaching learners about sources of information for answering comprehension questions. *Journal of Reading, 27*(4), 312–317.

Reutzel, D. R. (1985, November). Reconciling schema theory and the basal reading lesson. *The Reading Teacher, 45*, 194–197.

Roberts, T. (1988). Development of pre-instructional versus previous experience: Effects on factual and inferential comprehension. *Reading Psychology, 9*(2), 141–157.

Ronan, E. (1969). Analogy in elementary school. *Reading Teacher, 22*, 430–434.

Rothman, R. (1990, January). Decline at the top. *Education Week*, 34–35.

Russell, D. (1950). *Children's thinking.* Boston: Silver, Burdett and Ginn.

Schmitt, M. C., & Baumann, J. F. (1986, October). How to incorporate comprehension monitoring strategies into basal reader instruction. *Reading Teacher, 40*(1), 28–32.

Singer, H., & Donlan, D. (1980). *Reading and learning from text.* Boston: Little, Brown.

Smith, N. B. (1971). Reading research: Notable findings and urgent needs. (ERIC Document Reproduction Service Number 985 676)

Spires, H. (1990, November). Metacognition and reading: Implications for instruction. *Reading, 24*(3), 151–156.

Spiro, Rand, and others (1987). Knowledge acquired for application: Cognitive flexibility and transfer in complex cognitive domains. In B. K. Britton and S. M. Glynn (Eds.), *Executive control in reading processes.* Hillsdale, NJ: Erlbaum.

Sullivan, J. (1972). Liberating children to creative reading. *Reading Teacher, 25,* 639–642.

Sullivan, J. (1974). Receptive and critical reading develops at all levels. *Reading Teacher, 27,* 780–796.

Warner, S., & Shelton, N. (1972). Critical reading involves critical thinking, *Instructor, 81,* 61–62.

Wasserman, S. (1987, February), Teaching for thinking: Louis E. Raths revisited. *Phi Delta Kappan, 68*(6), 57–60.

Watson, J. R. (1974). Kids as critics: Can they evaluate? *Instructor, 38*(8), 40

Whitesitt, J. (1990, September). Writing study cards for understanding. *Mathematics Teacher, 83*(6).

Williams, G. (1959, May). Provisions for critical reading in basal readers. *Elementary English, 36,* 323–330.

Wittrock, M. C. (1981). Reading comprehension. In F. J. Pirozzolo and M. C. Wittrock (Eds.), *Neuropsychological and cognitive processes in reading.* New York: Academic Press.

Zarnowki, M. (1988, November), Learning about fictionalized biographies: A reading and writing approach. *The Reading Teacher, 42*(2), 136–144.

## *Chapter Seven*

Carbo, M. (1990, February). *Reading styles: Sharply increasing student motivation, self esteem and achievement.* Paper presented at ASCD Conference, San Antonio.

Corballis, M. C., & Morgan, M. J. (1976). On the biological basis of human laterality: Evidence for a maturational left-right gradient. *Behavioral and Brain Sciences, 2,* 261–336.

Denckla, M. (1985). Motor coordination in dyslexic children: Theoretical and clinical implications. In F. Duffy & N. Geschwind (Eds.), *Dyslexia: A neuroscientific approach to clinical evaluation.* New York: Basic Books.

Dewey, J. (1933). *How we think.* New York: D. C. Heath.

Dunn, R. (1990, February), *Children in crises: The learning styles of at-risk drop-out and multicultural underachievers—and how to increase their achievement.* Paper presented at National Conference of the Association for Supervision and Curriculum Development, San Antonio.

Freely, M., Perrin, J., Wilderson, G., & Butler, K. (1990). *Restructuring for individual differences: Using learning styles in all aspects of education.* Paper presented at Association for Supervision and Curriculum Development, San Antonio.

Glasser, W. (1990, February). The quality school. *Phi Delta Kappan, 71*(6), 424–435.

Greenberg, J. (1978). The brain, holding the secrets of behavior. *Science News, 114*(22), 355–365.

Hamachek, A. (1990, February). *Memory and study strategies for optimal learning.* Paper presented at CLDAA, Anaheim.

Hilgard, E. R., & Bower, G. H. (1975). *Theories of learning.* Englewood Cliffs, NJ: Prentice-Hall.

Hires, T. (1987). Left brain, right brain: Myth and importance for man and training. *Academic Management, 60.*

Hiscock, M., Kinsbourne, M. (1977). Selective listening symmetry in preschool children. *Developmental Psychology, 13,* 217–224.

Indrisano, R. (1982). *Independent application of SEARCH in reading and language arts.* Columbus, OH: Ginn. [Occasional Papers, 982].

Kohn, B., & Dennis, M. (1974). Selective impairments of visuospatial abilities in infantile hemiplegics after right hemidecortication. *Neuropsychologica, 12,* 505–512.

Luria, A. (1980). *Higher cortical functions in man.* New York: Basic Books.

Roswell, F. G., & Natchez, G. (1989). *Reading disability: A human approach to evaluation and treatment of reading and writing difficulties* (4th ed.) New York: Basic Books.

Singer, H., & Donlan, D. (1989). *Reading and learning from text.* Hillsdale, NJ: Erlbaum.

Skipper, B. (1986). *Study skills.* Arlington, TX: Skills of Studying, Inc.

Sperry, R. W. (1968). Hemisphere disconnections and unity in conscious awareness. *American Psychologist, 23,* 723–733.

Thatcher, R. W., Walker, R. A., & Guidice, S. (1987). Human cerebral hemisphere development at different rates and ages. *Sciences, 236,* 1110–1113.

Wade, S., Trathen, W., & Schraw, G. (1990, Spring). An analysis of spontaneous study strategies. *Reading Research Quarterly, 25*(12).

White, N., & Kinsbourne, M. (1980). Does speech output control lateralize over time: Evidence from verbal-manual time sharing tasks. *Brain and Language, 10,* 23–25.

Witelson, S. (1985, August). The brain connection: The corpus callosum is larger in left handers. *Science, 229.*

Witelson, S. (1987, June). Neurobiological aspects of language in children. *Child Development, 58*(3).

## Chapter Eight

Bakker, D., and others (1990, August–September). Hemisphere-specific treatment of dyslexic subtypes. *Journal of Learning Disabilities, 23*(7), 433–438.

Bruck, M. (1990, May). Word-recognition skills of adults with childhood diagnoses of dyslexia. *Developmental Psychology, 26*(3), 439–454.

Byers, J. (1989, Spring). AIDS in children: Effects on neurological development and implications for the future. *Journal of Special Education, 23,* 5–16.

Calkins, L., & McHarwayne, S. (1987). *The writing workshop: A world of difference.* Portsmouth, NH: Heinemann.

Carbo, M. (1988). The evidence supporting reading styles. *Phi Delta Kappan, 70*(4), 323–327.

Carbo, M. (1990, February). Reading styles: Sharply increasing student motivation, self-esteem, and achievement. American Society of Curriculum Development, San Antonio.

Carbo, M., Dunn, R., & Dunn, K. (1986). *Teaching students to read through their individual learning styles.* Englewood Cliffs, NJ: Prentice-Hall.

Cochran, J. (1980). *Differentiating interpersonal needs between regular and remedial readers.* Paper presented at the American Psychological Association, Toronto, Canada.

Collier, V. P. (1987, December). Age and rate of acquisition of second language for academic purposes. *TESOL Quarterly, 21*(4).

Corbalis, M. C., & Morgan, M. J. (1978). On the biological basis of human laterality: Evidence for a maturational left-right gradient. *Behavioral and Brain Sciences, 2,* 261–336.

Denckla, M. (1985). Motor coordination in dyslexic children: Theoretical and clinical implications. In F. E. Duffy & N. Geschwind (Eds.), *Dyslexia.* New York: Basic Books.

DSM-III-R Classification (1987). Washington, DC: The American Psychiatric Association.

Duffy, F. H. (1980). Dyslexia: Automated diagnosis by computerized classification of brain electrical activity. *Annals of Neurology, 7,* 421–428.

Dunn, R. (1990, February). *Children in crisis: The learning styles of at-risk children.* Paper presented at the American Society of Curriculum Development, San Antonio.

Dykman, R. A., Peters, J. E., & Ackerman, P. T. (1973). Experimental approaches to the study of minimal brain dysfunction: A follow-up study. *Annals of the New York Academy of Science, 205,* 93–107.

Feldman, D. (1984, April). A followup on subjects scoring above 180 IQ in Terman's "Scientific Study of Genius." *Exceptional Children, 50*(6), 518–523.

Galaburda, A. (1990). The testosterone hypothesis: Assessment since Geshwind & Behan, 1982. *Annals of Dyslexia, 40,* 18–38.

Geshwind, N. (1982). Why Orton was right. *Annals of Dyslexia, 32,* 13–30.

Gottesman, R., Belmont, I., & Kaminer, R. (1975). Admission and follow-up status of reading disabled children referred to a medical clinic. *Journal of Learning Disabilities, 8,* 642–650.

Greenough, W. T., Black, J. E., & Wallace, C. S. (1987). Experience and brain development. *Child Development, 58,* 539–559.

Hugdahl, K., Synnevag, B., & Satz, P. (1991). Immune and autoimmune diseases in dyslexic children: Erratum. *Neuropsychologia, 29*(2), 211.

Humphreys, P., Kaufmann, W., & Galaburda, A. (1990, December). Developmental dyslexia in women: Neuropathological findings in three patients. *Annals of Neurology, 28*(6), 727–738.

Hynd, C. R. (1987). Instruction of reading disabled/dyslexic students. *Teacher Education and Practice, 3*(2), 17–33.

Hynd, G., and others (1990, August). Brain morphology in developmental dyslexia and attention on deficit disorder. *Archives of Neurology, 47*(8) 919–926.

Jakupcak, J. (1973). *Job functions, roles and views of training of learning disability and remedial reading personnel.* Unpublished doctoral dissertation, University of Illinois, Urbana.

Jakupak, J. (1975). Areas of congruences in remedial reading and learning disabled. *Journal of Special Education, 9*(2).

Johnsen, B. (1990). *Acquisition of reading and writing: A neurolinguistic approach.* ED326864.

Johnson, S. (1985). Who are the gifted? A dilemma in search of a solution. *Education of Visually Handicapped, 18,* 54–70.

Karlin, R. (1984). *Teaching reading in high school: Implications for reading in the content area.* New York: Harper & Row.

Kaufman, A. (1979). *Intelligent testing with the WISC-R.* New York: Wiley.

Kendall, J. (1983, June). Values as the core of institutional commitment: Finding a common ground. *New Directions for Experimental Learning, 20,* 27–42.

Kimura, D., & McGlone, S. (1983). *Neuropsychology test procedures.* University of Western Ontario, London, Ontario.

Kirk, U. (1985). Hemispheric contribution to the development of graphic skill. In C. T. Best (Ed.), *Hemispheric function and integration in the child.* New York: Academic Press.

Klien, C. L. (1972). The adolescents with learning problems: How long must they wait? *Journal of Leaning Disabilities, 5,* 127–144.

Kolb, B., Whishaw, I. (1990). *Fundamentals of human neuropsychology* (3rd ed.). New York: W. H. Freeman and Company.

Krashen, S. (1982). *Child-adult differences in second language acquisition.* Rowley, MA: Newbury House.

Landwehrmeyer, B., and others (1990, June). Patterns of task-related slow brain potentials in dyslexia. *Archives of Neurology 47*(7), 791–797.

Levine, J. D. (1987). *Developmental variation and learning disorders.* Cambridge, MA: Toronto Educators Publishing Service.

Lewis, B. (1990, February). Familial phonological disorders: Four pedigrees. *Journal of Speech and Hearing Disorders, 55*(1), 160–170.

Lezak, M. (1989). *Neuropsychological assessment.* New York: Oxford University Press.

Luria, A. (1966). *Higher cortical functions in man* (2nd ed.). New York: Basic Books.

Marland, T. (1972). *Education of the gifted and talented: Report to Congress of U.S. by U.S. Commissioner of Education.* Washington, DC: U.S. Government Printing Office.

Matthews, C. (1991, February). Serial processing and the "phonetic route": Lessons learned in the functional reorganization of deep dyslexia. *Journal of Communication Disorders, 24*(1), 21–39.

Millichap, J. G., & Millichap, N. M. (1986). *Dyslexia: As the neurologist and educator read it.* Springfield, IL: Thomas.

Naidoo, S. (1981). Teaching methods and their rational. In G. T. Pavlidis & T. R. Miles (Eds.), *Dyslexia research and its application to education.* New York: Wiley.

Obrzut, J. E., & Hynd, G. W. (1986). *Child neuropsychology: Theory and research.* Orlando: Academic Press.

Orsini, D. L., Van Gorp, W. G., & Boone, K. B. (1988). *The neuropsychology casebook.* New York: Springer Verlag.

Pirozzolo, F. J., & Wittrock, M. C. (1981). *Neuropsychologist and cognitive processes in reading.* New York: Academic Press.

Presland, J. (1991, January). Explaining away dyslexia. *Educational Psychology in Practice, 6*(4), 215–221.

Roe, B., Stoodt, B., & Burns, P. (1987). *Secondary school reading instruction: The content areas* (3rd ed.). Boston: Houghton and Mifflin.

Rourke, B. P., Young, G., and others (1986). Adult outcomes of central processing deficiencies in childhood in neuropsychological assessment of neuropsychiatric disorders (pp. 244–267). New York: Oxford University Press.

Rudd, R. G., Holmes, J. M., & Pardes, J. R. (1988). *Assessment of developmental learning disorders: A neuropsychological approach.* New York: Basic Books.

Sarazin, F. F., & Spreen, O. (1986). Fifteen-year stability of some neuropsychological tests in learning disabled subjects with and without neurological impairment. *Journal of Clinical and Experimental Neuropsychology, 8,* 190–200.

Saul, R., Sperry, R. W. (1968). Absence of commisourotomy symptoms with ageness of corpus callosum. *Neurology, 18,* 307.

Smith, S., Pennington, B., and others (1990, March). Familial dyslexia: Use of a genetic linkage data to define subtypes. *Journal of Child & Adolescent Psychiatry, 29*(2), 204–213.

Snowling, M. (1991, January). Developmental reading disorders. *Journal of Child Psychology & Psychiatry, 32*(1), 49–77.

Sperry, R. W. (1968). Hemisphere disconnection and unity in conscious awareness. *American Psychologist, 23,* 723–733.

Templeton, A. B. (1969). *Reading disorders in the United States.* Washington, DC: National Advisory Committee on Dyslexia and Related Reading Disorders, United States Department of HEW.

Texas State Board of Education (1986). In newsletter, Scottish Rite Learning Center Publication, Spring 1990, 7.

Thatcher, R. W., Walker, R. A., & Giudice S. (1987). Human cerebral hemisphere development at different rates and ages. *Science, 238,* 1110–1113.

Thornton, J., & Bruner, D. (1993, May). *Media use with remedial, regular and talented and gifted readers.* Unpublished master's thesis, University of Texas, Permian Basin.

Vacca, R., & Vacca, J. (1989). *Content area reading* (3rd ed.). Glenview, IL: Scott, Foresman.

Vail, P. (1989). *Gifts, talents, and the dyslexias: Wellsprings, springboards, and finding Folley's rocks.* 40th Annual Conference of the Orton Dyslexic Society, Dallas.

Wolff, P. (1990, November). Rate variables and automatized naming in developmental dyslexia. *Brain & Language, 39*(4) 556–578.

Ysseldyke, J. E., & Algozzine, B. (1990). *Introduction to special education* (2nd ed.). Boston: Houghton Mifflin.

## Chapter Nine

*Advertising Age.* (1982). Crain Communications, Inc.

Armstrong, G. B., & Greenberg, B. S. (1990, Spring). Background T.V. as an inhibitor of cognitive processing. *Human Communication Research, 16*(3), 355–386.

Balajthy, E. (1987). What does research on computer-based instruction have to say to the reading teacher. *Journal of Reading Research and Instruction, 27,* 54–65.

Balajthy, E. (1989). Computer instruction and reading education. *Journal of Reading Research and Instruction, 28,* 49–59.

Becker, J. T. (1972, November). Language experience attack on adolescent illiteracy. *Journal of Reading, 16*(2), 115–119.

Bitter, G. (1989). Computers in education. *Arizona Statesman, 33,* 7.

Borton, T. (1971, February). Dual audio television. *Harvard Educational Review, 41*(1), 64–78.

Charren, P. (1990, December). What's missing in children's TV? *World Monitor, 30.*

Cochran, J., & Montando, M. (1978). *Using vocabulary games to raise SAT scores.* Paper presented at the Texas International Reading Association, Corpus Christi.

Collins, M., Carnine, D., & Gersten, R. (1987). Elaborated corrective feedback and the acquisition of reasoning skills: A study of computer-assisted instruction. *Exceptional Children, 54*(3), 254–262.

Cronin, C. H., & Hines, J. (1990, September). Integrating computers, reading and writing across the curriculum. *Educational Leadership 48*(1), 57–62.

Damarin, S. (1986, October). The classroom of tomorrow: The challenge of today. *Educational Technology, 26*(10), 23–28.

Elkins, R. (1986, July). Attitudes of special education personnel toward computers. *Educational Technology, 26*(7), 3121–3134.

Dalzell, P. (1988, spring). Media unit for secondary English. *English Quarterly, 16*(1), 7–12.

Darter, C. L., & Phelps, L. N. (1990, May). The impact of computer on the teaching of reading: A review of the literature: RIE.

Dees, A. (1990, January-February). Basic skills go high tech. *Vocational Educational Journal, 65*(1), 30–32.

Futrell, M., & Geisert, P. (1984). *The well-trained computer: Designing systematic instructional materials for the classroom micro-computer.* Englewood Cliffs, NJ: Educational Technology Publication.

Gattegno, C. (1964). *Toward a visual culture: Educating through TV.* New York: Educational Solutions.

Gattegno, C. (1973, September). Teaching reading via the medium of TV. *Educational Technology, 1*(9).

Geisert, G. (1990, July-September). Reading, learning styles and computers. *Journal of Reading, Writing, and Learning Disabilities International 6*(3), 297–305.

Golden, N., Gerstin, R., & Woodword, J. (1990). Effectiveness of guided practice during remedial reading instruction: An application of computer managed instruction. *The Elementary School Journal, 90,* 291–314.

Gortmaker, S., & Salter, C. (1990, Winter). The impact of T.V. viewing on mental aptitude and achievement: A longitudinal study. *Public Opinion Quarterly 54*(4), 594–604.

Grabe, C., & Grabe, M. (1985, February). The microcomputer and the language experience approach. *The Reading Teacher, 30,* 508–511.

Hamilton, H. (1975, April). Try TV tie-ins. *Instructor, 84*(8).

Hass, J. (1990, April). *The discourse of educational computing and the practice of teaching.* Paper presented at AERA, Boston.

Hassel, J. (1987). *An annotated bibliography summarizing and analyzing recorded research on the topic of CAI and its effects on reading comprehension.* South Bend: Indiana University Press.

Hoot, J. L., & Kimler, M. (1987). *Early childhood classrooms and computers: Programs with promise.* Urbana: University of Illinois.

Isaak, T., & Hamilton, J. (1989). Authoring software and teaching reading. *Reading Technology, 43,* 254–255.

Iyer, P. (1990). History? Education? Zap! Pow! Cut! *Time,* May 14, 98.

Jacobsen, P. (1987, November). Microcomputers: A medium of influence influenced by the media? *Educational Technology, 27*(11), 51–54.

Karger, H. (1988, December). Children and microcomputers: A critical analysis. *Educational Technology, 28,* 7–11.

Kinzer, C. A. (1986). Five-part categorization for use of microcomputers in reading classrooms. *Journal of Reading 30,* 226–231.

Long, C. (1985, May). How are today's elementary schools using computers? *Education Technology, 25,* 27–29.

Maginnis, G. H. (1970, May). *Captioned video cassettes: A source of reading material.* Paper presented at the Annual Meeting of the International Reading Association, Anaheim.

MecKlenburger, J. (1989, October). Technology in the 1990's: Ten secrets for success. *Principal, 69*(2), 6–10.

Nielsen Report (1979). *Report on TV.* Chicago: Nielson (AC) Co.

Packard, V. (1983, January). Warning: TV can be hazardous to children. *Reader's Digest,* 218–220.

Palmer, E. (1988). *Television and America's children: A crisis of neglect.* New York: Oxford University Press.

Proefriedt, W. (1978, November-December). Reading, writing, and philosophy. *Social Studies, 69*(6), 249–252.

Reinking, D., & Schreiner, D. (1985). The effect of computer-mediated text on measures of reading comprehension and reading behavior. *Reading Research Quarterly, 20,* 536–551.

Reinking, D., & Wu, J. H. (1990, Winter). Re-examining the research on television and reading. *Reading Research & Instruction, 29*(2), 30–43.

Reitsma, P. (1988). Reading practice for beginners: Effects of guided reading, reading-while-listening, and independent reading with computer-based speech feedback. *Reading Research Quarterly, 23,* 219–235.

Schaeffer, E. M. (1987). *Reaching writing with the microcomputer.* Bloomington, IN: Phi Delta Kappa Educational Foundation.

Schlich, V. A. (1973, April). Teaching English with TV. *American Education, 9*(3).

Siegel, M., & Missett, A. L. (1984). Adaptive feedback and review paradigm for comprehension based drills. *Journal of Educational Psychology, 76,* 310–316.

Smith, T. M. (1985, Spring). Computer-assisted video instruction: Promises and pitfalls. *Computers in Schools, 2*(1).

Snyder, T., & Palmer, J. (1986). *In search of the most amazing thing.* Reading, MA: Addison-Wesley.

Strictland, D., Feeley, J., & Wepner, S. (1987). *Using computers in the teaching of reading.* New York: Teachers College Press.

Swick, R. (1989, January). Appropriate uses of computers with young children. *Educational Technology, 29*(1).

Vermett, S., Orr, P., & Hall, M. (1986, January). Attitudes of elementary school students and teachers towards computers in education. *Educational Technology, 26,* 41–46.

Watkins, M. W. (1989). Computerized drill and practice and academic attitudes of learning disabled students. *Journal of Special Education Technology, 9*(3), 1967–1972.

Whitaker, B., Schwarts, E., & Vockell, E. (1989). *The computer in the reading curriculum.* New York: McGraw-Hill.

White, E. B. (1977). *Essays of E. B. White.* New York: Harper and Row.

Whitmer, J. E. (1987, September). *The effects of writing on reading abilities: A comparison of first grade writing programs with and without computer technology.* Paper presented at the Annual Reading Conference, Greeley, Colorado.

## Chapter Ten

Cranny, A. (1983). Two decades of adult reading programs. *Journal of Reading, 28,* 416–421.

Drabeck, J. (1980). Reading sequential competency system. *Resources in Education* (Educational Reproduction Service Number 210 493).

Gee, T., Olson, J., & Forester, N. (1989). A survey of content reading program development in U.S. schools. *Reading Research and Instruction, 28*(3), 30–44.

Glasser, W. (1986). *Control theory in the classroom.* New York: Harper and Row.

Kozol, J. (1986). *Illiteracy in America.* Urbana, IL: Scott, Foresman.

Madden, L. (1988, December). Improving reading attitudes of poor readers through cooperative reading. *The Reading Teacher, 41.*

Margolis, H., & McCabe, P. (1990). Using cooperative learning to faciltate mainstreaming in social studies. *Social Education, 54*(2).

Mark, J., & Mark, L. (1984, March). *Adult education: The fight against illiteracy.* Newspapers in Education Conference, San Antonio.

Martens, A. (1989). Allowing the unconventional. *Educational Technology, 29*(8).

National Academy of Education (1990). *Becoming a nation of readers: The report of the Commission on Reading.* National Institute of Education, Center for the Study of Reading, Champaign, Illinois.

Pascarella, P. (1987). Skills gap threatens our competitiveness. *Industry Week,* October 19, 235.

Pearson, P. D., & Samuels, J. (1987). *Changing school reading programs: Principles and case studies.* Newark, DE: International Reading Association.

Pipho, C. (1988, May). Sorting out the data on adult illiteracy. *Phi Delta Kappan, 630.*

Plawin, P., & Kainer, B. (1988, April). Educating our work force. *Changing Times, 42.*

Slavin, R. (1989/90). Here to stay or gone tomorrow? *Educational Leadership, 47*(4).

Smith, N. B. (1963). *Reading instruction for today's children.* Englewood Cliffs, NJ: Prentice-Hall.

Taylor, G. (1987, March). Adults who can't read: The enormous cost affects us all. *Readers Digest, 111*(4).

# INDEX